In the Night Sky

Hudson Valley UFO Sightings from the 1930s to the Present

Written by
Linda Zimmermann

*Dedicated to people everywhere who
have the courage to speak out.*

*And to the people of the Hudson Valley,
who share a long, strange history.*

To contact the author, email: lindazim@optonline.net

Or write to:

Linda Zimmermann
P.O. Box 192
Blooming Grove, NY 10914

For more information on the book and film, go to:

www.nightskyufo.com

www.BigGuyMedia.com

Cover by Big Guy Media

In the Night Sky
Copyright © 2013 Linda Zimmermann

Eagle Press, New York
ISBN: 978-1-937174-19-4

CONTENTS

This wonderful artwork by Thomas Ahearn illustrates how
UFOs have captured our imaginations for generations.

1
Full Disclosure

This book represents a journey.

For me, it was a journey of discovery, and a search for answers which ultimately led to more questions. For many residents of the Hudson Valley of New York, it was a journey into memories of past events that are still clear and vivid, even several decades later. For some people, whether local or global, this may be a journey from skeptic to believer.

However, I will attempt to refrain from ever telling you *what* to believe, but there will be times when I strongly suggest *what not* to believe. For example, if someone witnessed a silent, massive object, illuminated by bright, spinning, multi-colored lights, hovering just 100 feet above them, you should not believe it when officials claim it was a weather balloon, the planet Venus, or swamp gas.

On the flip side of that, I heard many reports of things that could easily be explained by conventional aircraft, meteorites, or yes, heaven help me, even the planet Venus. I have also seen some pretty bad photos and videos, and heard outlandish claims that pushed the envelope of credibility from here to the next galaxy.

In other words, the subject of UFOs—perhaps more than any other subject—is fraught with extremes. From official sources that adamantly deny and obfuscate, to people who suspend all reason and believe everything is alien, this polarizing topic is an intellectual mine field.

So why did I jump into this mine field feet first and hit the ground running? Because I was born and raised in the Hudson Valley, a hotspot of UFO sightings for generations. Because astronomy fascinates me, and the possibility of life on other planets would arguably be the greatest discovery in history. Because I love a challenge and gravitate to anything strange and unusual. And last, but certainly not least, because *I have seen things I cannot explain.*

I feel that anyone who writes a book such as this should state whether or not they are a skeptic or a believer. Well, the short answer is that I am both.

The long answer is, as a former scientist, I want hard evidence to come to any definitive conclusions. But short of the proverbial flying saucer landing on the White House lawn, what constitutes hard evidence when it comes to UFOs?

As a lifelong amateur astronomer, I am very familiar with the night sky and have spent countless hours observing. I have seen meteor showers, fragmenting bolides, comets, nebulae, planets, galaxies, satellites, and the International Space Station. But I know that a lot of people don't share my passion for space, and could easily misinterpret natural or manmade objects as something alien.

So in these regards, I am skeptical of the many alleged UFO reports, especially those that involve single points of light that appear to waver or change color—a common result of the tricks that stars, our atmosphere, and our eyes can play on us.

On the other hand, as an amateur astronomer I know that there are about *100 billion galaxies* in the observable universe. With *hundreds of billions of stars* with possible habitable planets in *each galaxy*, it would be sheer stupidity and intolerable arrogance to think that Earth is the only planet that harbors life. So in lieu of the staggering numbers, I fully believe there are countless intelligent beings out and about the universe.

While many scientists hold similar beliefs, they will argue that no alien race could possibly traverse the vast distances to Earth. I, however, have no problem with admitting that just because our technology has not yet found a way to do it, it doesn't mean that others haven't found the key to long distance space travel. After all, we are a species that went from the Wright Brothers' first powered flight to walking on the moon in the span of a mere 66 years. What will we be capable of doing in another 66 years, or 1,066 years?

Then there is my own personal sighting, which I might as well put out on the table from the start.

It was an evening in the late 70s or perhaps even 1980 or '81, and I was studying for an exam in my favorite red, furry bathrobe. The phone rang, and it was Harriet, the mother of my boyfriend's friend, Tony. Harriet was one of the most wonderful women I ever had the privilege of knowing, and several times a month we would go into Manhattan for the opera, classical music concerts, and museums. In addition, she worked in Waldenbooks at the Nanuet Mall and was as well-read as anyone I've ever met. In other words, she was educated, intelligent, and cultured.

So, when I answered the phone and she told me that three strange objects just flew over her house in Hillburn and were headed towards Nanuet where I lived, I didn't hesitate to run outside in my furry bathrobe and slippers and scan the skies. Sure enough, three bright, white, round lights, low in the sky and flying in a V-formation, were silently moving from west to east, roughly following Route 59. [Note: My boyfriend remembered that there were yellow flashing lights, I recall them as just white.)

Tony was at our house, and he, my boyfriend, and I jumped in the car and took off after them. The three lights then broke formation and headed off in different directions, and were soon out of sight. Rather than give up the chase, however, I remembered a Frank Edward's UFO book I read as a kid that had a photo of a classic flying saucer over Lake Tiorati in Harriman State Park, taken by Vincent Perna in December of 1966. I suggested we head up the Palisades Interstate Parkway to the lake.

We may or may not have been traveling at an excessive rate of speed up the parkway—depending upon the statute of limitations on issuing speeding tickets—but in about 20 minutes we were parked along the road at the north end of Lake Tiorati near the traffic circle. It was fall or winter, and I recall it being very chilly in the car, as I was still wearing nothing but that furry robe and slippers. At least I had thought to grab my 35mm camera, even if I didn't think to grab some clothes and shoes.

We sat in the darkness waiting, and waiting…until we saw a single white light in the sky coming from the north. A moment later, a light appeared to our south, and then one from the east. They all appeared to be moving towards one another. We fully expected there would be a terrible collision and crash of the three mysterious craft right over the 1,141-foot hill at the north end of the lake. I snapped as many pictures as I could, and held my breath waiting for the awful, inevitable collision.

And come together they did, but not in a manner any of us anticipated, nor could even understand. The three bright white lights came together in an intense burst of blue light, then slowly, in a controlled manner, descended as a single blue light on the top of the mountain. For

3

several minutes we watched that blue light pulsating through the trees. We were mesmerized, astonished, and convinced we had to hike up that mountain right then and there and see what this incredible object looked like up close.

At that moment a NY State Trooper pulled up. He approached our car and wanted to know what a woman in a bathrobe was doing with two men parked in a car in the middle of Harriman State Park!

Brimming with excitement, but trying not to sound drunk or high, I quickly explained the strange lights we had followed, how they had come together, and how they had landed on the mountain. He was clearly skeptical, and not at all amused, but he did turn to look and saw the pulsing blue light. His expression certainly changed—I would say from stern cop to freaked-out witness in a heartbeat—and he simply said something to the effect of, "Yeah, okay, move along now."

It was obvious there was no arguing with him. He wanted us gone, and he didn't want to be there either. In retrospect, hiking in the dark through the woods towards who-knows-what in nothing but my furry bathrobe wouldn't have been prudent anyway.

However, when the weekend arrived, my boyfriend and I returned during the day and hiked to the top of that mountain. At the summit was a bare, rocky area, and the trees around it had broken branches, as if something had landed. There was also some charred wood, but as hikers often make campfires, it could simply have been the remnants of firewood.

I recall that there was a newspaper article about the UFO sightings over Rockland that week, but unfortunately, I can't find the clipping. (I am a pack rat, which works both for and against me!) I also can't find my photos, which were either too dark to see anything, or just squiggly lines of light as I attempted to take long exposures without a tripod.

Still, I have no doubt about what we all saw that night, and in the years since, I have not been able to find a reasonable explanation. Was it super-secret military technology, or alien spacecraft? As a scientist, I do not have enough information to draw a conclusion. As an ordinary observer, my gut feel that night gravitated toward something out of this world…

2
In the beginning...

(Note: All locations in this book are in New York unless otherwise stated.)

From: (Name withheld)
Sent: Wednesday, June 20, 2012 9:06 PM
To: lindazim@optonline.net
Subject: ufo

I am a retired MD and was visiting one of my friends in lower Westchester when I was called for an emergency. I was traveling up the Taconic heading to my office when many cars were stopped in all lanes causing me to weave between them. My wife said, "Stop the car and look up in the sky." After pulling to the side we saw what looked like an object in the sky in the shape of a horseshoe crab. It was completely still and about 1/2 a mile to 1 mile away from us. In less than a split second it moved to another spot further away. We got back in the car and proceeded on the Taconic and got off on Rt 202. It was becoming night. On 202 many cars were on the side of the road. We pulled over. The UFO passed right over us not more than 100 feet over us. Its shape again was like a horseshoe crab. It was totally silent and the size of 2 football fields and surrounded by lights. It was awesome!!!! When I arrived at the office to see my emergency patient we called the police, who told us that they also saw it and had no explanation. Later, the paper said that it was ultralights traveling in formation, however, there was no noise whatsoever and ultralights could not move 1 to 2 miles in a millisecond. I hope this helps you.

———

This is just one example of the many emails and letters I received from doctors, nurses, lawyers, teachers, politicians, military personnel, librarians, and people from all walks of life. Some eyewitnesses, like this physician, insisted I keep their names confidential. Others had no qualms about having their names used, as I often heard, "I saw what I saw, and I don't care what people think." Several even consented to be filmed for the documentary, which leads me to the background of this project.

I have been lecturing throughout the Hudson Valley on a variety of topics for about 15 years. Whether I was speaking about astronomy, local history, or telling tales of the haunted Hudson Valley at Halloween, audience members would often ask if I ever spoke about UFOs. They asked, because they were not only interested in the subject, they claimed to have had their own sightings and encounters. My standard response came to be, "Sorry, I don't do UFOs."

That changed when an astronomy club asked if I could do another program for them. I had something of a reputation for, shall we say, "unusual lectures," such as my popular "Bad Astronomy" presentations, in which I brought humor to a field that often puts the average person to sleep. I had also done a program on "Astronomy X-Files," where I delved into some of the more esoteric or just plain weird aspects of our universe. So, as I had become the "go to" lecturer on fringe topics, it was not a giant leap, but a mere small step, for me to do some sort of a UFO program.

I mulled it over for a while and decided to take an approach I often use for other lectures—combining some of my varied interests. As I am a "space program baby" who grew up during the exhilarating years of the Apollo moon landings, I have always been enamored of rockets and astronauts. Over time, I had read about several astronauts having sightings of "bogeys" and other inexplicable things, so I put together a program entitled "Astronauts' Close Encounters." It went over well, and I was later asked to give the lecture at several other locations, after which I thought that would be the end of it, because, "I don't do UFOs."

Then in 2004, I was working on my second book about the history of the county where I was born and raised, *Rockland County Scrapbook*, and I was talking to a friend and long-time reporter for the *Journal News*, Scott Webber, about some of his memories of interesting news stories he covered. He is probably one of the last people I would have ever suspected to have a UFO story, but he took me completely by surprise when he shared his account of his 1979 sighting with me. I included it in the book, along with the story of the Vincent Perna sighting over Lake Tiorati in 1966, which had been my introduction to local UFO activity.

Years passed and I was at the New City library in October of 2011, giving my annual presentation of spooky stories. A friend of my husband came to the lecture, and afterward she asked that same question whether I wrote about UFOs. She then mentioned that her boyfriend, Gary, had confessed to her that he had had several encounters going back to his childhood. This was news to my husband, who had known this man since he was a boy. The woman then got an odd look, as if maybe she shouldn't have divulged this confidence. I assured her that the secret was safe with me, because after all, "I don't do UFOs."

Months passed, and as I was finishing up the manuscript of my latest novel, *HVZA: Hudson Valley Zombie Apocalypse* (I told you I gravitated to strange things), my thoughts turned to ideas for my next book project. Throughout the time since that night in October at the library, the tantalizing tidbits I had heard about the man with the lifelong ET encounters kept rattling around my brain. I finally decided that my next project would be another work of fiction, and this time I *would do* UFOs.

As I wanted to also place the setting of this book locally, I started researching sightings in the Hudson Valley. Having grown up here, I was already aware of a few sightings from the 1960s. And what local resident didn't know about the so-called "Westchester Triangles" of the 1980s? Then, of course, there was Pine Bush—the town that decided to embrace its reputation as the "UFO Capital of the East" and host an annual UFO Fest.

However, what I quickly began to realize was the incredible number of sightings stretching back generations. My scientific curiosity was piqued, and once that happens, resistance is usually futile.

How could so many people have seen so many things over such a long span of time? Could they all be hallucinating, misinterpreting something, or imagining things? Was the military using the Hudson Valley as a testing site for their secret aircraft? And if by some chance these *were* alien spacecraft, what the hell were they doing hanging around here all these years?

Even though I had already begun writing my novel and had most of the plot already planned out in my head, I contemplated the shift from fiction to nonfiction, or at least the addition of a nonfiction UFO book. One thing that would tip those scales to nonfiction would be if Big Guy Media (a production company in Rifton, NY, that I had enjoyed working with in the past) would possibly be interested in creating some sort of brief, companion video to the book.

So, on April 12, 2012, at 11:51am, I sent this fateful email to Felix Olivieri, who with his wife, Sarah, are the owners of BGM. I had sent him an email about a radio show, and added the following:

On another note, how do you feel about UFOs? We are coming up to the 30th anniversary of the wave of sightings in Putnam and Westchester of huge V-shaped UFOs. I'm kicking around a novel based on those sightings and all the other UFO activity in the valley. But I also think it would be cool to track down some of the witnesses of those sightings, and the ones in Pine Bush in the 1990s and do some sort of a show/documentary.

Little did I realize that email was like throwing gasoline on a fire. Felix emailed back that he had always wanted to do some sort of UFO documentary, he just didn't know what angle to take. When I explained that I wanted to see how these sightings had affected people during the decades following their experiences, the seeds of a documentary were firmly planted in Felix's brain, and knowing him, he had the whole thing planned in his head that night.

Things moved very quickly from there—press releases, articles in newspapers such as the *Putnam Examiner, Poughkeepsie Journal, Daily Freeman*, and online articles on several *Patch* websites. The ensuing flood of emails, letters, and calls, led to a long list of people to interview, both over the phone and on camera.

What soon emerged from these interviews were several recurring themes, some of which I will mention in later chapters, but there were two things that caught my attention right away. First, it was downright eerie how many people told me that they were glad to see the newspaper articles or hear about the project, because after decades of keeping silent, they had recently decided it was time to tell their stories. No kidding, it was simply bizarre how many people used the *exact same words* about feeling that *now* was the time to finally speak out.

Secondly, I was almost embarrassed by how many people were *thanking me* for taking on this project! These people had universally been ridiculed or ignored when they tried to tell their friends and families what they had seen. Some had *never told anyone*, or they only told their spouses, and often received nothing but scorn and derision from them. One elderly gentleman in his eighties was particularly grateful, as he had been waiting for a very long time to speak and be heard. The following is his story:

JPF: Albany, August 29, 1967

On June 27, 2012, I received a call from a gentleman who had been waiting for decades for someone to listen to his story of his 1967 experience. However, it wasn't just 45 years that JPF had been waiting, it was actually 65 years, as his first encounter occurred way back in 1947!

While serving in the National Guard after WWII, JPF was stationed at Fort Drum, which is near Watertown, New York. His job was to drive a 3/4 ton vehicle to run wire for communications. One night about three or 3:30am, he looked up and saw a "giant round thing" about 300-500 yards away. Its apparent size at that distance was similar to "holding a basketball at the end of your arm," and it was "very bright, all white" and "mesmerizing."

"I tried to think and nothing worked," JPF told me, trying to describe how completely captivating the brilliant object was. Finally, he remembered that he had binoculars in the vehicle. Turning for a moment to reach for the binoculars, when he turned back the object was gone.

"Two days later I went to see the commanding officer and I told him I thought I needed a mental discharge because I was going nuts. Then I explained whole thing to him. I didn't know how he was going to react, but he said, 'Relax! I had three other reports of the same thing that night.' I was so relieved to find out that the guards on duty that night also saw it."

When I asked him why he didn't report it that same night, he replied, "I waited two nights to see if I was going totally crackers."

One UFO sighting per lifetime is usually enough for anyone, but JPF was to get another opportunity twenty-two years later when he was driving a truck to the UPS facility in Albany, NY. When he told me about this second incident, he could neither remember the date or even the year, so how do I know it was August 29, 1967?

"The one thing I do know," JPF said, "was that it was the night the final episode of *The Fugitive* was on television. I'm absolutely certain it was that night because I tried to get the night off to watch the show, but couldn't."

A quick Internet search found that episode aired on Tuesday night, August 29, 1967. At that point, it was the most-watched television series show ever, with an estimated 78 million people watching the one-armed man meet his fate, and Dr. Richard Kimble finally being exonerated. While it "upset" him to miss the show after waiting four years for the exciting conclusion, this man was treated to a show in the night sky that beat anything Hollywood could produce.

After bringing his truck to the UPS facility off exit 23 of the New York State Thruway in Albany, JPF was walking across the long parking lot to go get some dinner at a nearby restaurant. It was about 1am, and the skies were clear. He happened to glance up at the stars and noticed something strange near the Big Dipper constellation. There was a bright, round, "star-like light" moving toward the Big Dipper, and it went "inside the top of the cup."

Then it got really strange. Over the course of about 45 minutes, the object slowly moved from star to star in the constellation, effectively "tracing the entire outline" of the distinctive pattern of stars. "It started at the top of the Dipper, went inside the cup, crossed the bottom, and then out the handle." He leaned against a fence watching the slow, but steady movement of this light which traced the Big Dipper, and was once again completely mesmerized by what he saw.

Although these sightings took place many decades ago, they are still very clear in his mind. One other thing is also clear after all this time, "No one ever seemed interested in hearing my story." After reading the article about our project in the *Poughkeepsie Journal*, he called the reporter, Maria Jayne, to get my phone number, and he was very grateful that he had finally found someone who would listen to his stories.

I expressed to him how grateful I was that he took the time to share his experiences, and told him that even though he offered to have me use his name, I suggested we just use his initials.

He then agreed, saying, "Yes, at my age if they hear you talking about such things they'll take you away in one of those white jackets!"

The "DUH!" Factor

One final note before I present the rest of the cases. Soon after beginning the interviews, I found that many people couldn't remember some very key elements about their sightings—things such as the month, the year, or even where they were. I thought this was inexplicable—how could anyone see something so remarkable, and not recall such basic facts? Well, to my embarrassment, I discovered that I was just as guilty of this "UFO amnesia," if not more so.

While working on the project one day, I got a call from my friend, Pauline Kranick. Pauline and I started working together at Fisher Diagnostics in 1978, and we have been friends ever since. She now lives in Florida, but I visit her every year. (I just happen to plan my visits to coincide with Mets' spring training games!)

I was telling her about all the UFO interviews, and mentioned a few stories. After one story, Pauline said, "That sounds similar to what we saw." I didn't know to what she was referring, and she explained, "You know, the thing you and I saw in Washingtonville that night when we were coming back from Walden."

At that moment I had absolutely no idea what she was talking about, and my memory rarely lets me down to this extent. The more she spoke about it, some fuzzy details did start to crystallize in my mind's eye. To help jog my memory, Pauline emailed me the following:

In the late 80s (could have been in August) we were coming back from a friend's house in Walden and had just turned on to Route 208 in Washingtonville. You were driving. It was starting to get dark as we approached an open area on the left, when I saw a band of bright lights in the sky. It wasn't a plane or stars. They stayed for a short time, then were gone. I've never seen anything like it before or since.

I thought hard about it, and then like finding an old photo in a drawer, the image of that night finally came into view. I asked Pauline if this object was to my left as we headed south on Route 208, over the fields before you get to Woodcock Mountain Road.

"That's it!" she replied. "That's right where we saw it."

Well, Duh! What took me so long to finally remember the large band of lights, and how it moved slowly and silently to the southeast and out of sight? How could I have completely forgotten such a thing? Why did it take such effort to coax the memory to the surface?

I don't know the answer, but from that day I certainly didn't judge anyone who said they couldn't recall crucial details of their sighting. After all, I had forgotten the entire thing!

3
The Triangles

I put a lot of thought into how I should present all of the cases in this book. I could have just done a straight chronology, but I think you lose something when it comes to trying to see patterns or similarities. I decided upon grouping stories according to what they had in common, where possible, and then put everything else in the Casebook chapter.

Of course, there is some overlap. For example, people who saw both triangles and discs, or various sightings in Pine Bush or Ulster County that are in their own chapters. And, although the appearance of triangular-shaped craft is something relatively recent in the whole UFO scheme of things, I opted to begin with this chapter as they have arguably been seen by the most people in the Hudson Valley, with estimates of 10,000 eyewitnesses in the 1980s alone.

While the majority of the sightings occurred during the early 1980s to mid-1990s, there were some earlier accounts of triangular-shaped craft. And, despite the common belief that these sightings are a thing of the past, there have been some recent ones, as well.

Dennis Sant: Brewster, March 17, 1983

Every time the 1992 *Unsolved Mysteries* episode on the Hudson Valley UFO sightings is rebroadcast, Dennis Sant gets a flood of letters from curious viewers and authors looking to write about his encounter in Brewster, NY on March 17, 1983. While he consented to be on several shows, for many years he has declined all offers—until now.

After reading about his experience in the book *Night Siege*, I also wrote Dennis a letter. In one of many delightful "coincidences" during my research, my letter to him happened to arrive just as he "had come to a point in my life that I wanted to connect all the dots" in regards to his UFO sighting and the influence it has had on his life.

As he began his first message to me:

"I received your letter today, with great interest, your timing is perfect and for the first time an author has caught my interest. Through the years I have received many letters like yours, and never felt compelled to get involved, for many personal reasons with a few exceptions."

So here again, was someone who now felt the time was right to speak, and after several email messages back and forth, I was convinced that I had to meet this man and interview him in person. Not only did he have a fascinating story to tell, but we had some interesting things in common— he was a kindred spirit, so to speak.

In another coincidence, on June 13, 2012, I happened to have a meeting in Carmel, New York—almost an hour from my home—with a producer for a Travel Channel show for which I was going to make a guest appearance. The producer wanted to meet at a restaurant called George's Place, which happens to be *right next* to the Putnam County office building where Dennis Sant's office is located! What are the chances? Dennis and I made arrangements for me to stop by his office as soon as my meeting was over.

In some ways it was like meeting an old friend, perhaps because I had already seen him on television and spoken to him on the phone, but more likely because we had many similar thoughts and viewpoints, not the least of which was our fascination with UFOs. He spoke about his sighting in great detail, and as with most of the other witnesses I've interviewed, Dennis recalls the event as clearly as if it was yesterday.

The story actually begins at 8:40pm with his neighbor, Linda Nicolletti, who saw a massive V-shaped object over an elevated section of Route 84, which was close to her property. The craft was lined with bright, multicolored lights, with a larger, brighter light underneath. Her initial thought was that it was a big jet about to crash, but when she opened her window she realized it was silent, and then she also realized it was moving so slowly it was practically hovering in place.

The V-shaped craft moved ever so slowly across the roadway to her house, then turned 90 degrees and headed for the house of Dennis Sant. As it reached his house, she could see Dennis standing in his yard looking up at the enormous craft, "and he was bathed in light" from it. She could also see him running into his backyard to keep pace with the craft and remain directly under it.

Nicolletti then called for her husband to come and look, and they saw Dennis and several other people in the neighborhood standing outside watching the UFO. They could also see that traffic had stopped on Route 84, as drivers sat mesmerized by the sight. She then called the Sheriff's office and was told they had many calls about the object. In fact, some State Police officers had witnessed it, but there was nothing to worry about because it was only an experimental military aircraft out of Stewart Airport in Newburgh. Subsequently, they denied making that statement.

From the perspective of Dennis Sant, who was an official for Putnam County, the event began as he was driving home from church with his children. As he came down the road, he first saw a "whitish light" near his house. By the time he pulled into his driveway, he and his kids could see that the object was about 120 feet long, and from his initial view, Dennis described it as L-shaped. It was drifting slowly over his house at a height of no more than fifty feet above the roof. They ran into the backyard, but lost sight of it. He then brought in the children to get them ready for bed, and thought that was the end of the sighting.

"Then I had a strong urge to go back outside," he explained, and when he did, there was the craft "about 100 yards away over Route 84," and only about 20 feet above a truck. He could see at least 30-40 cars stopped along the highway with their emergency flashers blinking, with all the people standing next to their cars, pointing at the object. He ran back in to get his father and kids, and they all watched the object together.

The ship was moving away, and Dennis thought to himself, "I wish it would come back so I could get a better look at it." Perhaps it was only a coincidence, perhaps it was something more, but at the moment he wished that the craft would come back over his property, the ship turned, and then started moving directly toward him! At this point, the massive object looked like it "was V-shaped with the center pointing down."

The huge ship had a sequence of multicolored lights and came within forty feet of where he was standing in front of the house, and it was no more than 20 feet over the telephone pole across the street. "It was so close that if I had a baseball I could have hit it." Dennis was in awe of the object that "looked like a city of lights in the sky."

The ship started to drift over his backyard and he was able to jog and keep pace with it. His children became somewhat frightened and went inside to watch from the windows, but he and his father continued to

15

watch the object at a very close distance. Once over the pond in his backyard, the ship stopped just at tree height, and the lights intensified threefold, lighting up everything in the area and reflecting brightly in the water beneath it. When he was closest to the object, he could just detect the slightest sound of an engine.

Dennis and I stand in his backyard by the marshy area where the ship stopped and its lights intensified.   Photo courtesy of BGM.

Dennis stood transfixed for two to three minutes, but then became afraid that the ship might actually land in his yard. At that point, it began to move and slowly drift away out of sight, as if it had read his mind.

But "as scared as I was, I was sorry when it left."

Dennis called the Sheriff's office the next day and told them what he saw. They tried to downplay the incident, but he was certain about what he—and hundreds of other people—witnessed that night over his house. A local reporter wanted him to give his account for the newspaper, and at first he declined, until they promised to keep his identity a secret. Unfortunately, as soon as the article appeared, the cat was out of the bag. The reporter had mentioned Dennis' position with the county government, where he lived, and just about every other detail of his life, except his name. That's a hell of a way to keep a secret!

Offers rolled in, and Dennis found himself on *Good Morning America* with Regis and Kathy Lee, *People Are Talking*, *Unsolved Mysteries*, and an HBO special. His story also appeared in the book, *Night Siege*, about the Hudson Valley sightings, and he was fortunate enough to spend a few days with its famous author, Dr. J. Allen Hynek, an astronomer who had been an adviser on Project Blue Book, the U.S. Air Force project to study UFOs.

Dennis Sant and Dr. Hynek share UFO stories at Dennis' home in March of 1983. Photo courtesy of Dennis Sant.

Over the years, he continued to receive requests for interviews, but he had no further interest in talking about his experience—until just before my letter arrived. Timing is everything, I always say, and I was delighted that we would be able to film this "celebrity witness" and his important case.

Sarah, Felix, and I arrived at Dennis' house on the hot day of June 29, 2012. It was exciting to see the actual location of a sighting I had seen recreated on the *Unsolved Mysteries* show decades earlier. (The house and roadway they used in the show were not the actual house and overpass on Route 84.) I have driven on that section of road countless times, and I knew every time I passed by there in the future I would picture that massive triangular craft hovering just several yards over the stopped traffic.

While all the cameras and lights were being set up, Dennis and I discussed more details of the sighting and what followed (while enjoying some of the delicious brownies his wife, Kathy, had kindly made for us). He said that in order to help his kids cope with the experience, he had them all draw what they had seen. I was anxious to see those drawings, but he said he had lent them to another author who never returned them.

Dennis also told me that a couple of weeks after the sighting, his entire family suddenly woke up at 2am for some unknown reason. They were all wide awake and ended up gathering in the kitchen to discuss the UFO.

Once the cameras were rolling, we went through the formal interview. Apart from the actual sighting, we discussed how it influenced or changed his life. His answers were thoughtful and direct. The appearance of that craft led him to question many things, become more open to life's mysteries, and try to "think out of the box." He gravitated to a more spiritual way of life in an effort to reach "a greater understanding" about the nature of things.

I asked if he thought something else unusual would happen in the future, and he wasn't sure, but he "wanted it to happen again." On the question of life in the universe, Dennis feels that it's "arrogant" to maintain that we are the only planet with life.

It was truly a pleasure speaking with him, as in addition to his kind nature and sense of humor, Dennis possesses a rare quality I would characterize as a special type of wisdom. Whether or not he would have gained that wisdom had he not had that amazing experience in 1983 is a debatable point, but the fact remains that he saw what he saw, and his life changed for the better.

Unfortunately, our pleasant conversation came to an end when it was time for the outdoor filming. It was 97 degrees with high humidity, and decidedly unpleasant. But we all kept our senses of humor and trusted that Felix's wizardry with the cameras would all make it worth the dehydration factor. And I have to admit, despite the heat, it did give me a chill to stand exactly where Dennis stood almost 30 years earlier and witnessed something almost beyond description. I was also a bit jealous that I never had a close encounter like that! All in all, it was a privilege to interview Dennis at his home and experience this incredible case vicariously through his vivid recollections.

Will Dennis Sant ever encounter something like this again? Maybe. Maybe not. But if he does, regardless of the nature of the event, he will most likely learn from it and turn it into a positive experience. And what more could we ask from life than that?

Dennis and I on the spot where he was so close to the massive triangle he could "have hit it with a baseball." Photo courtesy of Dennis Sant.

19

The Three Teachers:
Yorktown & Mahopac, March 24, 1983

The following is based on a phone interview I conducted with Debra Carbone:

On March 24, 1983, between 8:30-9pm, Debra Carbone and two of her friends, Doris Acosta-Krawiec, and Jackie Worthington, were driving north to Yorktown on the Taconic State Parkway on their way home from Fordham University, where they were all taking graduate classes. They saw a strange light in the distance, and when they reached Yorktown "everyone had pulled over to the side of the road and not a single car was moving in either direction."

Doris also pulled over, because that distant light turned out to be a "pitch black" triangular craft "the size of two football fields hovering just above the trees." On the back edge they could see red, blue, green, and white "rotating lights" that illuminated the outline of the enormous craft. It was totally silent and motionless.

When I asked how far away she was from this craft, Debra replied, "Almost directly underneath it." And how long did this craft hover at that spot? "At least 20 minutes," she replied, to my surprise.

Debra admits she was "spooked" by the size and proximity of this "unidentified flying object." And she was laughing when she told me that during the sighting she thought about "the music from Close Encounters."

After those 20 long, exciting minutes, it suddenly "took off fast," heading southbound down the Taconic. The three friends then continued north to Mahopac. As Doris turned down Debra's street, Debra saw the same exact craft moving directly over her house! Debra ran in to get her husband and son, but by the time they got outside it was gone.

This part definitely raised an eyebrow and I asked for further clarification.

"I'm sorry, but I thought you said the triangle headed south, but then later it was going right over your house in Mahopac…to the north…*just as you got home*?"

"Yes, it must have returned to the north. I heard people at Lake Mahopac saw it that night, so that's where it must have been heading," she replied.

She was missing my point.

"Don't you think that's a remarkable coincidence? It was hovering over you for 20 minutes, and then headed south, but then was right over your house to the north *just as you arrived*?"

"All three of us had just gotten out of class. We weren't drinking or anything," Debra replied, still not seeing what I was driving at.

"I don't doubt your story. I just think this may not be a coincidence. Did you ever consider that it may have been looking for you?" I finally asked, getting to my point.

Clearly, Debra had never considered that, and could only offer that "it just happened to be there" when she got home. Perhaps it was that simple. Perhaps not.

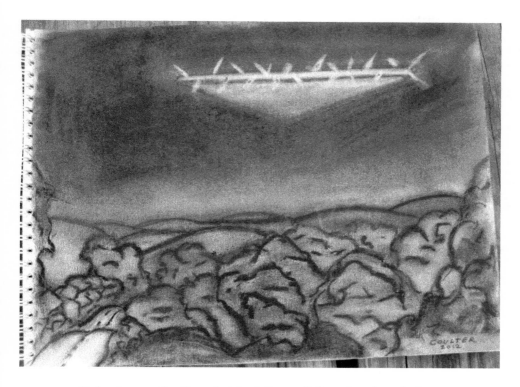

Debra's son, Coulter, sketched the craft from her description.

In any event, she immediately called the Yorktown Police to report her sighting. The officer who answered told her they had "received hundreds of calls" that night. She was surprised that he was actually nice to her and "didn't try to make any excuses," like it being a formation of ultralights. What he did do, was give her the phone number of NUFORC, the National UFO Reporting Center in Seattle. She called immediately to report her experience.

Debra admits the encounter made her so "excited and enthusiastic I had to tell people about it, and not just anyone, people of authority!"

Later that year during the summer, while driving along Peekskill Hollow Road, she and her husband saw the same triangular craft, although "it was much higher in the sky, but it had the same rotating lights."

Debra is now a retired school teacher (she and both of her friends became teachers), and looking back she can compare and contrast her sightings to other things she saw over the years. For example, a few months after the first sighting, several times she and her husband saw a formation of ultralights flying at night over a field in Mahopac.

"They were definitely individuals trying to fly in a V-formation and they clearly weren't hovering, they were moving, and they were definitely noisy. There was no mistaking what they were, and they weren't anything like the triangle we saw."

Years later, her family was in Virginia Beach when they heard a deep, rumbling sound. They looked up and a stealth bomber was passing overhead. "The shape looked something like the triangle, but it shook the ground and we had to cover our ears it was so loud." Again, it was nothing like that silent, motionless, black triangle the size of two football fields.

So, what does Debra think she witnessed and how did it influence her life?

"It was definitely an unidentified flying object," she repeated, but then added. "Not necessarily alien, it could have been from our government, but maybe I'm just second guessing myself with that.

"It opened me to the thought that there are likely other beings, but I didn't necessarily want to meet them that night!"

Ever since then, Debra is "always looking up in the sky. Always."

After speaking to Debra and writing this story, I spoke to Sarah and Felix about possibly interviewing all three teachers near where the

22

sighting occurred. They agreed that it would be good to film these credible, multiple eyewitnesses, so we all arranged to meet the morning of August 1st.

We all met in the BJ's parking lot on Crompond Road in Yorktown Heights. Before the teachers arrived, Sarah, Felix, and I had a very unusual exchange of objects. Felix wanted some UFO, space, and alien props for the film, and as I have a collection of all things space-related, factual and fictitious, I was able to bring him boxes of stuff. I also brought the almost 4-foot-tall ceramic alien that usually stands in the "Galaxy Diner" in my home, wearing a miniature Mets batting helmet. (You can't make this stuff up!) I wondered what people thought as I pulled the blanket-draped alien body out of my car and handed it to Felix!

After everyone arrived, we drove to a spot on the Taconic where we could park on the shoulder near a grassy area, but it didn't seem to be a particularly safe, quiet, or scenic place to film. It was then decided to go to FDR State Park nearby, which turned out to be an ideal location. I sat on one side of a picnic table, while Debra, Doris, and Jackie sat on the other side. Debra's husband, Glenn, was nice enough to take photos for me.

The following are Doris and Jackie's recollections, and some additional information from Debra:

Doris: I was driving, and I remember first of all everything got very, very bright. And everyone in front of me was moving over to the right, past the shoulder and the grassy area. So I pulled over like everyone else, and I was just amazed at how everything was bright. I don't remember details like Debbie does, but I remember I wanted to stay. I was like, overwhelmed by it, I was in awe of it. And Jackie said, "Let's just go home!"

And I couldn't sleep that night. I was just waiting for it to come back. I was waiting for something more to happen. You know, I just couldn't sleep, I was just so awed by it. But, I remember there was no sound, and it was bright, like beyond daylight bright. Like a white, very bright, bright. So, that's what I remember.

Jackie: Okay, what I remember is somebody said, I think it was Doris who said, "Do you have apartments in Mahopac?" and we didn't know. And she said, "What are those lights?" And then we all focused on the lights, and they were coming down the parkway towards us as we were going north. Then we noticed there were cars pulled off everywhere on the sides, so the next grassy area we pulled off.

And we waited, and it was shaped like a boomerang. I remember colored lights, but I remember them being round and on the sides. And when you looked up, it was above the tree line, and I don't know if it was a hundred feet, but it wasn't high in the sky, and it just hovered there. I had the feeling that it was eerily quiet. There was not a sound. The people were not making sounds, there wasn't any talking, and that object was quiet.

We stood there for I don't know how long, maybe 20 minutes, and I just thought I wanted to go home, I had it. I was curious to see where it would go or what would happen, but it was just so eerily quiet that we left.

We watched in the background, we watched through the rear window and turned around, and eventually the lights disappeared.

Zim: About how many people do you think were standing outside their cars?

Jackie: There had to be a hundred. The parkway at the time was only two lanes, and there were more grassy areas, and on different grassy areas there were people pulled over. But there were probably, maybe not a hundred, but 25 cars with two to three people per car. There were a lot of people there.

Zim: And nobody spoke to one another?

Jackie: Nobody spoke, it was quiet. They were quiet, it was quiet.

Doris: I was just in awe. It was just an awesome…I was almost paralyzed with it.

Zim: How did that affect you in the years since?

Jackie: Interestingly enough, you get teased about such things, but enough people saw it that there was some credibility to it. If I had seen that by myself I think I would probably say, "I think I saw it," but there were so many people. And I can still see it. I can still see it my mind's eye. And over the years, most people I've talked to wish they had seen it. That's the bottom line.

Doris: Yes, about the same thing. I don't really talk about it unless I'm with Deb or Jackie, who I haven't seen in a while, because I kind of feel like it's taboo. And also, I don't remember as much detail as Debbi does. I don't want to elaborate on it. I just remember it being really awesome and bright and light, you know, almost transformative somehow.

Doris, Jackie, and Debra.

I asked if overall, this had been a positive experience, and all three women said that it was. Debra then showed us a sketch her son, Coulter Young, had drawn from her description, along with an entire folder of newspaper clippings from the time. One the clippings had an amazing photo taken by then 17-year-old Jeffrey Salmonese, which clearly shows a very bright triangle of lights, with a single beam of light shining down to the ground.

After some more discussion, I thanked the three teachers and said that they added a lot of credibility to this sighting. They had never been interviewed before, and they clearly had no agenda, other than to finally share what they had seen 29 years earlier.

Interviewing the three teachers as Sarah films.

The following are some of the 1983 articles Debra Carbone has collected:

The Evening Star

Serving Peekskill, Cortlandt, Yorktown, Putnam Valley, Mahopac and Philipstown

VOL. LXI - 84   PEEKSKILL, N.Y., FRIDAY, MARCH 25, 1983   USPS 181 - 320   25¢ a copy

Weather
Clear and cold
Details on Page 1

Look! Up in the sky...

By ROSE SPADARO
Staff Reporter

What many area residents saw in the skies last night may well have been UFOs, but, as one report says, it might also have been a flight of five propeller-driven aircraft flying in military-type formation.

Yorktown, Putnam Valley, and Carmel police were deluged with phone calls last night from area residents contending they saw strange lights in the sky. The calls came in to the departments between 8:30 and 9 p.m.

Yorktown police reported many people traveling in the vicinity of the Taconic Parkway stopped their cars in the middle of the road blocking traffic as they gazed skyward with unbelieving eyes.

One report Yorktown police had was from a witness who told them the suspicious sight was not suspicious at all, but that they were five propeller-driven airplanes flying in formation.

Yorktown police, attempting to confirm this report, called the Westchester County airport and as of this morning it is not unclear as to who, what or why the formation was flying over Yorktown, according to Sgt. Anthony Mari.

A spokesman for the Air National Guard Tactical Air Support Group at the Westchester County Airport, said the planes could not have possibly been there as the unit has night drills on Wednesdays.

Lt. Col. John Fenimore indicated their night flights are three planes at a time and they do not fly in formation and never in military exercises.

"What we are basically is flying air traffic controllers," said Fenimore. He says the unit does fly in formation only during daylight hours, never over populated areas, but over Long Island sound or other large bodies of water.

"It is not for safety, but to minimize noise," he said. The planes they do fly out of Westchester were described as small Sky Master jet aircraft.

A spokesman for the Federal Aviation Administration station out of Westchester County Airport, said that it may never be known what these planes might have been doing flying over Northern Westchester and Putnam Counties last night.

He said that 90 percent of the people flying cars not required to use lights, plans likely the were flying instrument.

"The show before, to the Westchester police. Do you like a plan when you get into your car?" he asked.

A clash with attitude as long-get Airport, outside to heads to go individuals they did not have five planes take off or land at the time in question.

This was confirmed by Robert Weeks, the supervisor in operations at 8 on air.

What was that brightly colored object reported in area skies Thursday?

A UFO?   Drawing by Antonio Leavitt

By SETH BENGELSDORF
and STEVE FRAIOLI

IN THE SKY — "I would never have believed in a million years that I would say to someone that I saw a UFO," said a New Castle resident who is now a believer.

Something unexplainable in the spring sky was viewed as far north as Yorktown and as far south as White Plains shortly before 9 p.m. Thursday. Police in Yorktown and New Castle, as well as residents in Mount Kisco and Chappaqua, reported seeing it — unexplainable lights in the cosmos. Observers said the arrowhead or V-shaped array containing "green and white lights" made no noise and "hovered. . .It moved very slowly." The woman, who claimed three planes joined her while watching the object outside

Horace Greeley High School, said the sighting lasted about five minutes.

Alternating colors between white and green, it moved from the south, halfway across the sky, returned to its original position, then moved completely across the sky, zigzagging toward the north, she said. "We looked back and it was gone."

Mount Kisco Sgt. Robert Cercena said one call to the desk stated that the unidentified flying object appeared "like a whitish owl" and was "heading toward the police station."

John Tower, supervisor for the Westchester County Airport, said calls began coming in at about 9 p.m. "I really don't know what it is, but I believe there is a logical explanation," he said. Tower offered two theories.

He suggested that it could have been several aircraft flying in formation. That, he said, is what the

(Please turn to Page 3)

Theories abound for lights in sky

By E.B. Walzer
Staff writer

In the week since hundreds of people reported seeing strange lights in the night sky over Westchester and Putnam, officials investigating the sightings have come up with a number of theories, but no firm explanation for the phenomena.

It has been speculated that the lights — invariably described as being in a V-shape — were from planes flying slowly and close together or from a dirigible, or

that they were caused by atmospheric disturbances. But so far, none of the theories has been confirmed.

"We've come up with nothing at all," said Robert Fulton, a spokesman for the Federal Aviation Administration. "We learned that some Air Force aircraft went through there the following morning, but for the time frame in question there is no rational or reasonable explanation."

Fulton said checks with the military and the FAA's long-range radar center showed no aircraft were in the Putnam-

northern Westchester vicinity at the time of the sightings. He could only speculate that the lights, which stopped many motorists in their tracks and resulted in a flood of calls to police, were the result of "occlusions," in which different layers of the atmosphere interact violently and cause disturbances.

The sightings — on the nights of March

Please see LIGHTS
on page A17

27

Jeffrey Salmonese: Mahopac, March 24, 1983

Gannett Westchester Newspapers
Sunday, April 3, 1983

Section A

UFO SIGHTING — Jeffrey Salmonese, a 17-year-old Mahopac High senior, said he took a picture (left) of what he described as a large V-shaped set of lights in the sky over Mahopac at 8:45 p.m. on March 24. The Mahopac High photography club president said he took the picture from the front lawn of his Butterfly Lane, Putnam Valley, home. Salmonese said the object — which looked like a humongous boomerang with lights, gave off no engine sound, but emitted a humming noise — was moving south (left to right in the photograph) and had red lights that changed to green and white by the time he snapped this picture. Hundreds of people reported that night seeing the lights in the sky over northern Westchester and Putnam.

This article was in Debra Carbone's collection, and describes high school student Jeffrey Salmonese's sighting of the craft he saw on the same night of March 24, 1983. I was struck by his remarkable photo of the object which is triangular in shape, and is beaming a light straight down.

I tracked down Mr. Salmonese and gave him a call. He was naturally surprised to hear that someone was interested in his photo from almost 30 years ago. I told him how impressed I was by the image, and asked if he still had it, as I considered it one of the most important Hudson Valley UFO photos. He said he would go through his attic and see if he could find it.

However, he couldn't understand my interest, because at the time he had been told it was nothing more than a group of ultralights flying in formation!

The next time I called, he said he had found the original photo, but his kids must have moved it, so he didn't know where it was. I waited, and waited, and finally wrote a letter in hopes that he would realize the importance of his photographic evidence. I never heard back, and I can only hope the photo and the negative are safe and sound, so that someday photographic experts can examine it.

A close-up of Jeffrey Salmonese's photo. Note the beam of light which appears to be coming from the center of the craft and is illuminating the ground beneath.

Carla Taibi and Bill Pollard: Kent, mid-1980s

Carla lived on top of a mountain on Farmers Mills Road in Kent. There were two houses on their 48 acres of property, and she said they were so high up and far from the road that they "heard more planes than cars."

Carla lived with her boyfriend and a roommate in one house, and a mechanic, Bill, lived in the other house. During the early to mid-1980s, from her excellent vantage point on the mountain, she saw the planes flying in a V-formation (supposedly from Stormville Airport) that were pretending to be UFOs. However, "they didn't fool anyone. Their engines were really loud and they bounced all over the place."

These planes were nothing like the silent triangles she saw on several occasions. Carla admits these sightings "were kind of scary because they were so low and completely silent." These triangles had white lights, "were big, but not huge," and were seen by thousands of people in the area over the span of several years.

Then one night Carla's roommate shouted for them to come upstairs. They ran to his second-story bedroom and saw an amazing sight. On the top of the mountain across the road "there were red, green, and white rotating lights." They called their neighbor, Bill, who quickly joined them. They "watched for quite a while—at least a half an hour, maybe even an hour. We were all excited, and scared." Then the lights just went out.

"We couldn't wait for daylight to hike to the top of that mountain. There weren't any houses up there, and there weren't any roads. When we got to the top, we found all the grass and vegetation had been tamped down and flattened, and there were broken trees and branches"—as if something large had landed there.

Carla can't say whether or not this craft had been one of the triangles, as they only saw the lights. She also doesn't know how long it had been sitting on the mountain; she can only attest to the hour or so that the four of them watched the rotating lights. The only other thing she was able to add to the story may or may not be related—there were many of those mysterious stone chambers in the area where they lived, and many sightings had occurred. (See Chapter 14)

I asked if she was still in contact with any of the other three people from that night, and she replied that she wasn't, and didn't know where to find them. However, later that night, she recalled the last name of her neighbor, Bill Pollard, and had tracked down his business number. The next day I called him at work, and here's how I began the awkward cold call:

"This is probably a blast from the past, but I got your name from Carla, from the Farmers Mills Road house in the 1980s," I said, having no idea what to expect.

There was a pause, and then Bill said, "Wow, that is a blast from the past!"

So far, so good. Now for the bombshell.

"I'm writing a book about UFOs in the Hudson Valley, and Carla told me about the sighting you all had, and I was wondering if you would share your side of the story?"

There was another pause, and then Bill started to laugh, which put me at ease. It was clear he was willing to talk, but I had to give him a moment after hitting him with an almost 30-year-old blindside. However, he was to return the favor with a blindside of his own—he happens to be something of an expert on the stone chambers, and had studied them for decades! That information is in Chapter 14, but his UFO stories follow.

Bill's father had been an airline pilot, and he also learned to fly, so he was quite familiar with planes and their flight characteristics. So when he was driving on Route 84 toward Danbury one night, and saw a field brilliantly lit from red and green lights on a large aircraft very low in the sky, he thought at first glance that "it was an airliner about to crash in the field." However, instead of the craft impacting with the ground, it "suddenly rose straight up and starting tumbling through the sky."

I asked for some clarification, and Bill explained that it was a large, black triangle "with lights in the corners that all changed colors simultaneously. It tumbled slowly, end over end, unlike any conventional aircraft I ever saw. It headed toward Connecticut and I lost sight of it. Later, it returned, heading west and following the path of Route 84." He has no explanation as to how this triangle was able to fly with such a bizarre motion.

On another night, he was driving west on Route 84 and had pulled over at the rest stop near Fishkill. As he was exiting the restroom, he heard people shouting, "Look, there's the triangle again!" To be honest, so many people had previously seen them, "it was getting old" and Bill first thought, "What's the big deal?" Then he looked and saw that it *was* actually a group of ultralights.

"What the hell…" he wondered as he looked up, realizing that "they were trying to duplicate the triangle, but couldn't't."

The ultralights were noisy, couldn't stay in formation, and when they tried to change the colors of their lights, they switched at different times. In other words, they made a pretty pathetic UFO lookalike, although they did manage to fool some people at first glance.

When Bill heard that this wasn't the first time the ultralights had flown at night, he "started to pay attention" and found that they "flew every Tuesday and Thursday night for months." At first he just "thought they were a bunch of wacky pilots having some fun," but then he began to suspect that this went far beyond a mere joke. Flying ultralights at night in formation was something "that was so dangerous and stupid," not to mention illegal, that he couldn't imagine the flyers were taking so many risks on so many occasions, just for a laugh. He believed "that something big was behind it, some concerted effort," possibly "to hide secret government aircraft." I mentioned that there was a story circulating that the CIA had paid the flyers, and he replied "that it was the first explanation that made any sense."

When the local paper announced one day that the "Mystery Was Solved," as the giant, silent, solid triangles everyone was seeing were actually just these noisy and erratic ultralights, Bill was very annoyed. The idea was obviously so wrong on so many levels, but the misinformation campaign was good enough that some people still believe it to this day.

As for the sighting he had with Carla that night at her house, Bill confirmed that although the mountain was heavily wooded and they couldn't see the shape of the craft, there were red, green, and white lights, similar to those he had seen on the tumbling triangle. He also recalled that the lights all turned the same color simultaneously, and then just went out. He was not with the others on the hike the next morning, so he couldn't speak to the flattened vegetation and broken trees.

Bill also shared some secondhand stories. One night two friends were driving on the Sprain Brook Parkway and dozens of cars had pulled over near a bridge. They also stopped and got out, and witnessed a UFO hovering, beaming down a bright blue light into the water.

Another story involved his cousin. One night in the 1960s, she was driving on Drury Lane, by what was then Stewart Air Force Base. A triangular-shaped craft flew over her car, and as it passed overhead the radio turned to all static, and her car stalled. After the craft had passed, the car started up again and her radio station came back on. Not only is this a "classic" car stalling/radio interference story, but it's the earliest account I've heard of a triangle UFO! And I doubt that its proximity to Stewart AFB is a coincidence.

Even with all his personal experiences and the stories he has heard, Bill still maintains that these sightings are of our own secret military craft. He again cited the dangerous and prolonged attempts to fake the triangular

UFOs as evidence of a cover-up. While I fully agree with the idea of a cover-up, I can't say whether or not the government is trying to conceal their own secrets, or secrets of cosmic proportions…

Mike Hartnett: Mahopac, mid-1980s

Mike Hartnett is a keen observer and "always searching for facts"— skills he utilized in the military when he served in Southeast Asia. He also got his degree in chemistry, and as a Deputy Chief for the New York Fire Department (now retired), the combination of his education and skills also served him well, as "fighting fires is half science and half art." In the military and the fire department, paying attention to details is what keeps you alive, so when someone like Mike has a sighting of something he can't explain, I sit up at take special notice.

It was the mid-1980s and Mike was driving home from work one night. He was on the Taconic State Parkway, near the old Hawthorne Circle (where the Taconic meets the Saw Mill River Parkway and NY 100) when he saw a triangular-shaped craft with white lights around its perimeter, moving from the southwest to northeast. It was "huge, and had white lights that were not blinking." On another night, he was driving home and was farther up the Taconic when he saw the triangle again, observing that it was taking the same southwest to northeast path. As both times he was driving, he was unable to get a long look at it, but as they say, the third time is the charm.

He was at his home in Mahopac, which is on top of a hill in a "very quiet location." The phone rang and it was his neighbor. She excitedly said, "They're coming!" Mike and his wife ran out onto their deck, and the neighbor joined them. There was the triangle again, moving directly over his neighbor's house toward his.

"It was moving slowly, so slowly. It was astounding how slowly it was moving," Mike said. "And it was silent. I strained to hear something, anything, and even went to different places in the yard to see if I could hear any sound. I grabbed a tape recorder and put it on the deck, and when I listened to it later there was complete silence."

33

The craft was at an elevation of roughly 400-500 feet. Mike tried to judge the size of it when it was directly over his house, by comparing it with his property, and concluded "it was at least a football field in length." And he couldn't be certain, but the massive craft appeared to slow down even more when it was overhead, as if it was almost stationary for three or four minutes.

"And here's the really strange part," Mike said, as I laughed and realized that for many residents of that area during the 1980s, these triangles were almost "normal."

Mike had a 2 million candlepower spotlight which he shined directly on the craft, but even with the bright light he was unable to see any structure. Then his curiosity compelled him to try a little experiment. He flicked the light on and off several times. In response, all of the white lights on the craft dimmed for about five to seven seconds before returning to full brightness! I guess you don't spend your career as one of New York's Bravest by being timid!

Mike also observed that as bright as the lights were on the craft, "they never propagated to the ground." In other words, for some reason the lights did not illuminate anything beneath them. The triangle ever so slowly and silently moved off—again in that southwest to northeast direction—and finally went out of view. The entire sighting lasted at least ten minutes.

While that was the last time he saw anything in the sky, after that night strange lights began appearing in the woods behind his house. There were no buildings back there, so he couldn't account for the "greenish-white glow" through the trees. From his time in Southeast Asia, he had learned to move quietly through the woods, and he attempted to get close to the source of the light. However, as careful and silent as he as was, as soon as he got close, the light went out. He went back to the area in daylight, but was unable to find anything unusual, or any sign that something had been there.

This glowing light continued every night for about a month, and several times Mike tried to sneak through the woods toward it, but each time the light went out before he could see what it was. Finally, the glowing light stopped appearing altogether, and he had no further sightings, although he heard many other stories from people in the area.

"I'm a factual person," he reiterated. "These objects obviously wanted to be seen. They were seen throughout the area for years, and then it all stopped suddenly.

"What I saw can only be classified as a UFO. And by that I mean it was flying, it was an object, not my imagination, and it was unidentified. So it was a UFO." Beyond that, he really can't say what it was with absolute certainty, although his three sightings have made him a believer.

The facts are there. How you interpret them is up to you.

Darlene Donofrio: Saugerties, 1985

From: darlene donofrio
Sent: Sunday, October 07, 2012 10:38 AM
To: lindazim@optonline.net
Subject: ufo

Hello Linda,
My friends and me saw something in the sky on route 32 in Saugerties. The year was 1985. I wrote my mom a letter the next day about the experience. My mom passed away in 1992 and I got her box of letters and cards that she saved. In that box was my letter. I would be happy to scan and email it to you or if you would rather I can photocopy and mail.

We were driving south on 32 from Palenville. I did give exact locations and even made drawings. I was 20 years old at the time.

Hope the research is going well.
Darlene Donofrio
Saugerties, NY

I requested that she send me scanned images of the letter, the excerpts of which follow. I think this is a fantastic example, as it captures the excitement of a sighting that had just occurred the night before. Darlene also thought to include two sketches while the images were fresh in her mind. Critics often claim that people don't remember sightings clearly after so many years, and embellish details, but thanks to Darlene's letter, we have a record written within hours of the event.

Dear Mom,   Oct 30, 1985

[Darlene begins by explaining why she decided to write the letter.]

I was driving to Saugerties to pick up Jennifer (I don't know if you remember or not, but we've been friends since H.S.). Anyway, I had 2 passengers—Melissa & her sister Kristy. Anyway, we were just a few feet past Red's junk yard when I saw this huge BRIGHT light in the sky. Conversation goes as follows—

Me—What the hell is that?
Melissa—It's the Christmas star.
Me—Chuckle, chuckle. It's not a star, Mis. It's too big. Next to it is a star. Maybe it's a planet—Venus or something.

I was driving and by this time we were still watching this planet while driving and now we're by HOJO's and—

Me—Oh my God, it's moving.
Kristy—No, it's you who's moving.
Melissa—They're both moving.
Me—No. Where's another one?
Melissa—Right there.

I then pulled over and what was moving was this big ball of white fire. (There was only one, Melissa thought the star was moving.) Here's the difference in the sizes.

a difference in t
Star ↗   ↖ UFO
Anyway this thi

36

Anyway, this thing started moving up and down. Then it shot across the sky. Mom, it went so fast and it got so small until it was the size of the star. I got a great view. (I had my shades on.)

The triangle was underneath. The circle was the glow. The two dots were these lights it had. I thought it had more lights but it was just a glimpse so I can't draw them.

[Darlene and her friends discuss whether it could possibly be a plane or a helicopter. At this point a plane goes by, but Darlene can easily tell the difference.]

..[the object] went much faster, real fast, Ma. I can't ever explain it as it was that moment. But I was as accurate as I could be. It happened within minutes, but I tried to describe it fully. It seemed to last forever, but in actuality it didn't.

So we concluded it was a UFO.

Pretty exciting, huh? I wish I had a 35mm so I could have taken a picture.

Well, that's my story. I hope it excited you.

I love you and miss you.

Love,
Dar
XXOO

Sorry it's so sloppy but my brain was moving faster than my hand.

Maureen Davis: Yorktown Heights, November 1985

On June 16th, I received the following email from Maureen Davis, who is a reference librarian in Putnam County, NY. Her account really caught my eye because she actually *saw inside* the craft!

Dear Linda,

I have read your article about witnesses to the UFO sightings in the Northern Westchester area, and I'm writing to tell you that I was one of those individuals. I never did report it, because I was too afraid that the police would think that I was a crazy pregnant woman. (At the time I was expecting our first child.)

It was an Autumn evening, the exact date escapes me -- but I believe it was in November. I was parked at the corner of Route 132 and Oakside Road in Yorktown Heights -- waiting for my husband to get off of the bus. Something strange in the sky to the northeast caught my eye. It was an enormous Isosceles triangle-shaped "thing." It was interesting to me because I could not hear that it was making any sound -- nor was it moving. It was just hovering. I have been familiar with this area since I was a child, as my family had a summer home in Lake Baldwin -- and to me the craft looked like it was hovering over the area of Lake Osceola. I continued to watch in amazement as the bottom of the craft opened. It was a circular opening -- and I could see many levels of lights inside of it. After about three minutes, a pulsating red light flew up behind it and flew up into the opening. This "hatch" then disappeared -- although I didn't see anything like a door shut or slide closed -- it was just there one second and gone the next. Then this LARGE triangle whooshed out of sight. It just sped away so fast that it left me doubting whether I had really seen anything at all -- but yet I know what I saw. To his credit -- my husband did not pooh-pooh my story and think that my pregnancy was affecting my brain.

Since that night, I have seen some flashing twinkling lights that seem to dance around the sky then zoom out of sight, but nothing on the scale of this sighting.

I should add that I am a wife and mother of three with a bachelor's of arts in history and a masters of library science degree. I have been a librarian at my town's public library for the past 25 years. I have told my story to some family and friends, but I have never mentioned it outside of that circle.

I emailed a few questions back to Maureen, and she responded with this:

I would be happy to tell my story -- I don't mind going public with it -- I saw what I saw! It was November of 1985. And it is difficult to estimate the size of the ship because of the altitude and distance, but the closest I could guess would be like a football or baseball stadium -- really big. But very quiet.

Maureen Davis

What's not to love about this story? A highly credible, educated, librarian and mother, who has never spoken publicly in these past 27 years? And this craft was not the size of football field, but a *football stadium*! I knew we had to interview Maureen in person, and that interview took place on a baseball field in Yorktown Heights on August 8th.

This was a very busy day, as we had interviewed Scott and Art DiLalla down in Congers earlier that day. As it was another brutally hot and sunny day, I had driven home to shower and change, and grab a bit to eat, before hitting the road again for Maureen's interview.

When I arrived, Sarah and Felix were already there, and despite being tired, Felix had a certain sparkle in his eyes, something of a "cat with the canary" look. But it wasn't a canary he had just gotten between film shoots, it was something much better—a flying drone with HD cameras for aerial filming! Had the drone come with charged batteries, I guarantee it would have been in the air for this interview, but unfortunately it would have to be a strictly terrestrial interview—with a possibly extraterrestrial subject.

Maureen, Felix, and Travis Hastings.

The following are some of the highlights and additional details Maureen provided that day.

The object Maureen saw that night was "darker than the night sky, dark black. It was enormous and shaped like a triangle. It had lights across the back. Some lights underneath, like at the points of the triangle. And it was just hovering."

She "opened up the window to see if it was making any noise. I could not hear a sound."

And how did this sight make her feel?

"I just sat there mesmerized. I wasn't frightened."

Maureen watched this enormous, silent, motionless craft for several minutes, then something even more extraordinary happened."

"A small ball of light came from behind it. It flittered in. In was like a red, blinking orb of light and it came underneath the triangle. All of a sudden, a hole appeared in the triangle. It was flat, there was nothing there, and then all of a sudden there was this opening in the vehicle.

"I could see into it. It was lit, like it had strata of light that went up into it. I couldn't really see past that opening, like I couldn't see into the corners, but I did see, like different—it almost looked like the outside of an apartment house with the terraces, and everything was lit all the way up.

"The little red orb went right up into it, there was no hole. I didn't see anything slide, it was just there, and then it wasn't there. And then the vehicle was gone. It was there, and it was so fast that I blinked and I looked, and I said 'Was that really there? Did I see what I just saw? Yes, I did see what I just saw!' But why did I see it?

"It was fascinating more than frightening."

I asked what direction the craft went when it moved away, and she replied that it had gone north. "And it was gone just like that," Maureen said, snapping her fingers. "In a blink."

I then asked if that had been the only incident she had, and she said there were others.

"A couple of years later, my husband and I were looking out our bedroom window. We saw—I saw it first—what looked like a cigar-shaped blinking light. Very, very high in the sky. It was just blinking and flitting around, and I thought it was a star, but it was moving too fast for it to be a star. It wasn't stationary at all.

"So I woke my husband up, of course, and I decided to tell him to look out that window and tell me I'm not seeing things. He looked out the window and he said, 'That's not a star, that's something moving very, very quickly.' And it flitted around, and just as dawn broke, it was gone. It just shot out of the sky, but straight up.

41

"And then a few years later, I was sitting on my front stoop with my son. He was 6 at the time, he is now 19, my middle son. And we were looking at the sky and noticed there were these two little stars that looked like they were dancing with each other. And they would actually orbit each other, and then twinkle over here, and then move to another section of the sky, twinkle a little bit, and then revolve around one another, and I said, 'Do you see that?' And he said, 'Yes I do. What is that?' And I didn't want to tell him what I thought it was at the time, because I didn't want him to be frightened. I said, 'I think that's something a little strange. Let's watch it.' We watched it for about 15 minutes, then again, it zoomed back off into the sky, just straight up."

I asked if she had ever been afraid during any of these sightings, and she replied, "Never. Just kind of fascinated by it all and kind of intrigued."

"How has this affected your life?" I asked. "Or has it?"

"It just kind of makes us know that there's something else," she replied. "We can't be the only life forms in the universe. There has to be something else, somewhere else, that's as curious about us as we are about them."

I asked how her family and friends reacted to her sightings, and she said that because she is "very grounded, when I tell people I've seen things they believe me."

I then asked what she would tell people who have had sightings and might be hesitant to speak about it, and she offered some excellent advice.

"If you are hesitant to speak about it, don't do what I did. Go home, write down the date, write down the time, write down the place. Even if you don't want to share it right away, you never know when somebody will say to you, 'Did you see this in the sky that night?' They may be as reluctant to tell you what they have seen, as you are reluctant to tell somebody else.

"So if you're reluctant, it's okay to keep it to yourself, but write everything down so you have a journal, and you can go back at a given time and say, 'Yes, this is when I saw it. You were right, I saw it in that same place, too.' This way you can share, and I think sharing the knowledge is a very, very important thing."

Finally, I asked if there was anything else she wanted to share with us, and she replied, "I wish I could see it again."

Sherry: Poughkeepsie, March, 1983 & Hyde Park c. 1987

The following story about Sherry from Poughkeepsie caught my attention in particular, because of how her sightings provoked a fear that has lasted thirty years. Here is her initial email, and after I asked some questions and received a follow-up message, we spoke on the phone on June 28, 2012, and met on August 13, and the contents of those conversations are summarized below.

From: Sherry
Sent: Monday, June 25, 2012 12:32 PM
To: lindazim@optonline.net
Subject: UFOs

Read the Pok. Journal article on your UFO investigations/stories. I also was a witness to the sighting in March '83. Was with my mother and it was approx. 10pm at night. Another time was in late 1987 or mid '88. If you'd like to hear my story let me know. I am so glad others have come forward. I have told my story to many people over the last 30 yrs., and they all have thought I was crazy....seriously crazy. My 1st sighting initiated an "in awe" kind of feeling. I was young. 2nd time around a fear rose up that had me fleeing in tears. It still impacts me today, esp. if I must drive at night. It's always in "the back of my mind." Can't wait to read the book!

In the 1970s when Sherry was about 14 or 15-years-old, her father awakened and said she had to come outside because there was a UFO. In her groggy state, she mumbled that she wasn't interested and went back to sleep. Today, she wishes she had gotten up to see what it was.

Then in the early 1980s, her sister came home late one night "as white as a ghost and trembling like a leaf." She had just dropped off her boyfriend at his house, and on the way home she really had to go to the bathroom so she pulled her car over in a secluded spot. Just as she started to go, a super bright light shined down on her from above. Jumping in the

43

car, she sped off, but the bright light followed her. By the time she got back to her house, she was absolutely terrified and kept saying, "A UFO chased me home!" Sherry didn't believe a word her of her sister's story, and told her so.

It's remarkable how quickly skeptics become believers—often in the blink of an astonished eye or the span of a single rapid heartbeat. That moment came for Sherry in March of 1983, when she was 24 years old.

Sherry had just worked out at Allsport in Fishkill, and her mother was driving her home. It was about 10pm as they pulled into their development. Sherry remembers what happened next "like it was yesterday" as the events is still "so vivid" in her mind.

"My mother suddenly asked, 'What's that!?' There, just above the trees in front of them were two *huge*, intense lights. My mom yelled, 'What do I do?' When I realized there was absolutely no sound coming from this thing I yelled, 'Take off!'"

The object was so close she couldn't make out the shape, (although her mother believes it was circular) only that it was made of dark, gray metal and had those two, intense lights. Her mother hit the gas pedal, and had to actually pass directly beneath the craft to get to their house on the other side. Sherry could see neighbors standing out on their lawns. One man had fallen off his motorcycle. As she passed one group of neighbors she shouted out the window, "We're being invaded!"

The massive craft slowly moved over their backyard to the large Central Hudson electrical line tower and stopped so close above them that it looked like it was sitting on the tower. As soon as her mother parked the car, she ran screaming into the house and started closing all the drapes and curtains. While her mother was clearly terrified, Sherry was just "in awe" and was so intent on staring at the object that she "fell over the garden hose."

When she entered the house she told her mother, "I'm going out on the back porch because I want to meet them."

Crying hysterically, Sherry's mother grabbed her by the shoulders. She shook her for about 30 seconds, screaming at her to not go outside. Her mother was repeatedly yelling that, "You don't know what they will do to you!"

Finally, her mother's message sank in. They were NOT human! At that moment, she began trembling and was "petrified" by the object. They

The massive UFO hovered over these power lines in Sherry's backyard.

closed all the curtains and then stayed away from the windows. Sherry then decided to call the State Police and told them a massive craft was on the power lines tower. The officer replied, "Are you drunk?" and then hung up. Twenty minutes later the craft was gone.

When Sherry went to work, she told everyone what she and her mother had witnessed. "Everyone said I was crazy," she told me. "People really thought I was insane." Years later, even her fiancé doubted her story, until her mother confirmed everything Sherry had told him. And it's a good thing he believed her, because the last thing a prospective son-in-law should do is call his future mother-in-law a crazy liar!

About three months after this sighting, the *Enquirer* newspaper ran an article about the UFOs that had been seen in Putnam and Dutchess Counties. Sherry brought the article to work and stated, "See, I'm not crazy!"

(Author's note: I asked if she could speak to the neighbors to whom she had shouted that they were being invaded, but she said within a couple of months after the sighting they moved away! Also, the computer in her mother's new car suddenly malfunctioned after the sighting and the dealer said it "was fried" and must have "been a lemon" and they replaced the car.)

The second sighting occurred in 1987 or '88 on Fallkill Road in Hyde Park. Her boyfriend was driving and they came upon a section of the road where at least 20 cars had pulled over. Everyone was looking at a brightly lit craft over some sort of government installation that supposedly has radar or communications devices.

Since her last experience, Sherry had been reading up on UFOs and close encounters. She had read somewhere that aliens communicate telepathically, and she suddenly became very fearful that they "had singled" her out and were trying to communicate with her.

"I yelled at my boyfriend to take off, and in my mind I kept repeating, I don't want to meet you! I don't want to meet you!" A short time later, they saw many jet fighters chasing this object, so she knows "the Air Force must have a record of it."

She tried to report the sighting to Stewart Airport, but only got a recording. She called the local police, and once again they asked if she was drunk and hung up.

Isn't it comforting to know that members of our law enforcement are on top of the situation? After all, who cares if strange craft are hovering over power lines and government installations!?

The result of these two traumatic sightings is that even 30 years later, Sherry "still freaks out" when she sees a light in the sky. Her husband and children constantly kid about her reactions to lights in the sky, and tell her that what she is seeing is only a plane or a bright star. However, her family's reassurances don't help.

"Even when I take out a bag of garbage at night I always look up at the sky first. Wherever I go out at night, I'm always looking up. I'm still scared."

Felix directs the drone to get some aerial footage on the street where Sherry and her mother had their sighting in 1983.

Chris Griggs, Sleightsburg, c. 1984-87

Here's another response generated by the *Daily Freeman* article. What I found particularly interesting with this account is the "IBM Excuse." Hadn't heard that before!

This was also the case of another strange coincidence: After reading Chris' first email, I looked to see where Sleightsburg is, and Google indicated it's where the Rondout Creek meets the Hudson River. Not ten minutes earlier I had just finished writing the story of the person on the boat seeing a circle of lights under the water in the Hudson, right where it meets the Rondout.

From: chris
Sent: Friday, October 12, 2012 3:30 PM
To: lindazim@optonline.net
Subject: sighting

Not a biggie....but approximately 25-28 years ago, my son and I spotted a large triangular shaped object hovering above us in the Sleightsburg, NY area. It had lights on each end, rotated around once very slowly continued to move slowly and then shot off like a bat out of hell towards the Kingston, Whittier area...which does coincidentally cover the south RT 32 area of Saugerties.

The Kingston Daily Freeman did cover the sighting in the paper the next day and stated, if I recall, that IBM was testing something.

It was huge and so low in the sky I swore I could reach up and touch it. To this day, I know it was not an IBM test of any kind.

Anyway - nothing big, just another unexplained occurrence when it comes to sightings.

Chris' second email:

When my son and I looked up at the item, I swear it seemed to cover almost my entire view of the sky. I know it was not that huge, but I would say at least a football field. I am also pretty sure that IBM testing was the excuse for what was seen. I know my son was ridiculed by his teacher, but

I believe she did apologize when the article came out in the paper. There was never any other follow up, nor did I ever see it again.

It's unfortunate that Chris' son was ridiculed by his teacher—certainly something a child will never forget—but at least she had the decency to apologize. I can't help but wonder how many other witnesses remain silent for that same reason.

William Gallaher: Peekskill and Buchanan, Late 1980s

From: William Gallaher
Sent: Wednesday, June 13, 2012 5:19 PM
To: lindazim@optonline.net
Subject: UFO

My daughter asked me to email you in reference to a UFO sighting in Peekskill, NY in the late 1980s. I have witnessed something out of the ordinary on 3 different occasions. The first was what appeared to be something very huge. It traveled from the southwest over my house (or I should say neighborhood), toward the northeast. At first you would have to think it was some kind of lite aircraft spaced far enough apart to give the impression of one large ship. If it was lite aircraft, they did not deviate from their course and they were silent. 5 other people witnessed this. We got into 3 cars and tried to chase this thing. I went east to the top of Frost Lane, thinking that higher ground would give me the best chance to see this thing, I went the wrong way and did not see it again. My cousin and brothers followed it to Putnam Valley until they got scared and turned back (probably because of the remoteness).

The 2nd time I saw something unusual was from Tompkins Park, in Peekskill. I had a 4 inch telescope set up on the baseball field to look at the planets. Looking west over the Hudson River I noticed 5 or 6 lites in the shape of a boomerang. I was able to get my scope on them and they were separate aircraft.

The 3rd time was at Lents Cove softball field in Buchanan, right next to Indian Point power plant. We had just lost the town of Cortlandt softball

49

championship game. It was a nite game and as I was leaving the field, I happened to look up and there was that boomerang. This time it looked like accounts I have seen on t.v.

Being disappointed at losing the game I didn't say anything and as far as I know the other 100 people that were there didn't even see it. It was very bright lites, seen right through the glare of the field lites.

From: Linda Zimmermann
To: William Gallaher
Sent: Thursday, June 14, 2012 6:57 AM
Subject: RE: UFO

Thank you very much for these accounts. So just to be clear, you believe you saw those planes flying in formation to fake a UFO, and something very different that was silent and solid?
Would it be alright to use this material in the book, keeping your identity anonymous if you choose, using just Bill or Bill G?

From: William Gallaher
Sent: Friday, June 15, 2012 10:03 AM
To: Linda Zimmermann
Subject: Re: UFO

It's ok to use my name. The 1st account seemed to be solid over a great expanse of sky (the size of a small neighborhood). I remember asking my brothers if they saw any stars in between the lites, no one did. The 2nd account was definitely 5 or 6 planes (seen through my telescope from a couple of miles away). The 3rd account was directly overhead from the softball field. I guess because of what I saw in the 2nd account, I didn't pay much attention, but there was no way to tell that they were planes with the naked eye. I have seen re-creations of this on Unsolved Mysteries (seen by members of the Yorktown police department).

To: William Gallaher

From: Linda Zimmermann
Sent: Friday, June 15, 2012 10:19 AM
Subject: RE: UFO

Thanks for the clarification. It's important because some officials tried to explain away every sighting as airplanes in formation. You appear to have seen both the planes and the object and could easily distinguish between the two. Would you be interested in being filmed recounting your observations?

———

Unfortunately, it didn't work out with scheduling to meet and film Mr. Gallaher, but I did go to the baseball field in Buchanan to look around. It is indeed very close to the Indian Point nuclear facility—just a couple of thousand feet away on the other side of a patch of woods. (In fact, I couldn't help but think if something went wrong with a reactor, I would be a carbon smudge on the ground.)

Indian Point has been the scene of numerous UFO sightings, but without a specific date, I can't say if these sightings are related to any others in the area. Of course, the similarities are there—massive, silent craft.

The view of Indian Point from the west bank of the Hudson River.

This account is very important, as it is an example of how hoaxers muddied the waters with their stupid pranks. Here was a man who, along with five other people, saw something extraordinary. The craft was directly overhead, solid, and so huge it covered the *entire neighborhood*!

Then, during his second sighting, thanks to his telescope, he was able to identify separate planes flying in a boomerang formation a few miles away. If these pilots intended to desensitize people to V-shaped or boomerang-shaped lights in the sky, then they certainly accomplished their mission, as the third time Bill Gallaher looked up and saw something unusual, he didn't bother to pay much attention to the object. It could have been the hoaxing pilots again, or it could have been something *very* different. We will never know.

We can only hope that in the grand scheme of things, what goes around does come around, and people who commit such fraudulent acts somehow get a taste of their own medicine.

Jesse W.: Port Ewen, 1990 & 2000

Email message:

I am Jesse W. Grew up in Port Ewen, just below Kingston on Broadway by 9W. In Jan., 1990 I was 9 yrs. old.

It is strange to see a black triangle blocking out the stars. Stranger still that I only noticed it because of an ominous feeling coming over me which inexplicably made me look up into the sky without another "normal" indicator, i.e., noise, lights, to suggest something was passing overhead for me to look up.

On each point of the triangle was a white point of light. There were also lights on the sides of the craft, two to a side, at one- and two-thirds points, and a light in the center at the back of the craft; each light was the same in strength of illumination. I remember these details because in my childhood it was a hobby to look for aircraft upon hearing an engine or seeing an exhaust trail in the sky, to look for its origin, and I had never seen aircraft of this shape before or since until the age of 19.

The time was around 11:45 P.M., a Saturday, and by way of explaining why I would be up at this time of night, I was fetching wood for our wood stove as an excuse not to go to bed. I only told my mom at the time, but the experience sparked my curiosity, and has kept me looking in the night sky since.

When I was 19, I saw the UFO the 2nd and last time, oddly enough 10 years after the first sighting and around the same time at night. In the end of a rerun of X-files, no less, which had been produced in 1992.

Tami Vertullo: Rockland County, 2000

I received the following email on August 10:

I was driving home from work one night and above my car was a giant triangular shaped flying object. I opened the window thinking it was going to be really loud. Not a sound at all. It hovered above my car as I drove slowly. I looked down for a split second and it was gone. Just disappeared completely. It had blue and red lights on it and it was so big it scared me. The location was on Spook Rock Road going towards Pomona and Mount Ivy New York.

I asked the year and date, and her response was:

I believe that it had to be 2000. I really don't know the exact date but I think it was fall. The window was closed and it was chilly out but not freezing. I remember just moving to Tomkins Cove and my route home from work was different than before. At the end of Spook Rock Road where it meets 202 is where I saw this weird craft. It hovered over my car. Scared the crap out of me!

Triangle, Florida-Style, 1992

Although the focus of this book is obviously the Hudson Valley, I was intrigued by the following report of a massive triangle in the state of Florida. The similarities are striking to sightings in New York. (And I'm just waiting for officials to claim that this was also just a formation of small planes out of the Stormville Airport!)

From: Dennis
Sent: Thursday, September 20, 2012 5:52 PM
To: linda@nightskyufo.com
Subject: Post Hurricane Andrew Sighting

Ms. Zimmermann...My girlfriend told me of a huge triangle UFO her and her ex-husband experienced after hurricane Andrew hit their area. This was on the west side of Miami in 1992. She is not one to make up stories and what she told me was a shocker. She told me that the size alone was tremendous since it took up most of the sky.
Not sure you want to hear about this one or not. If so I will have her tell me about the experience again and I will provide you with as much info as I am able to obtain.

As I was very curious to hear the details, I asked Dennis to provide additional information. The following was his reply.

From: Dennis
Sent: Wednesday, October 10, 2012 10:40 PM
To: Linda Zimmermann
Subject: Re: Post Hurricane Andrew Sighting

I talked with my girlfriend tonight (10/10/12) about the triangle sighting that took place after hurricane Andrew. I decided to list the info in sections.

DATE: After Hurricane Andrew 1992....perhaps August - Sept.

LOCATION: Next to the last paved road next to the Everglades, Homestead, FL

SETTING: My girlfriend and her ex-husband were living in a RV close to their hurricane destroyed home. Most of the homes were destroyed and very few if any people were still present in the area. They had electricity but most of the area was without power so there were no other lights in the area. What first alerted both of them was a low humming sound. It also sounded like a plane in the far distance. My girlfriend was in bed and her ex was watching TV. After they found out that neither one was responsible for the sound, they went outside and looked up to the sky. They then stood in amazement at what they were viewing.

SIZE: Apparently close to the ground because it took up a good portion of the sky. When I asked her the approximate size she stated it was bigger than a football field.

SPEED: First hovering directly overhead for a while and then it moved north.

COLOR/LIGHTS: Lots of lights of all sizes...some bigger...some smaller. Some brighter and some dimmer. Some seemed to sparkle or twinkle. No pattern to the lights. She stated that some may have had color but wasn't sure on the color property.

SHAPE: Broad arrowhead shape that she thought was somewhat rounded in the front and perhaps concave in the back.

EXTRA INFO: Homestead Air Force Base was less than 10 minutes away. She stated it also was devastated from the hurricane and never reopened. [Note: It wasn't until 1994 that the base reopened as the Homestead Air Reserve Station.]

The info she provided me was pretty much the same as she stated to me the first time she told me about the sighting. She is not one to make up stories and is very level headed. Not what I would call an UFO fanatic. Not sure any of this corresponds to other sighting reports you may have collected in the Hudson Valley area of New York.

If I can be of any further help, don't hesitate to contact me.

4
The Hoaxing Pilots

Let Us Tell You What You Really Saw...

It's unfortunate that any book of this nature needs to devote any time or space debunking something so ridiculous, but it's essential to introduce some facts to the idea that witnesses didn't really see what they thought they saw.

The time-honored tradition of lying to anyone who tries to file a UFO report—telling the witness that what they saw was actually a weather balloon, swamp gas, etc.—reached an absurd apex in the 1980s, when police tried to tell callers that the massive, motionless, silent triangles they saw were just formations of ultralight planes. Indeed, there was at least one group of pilots trying to fool people, but let's try to take a rational approach to the subject of ultralights.

An Ultralight Point of View

In my quest to prove that a formation of ultralight planes flying at night could not explain the countless sightings of silent, hovering, solid craft, a friend got me in touch with someone he knew who has been flying ultralights for about 18 years. He requested anonymity, so I will just call him Mr. M.

I began our phone conversation by explaining our book and documentary project. Once he confirmed that ultralight planes *were not silent* and *could not hover*, I asked him some specifics about the aircraft, its flight characteristics, and any pertinent regulations. Mr. M was a wealth of knowledge, and he also added some very interesting stories.

An ultralight designation is given to any aircraft weighing less than 254 pounds. The top speed is a little over 50 mile per hour. The minimum air speed necessary to remain flying is about 28 mph. To be objective, a headwind of only 10 mph could make an ultralight traveling at a low speed appear to be stationary from a distance, and a strong gust could actually send the aircraft backward, which could confuse witnesses.

Ultralight aircraft at the Sha-Wan-Ga Valley Airport in Bloomingburg, NY.

On the subject of wind, Mr. M stated that an ultralight is very much "like a rowboat on the ocean that struggles against the waves." An ultralight is "at the mercy of the winds," so pilots look to fly only in calm conditions. That usually means they fly in the early morning or close to sunset, when winds are typically the calmest.

On the question of flying an ultralight at night, Mr. M confirmed that it is illegal. However, there is "a half an hour grace period after sunset" if you have a strobe light on your plane. It is simply too dangerous to fly in the dark.

Next, he covered formation flying. Again, from the perspective of someone on the ground, ultralights at a distance may appear to be close to one another, even if they are as far as ¼ to a ½ mile apart. When I asked him about the explanation officials had offered that these ultralights were flying in the dark just a few feet apart, maintaining their distance from one another even when turning so they appeared to be one solid craft, Mr. M basically said that would be almost impossible, not to mention that no one in their right mind would attempt such a foolish stunt.

Mr. M then shared a fascinating story with me. Years ago, he was flying along the ridge of the Shawangunk Mountains, when a small, bizarre aircraft went right past him. He was traveling about 40-50mph, and this 12-15 foot, metallic vehicle just whizzed by. It was unlike anything he had seen—it appeared to be much too small to have a human pilot, and at first he thought it must be a UFO.

Only later did he learn about unmanned aerial vehicles, popularly known as drones, which look just like what had flown past him. Mr. M is now certain that it was a military drone that flew past him that day. I asked where he thought drones were being launched in this area, and he replied, "That's the million dollar question."

Rumors about secret military and CIA "training facilities" in the area have abounded for years. He and other pilots believe that the government has also used the Hudson Valley to test various stealth aircraft, as they have seen a lot of "suspicious and spooky" things in the air. Mr. M actually saw a stealth aircraft at an air show that he said would have made him "swear in court" that he "saw a spaceship," had he not known what he was looking at.

This raises a crucial point—if branches of our government have been using the Hudson Valley to test drones and stealth aircraft, how many of these thousands of sightings over the decades can be attributed to these secret experimental vehicles? There is no doubt that some people can mistake what they are seeing, even in broad daylight.

Case in point: Mr. M and fellow pilots used to carry CB radios with them to communicate to one another in the air. One sunny day, he and a friend were flying when "all kinds of chatter came over the radio about UFOs." People were excitedly telling others where to look in the sky to see these alien spacecraft.

"I said to my friend, 'Hey, that's where we are,' so we started to look all around us for the UFOs. I didn't see anything, and then it dawned on me, they were talking about us! I asked my friend, 'When did we become UFOs!?'"

If people could mistake two noisy ultralights for UFOs in daylight, it is certainly possible for them to confuse what they are seeing at night.

So is it possible for several ultralight aircraft, flying under the cover of darkness and equipped with extra lights, to fool some people into thinking they were seeing alien spacecraft? At a distance, they absolutely could think that, and probably have many times. However, it is highly unlikely to be fooled by these loud aircraft if they are close, and impossible if they were directly overhead at low altitude. Additionally, some of the nights that UFO sightings were reported had winds up to 35 mph, poking even bigger holes in the tight formation of ultralights explanation.

Are the craft that people in the Hudson Valley have been witnessing secret military vehicles or alien spaceships...or both? I can't say, but I can say they were NOT all ultralights!

Being There

For many years, I have been writing and lecturing about the Civil War. One thing I learned early on is that you can spend 50 years reading about something, but it all doesn't hold a candle to 5 minutes of *experiencing* something.

For example, I had read stacks of books about the battle of Gettysburg, saw documentaries and photos, and thought I had a pretty good understanding of how the events unfolded and progressed, and what the soldiers faced—until my first visit to Gettysburg.

Until you stand along the lines where the Confederate troops began the famous and fatal Pickett's Charge, and gaze across the mile-long field they marched over, exposed to a hailstorm of shot and shell, you absolutely can never appreciate what it must have been like there on July 3, 1863. No amount of books and videos can replace actually being there, treading the same soil as the soldiers, seeing the vast expanse of open field that for so many marked their final moments of life.

Okay, so maybe this is a rather dramatic example compared to something as benign as a recreational plane, but I wanted to drive home the point with the force of the butt end of a Model 1861 Springfield musket—don't try to tell someone that what they saw had to be a formation of ultralights, and don't believe anyone trying to tell you what you saw was ultralights, if you've never even seen an ultralight!

In this spirit of experience being the best teacher, Mr. M got me in touch with Joe Acoveno, a former ultralight flight instructor with the United States Ultralight Association, and certified mechanic for these planes. Joe has been flying for 32 years and is a member of the South Mountain Ultralights group that flies out of the Sha-Wan-Ga Valley

Airport in Bloomingburg, New York. Just with ultralight planes, Joe has about 1600 hours of flight time!

Joe Acoveno was kind enough to share his expertise with us.

On Saturday, September 1, 2012, Sarah, Felix, and I, met Joe and other members of South Mountain Ultralights at the small Sha-Wan-Ga Valley Airport on a beautiful afternoon. Joe is like a walking aviation text book, and he was kind enough to share his extensive knowledge on-camera to help us better understand these aircraft and their flight characteristics.

For example, his two-seat plane used to be an ultralight trainer, but after new regulations were adopted about twenty years ago, it was reclassified as an experimental sport plane. While this seems to be just a question of semantics, the point is that when the regulations were changed for the sake of greater safety, it put a damper on the sport as it became increasingly more difficult to find an instructor and training aircraft. The height of the ultralight sport was really in the 1980s, before the new rules went into effect. Of course, this wasn't entirely a bad thing, as it prevented a lot of people with homemade planes and no experience from killing themselves.

We stood in the hangar for the interview, and—what a surprise—it was an unexpectedly hot day. (I became convinced that if we planned an interview in January it would be 92 degrees with 100% humidity.) After introducing himself, Joe explained that it was illegal to fly an ultralight at night, but also said that there was a half an hour grace period after sunset if you had a strobe light.

As for flying in formation, he said, "You can fly in formation if you have been properly trained do that. It's also a little bit of teamwork, obviously, and it requires communication with the three or four planes flying in this formation. And we've done it, but we've done it in a safe manner, planned ahead, and during daylight hours and proper weather conditions to do this."

I asked how close two planes could safely get to one another, and Joe said you wouldn't want to get much closer than 30 feet apart from wingtip to wingtip. When flying in a formation such as that, it may appear to people on the ground that the planes are much closer together.

We then discussed stall speeds, or how slow you can go "without dropping out of the air," as I put it. On a calm day, Joe explained that his plane's stall speed was about 22 mph, but each plane has different characteristics, although all basic ultralights are in the same ballpark. However, like the math problems we all knew and disliked in school, he explained that he could be flying at 22 mph into a 10 mph headwind, and from the ground the plane would appear to be creeping along at a mere 12 mph. And at higher altitudes with stronger winds, it does become conceivable that a quick glance might convince an onlooker that the vehicle is stationary.

Speaking of wind, Joe said that the maximum wind speed he would suggest flying in is 15 mph, for an experienced pilot, and much less for beginners, with 10-12 mph being a more suitable range. This confirmed that on those nights where sightings took place in 35 mph winds, sane ultralight pilots wouldn't even think of taking off.

As for the time and distance a fully fueled ultralight can travel, they are allowed to carry a maximum of 5 gallons, and under ideal circumstances will fly safely for about 1.5 hours, at an airspeed of 55 mph. That gives an overall distance of about 80 miles on a tank of gas. This is important when trying to pin down where the hoaxing fliers took off and landed, as it would have had to be within a 40-mile radius from where they were seen in Putnam County. While the number of conventional airports is limited at such a distance, remember that these are unconventional aircraft that can take off on as little as 75 feet of a field, so private property also comes into play as a "home base" for hoaxers.

We then discussed the 48-55 horsepower, two-cycle Rotec engines that power these aircraft. When I asked about the sound they make, Joe said he would "compare it to some weed whackers. Some of them are quieter because of the prop. If it's a wood prop it will be louder than a composite prop, most people feel. There are restrictors for the exhaust, where you can actually slow the sound of the exhaust, like motorcycles that have a loud pipe that you can put mufflers on to restrict them down to make them even quieter."

However, if this sounds like you can make an ultralight very quiet, remember that quiet is a relative term here, as was made clear by what Joe said next.

"So therefore, earplugs are a must."

My final question to Joe was this: In his opinion, would it be dangerous and foolhardy to fly ultralights in formation at night? He promptly replied, "Yes."

It was now time to let experience be that teacher, as one of the pilots, Frank Hauser, a retired NYPD lieutenant, readied his plane for takeoff. We stood behind his plane at a distance of maybe thirty feet, and the noise was quite loud. There was also a considerable amount of wind generated by his propeller being blown back onto us. That brings up the subject of turbulence created by a group of ultralights flying in formation. All of those propellers would be creating turbulence for the planes behind them, making it even more difficult to fly in a tight, steady formation.

Frank Hauser gets ready for takeoff.

After Frank taxied out to the runway, he opened up the throttle and zoomed down the runway, and was up in the air so quickly it was amazing. He circled overhead several times at various altitudes so Felix could film him. The noise of this one plane was substantial, so clearly, five or six of them at an altitude of 100-200 feet would be deafening.

It was fun watching these simple and efficient aircraft, but the true researcher always takes that next step—she straps in and goes for a ride! Joe was generous enough to offer to take me up in his plane, and I have to admit I was a bit apprehensive at first. You see, roller coasters and I don't mix, as I get quite nauseated, so I warned him that if this was anything like an amusement park ride my stomach would not be a happy camper.

He reassured me that it would be a smooth and nausea-free experience, so I popped in the earplugs, donned the helmet, and took a seat. It seemed almost impossible that this collection of metal tubes, wires, fabric, and a big weed whacker engine was going to get us up in the air—and more importantly, keep us there—but I was excited to leave the surface of the earth ASAP.

Joe explained all of the controls and some of the preflight things that should be checked. As we taxied over to the runway, it reminded me of a go-kart bouncing along. Then the engine roared even louder, and we shot forward. Before my mind could process the speed, vibration, wind, and noise, we were off the ground! The rattling instantly stopped and we slowly climbed several hundred feet in the air.

I have to say, it was the closest I ever felt to flying. What I mean is, it wasn't like sitting in a jet or small plane or even a helicopter that was flying, it was like *I was* flying! There was a tremendous sense of freedom as the landscape just opens up beneath you. I admit it, it was love at first flight!

We circled the airport a few times, and I felt as if I could do this all day. I instantly understood why people have been flying ultralights for decades. Even the landing was exciting, as the ground rushes up under your feet.

As exhilarating as the experience was, I still tried to keep focused on shooting some footage of the flight, paying attention to how the aircraft handled, and what things looked like at different altitudes. And all the while , the one thing I couldn't neglect was the noise! Even with earplugs and headsets, it was still very difficult to hear Joe speaking to me.

63

This reminded me of what one woman said about seeing the formation of ultralights over Putnam County. In addition to the engine noise, she could actually hear the pilots shouting. They must have been shouting over their radios to be heard! (Another strike against the ultralight explanation.)

Joe and I ascending just after takeoff, and me thoroughly enjoying the flight.

Pumped up with adrenaline after landing, I give the thumbs up to the exhilarating experience of flying in an ultralight.   Photos courtesy of BGM.

After I landed, Sarah took a ride, as well. Felix was content to stay on the ground, because as he said, they don't make ultralights his size.

I really couldn't thank Joe enough for sharing all his expertise and giving me an opportunity to experience one of these amazing aircraft firsthand. If you have never tried one, seek out the nearest airport to take an ultralight ride.

Just do us all a favor. If you do become a pilot, please don't try to pretend to be a UFO!

In Conclusion:
Where Officials Can Stick Their Ultralight Excuse

In the 1980s, thousands of eyewitnesses in Dutchess, Putnam, Westchester, and Rockland Counties saw massive, triangular, *solid* craft, *hovering silently* and *motionless* in the sky, sometimes as close as a mere 100 feet above their heads.

Those people who had the courage to report their sightings to local police, state police, airports, or to other government officials, were often told that what they had really witnessed was a group of ultralight airplanes flying in formation.

Really? That was the best excuse they could manage? Let's take a moment here to explore just how stupid and insulting that excuse really was.

- Fact: There were groups of pilots perpetrating hoaxes by flying their ultralight aircraft in formation. (There were also groups of pilots flying small planes in formation, allegedly out of Stormville Airport, but much of the following applies equally to them, as well.)

- Fact: Ultralights are not silent. They are quite the opposite of silent. They sound like weed whackers. Therefore, a group of ultralights flying in formation would make as much racket as a flock of weed whackers. In fact, the noise would even be louder, because ultralights are in the air above you, so unlike a weed whacker, the sound would not be muffled by the ground, trees, hills, or buildings. It is impossible for anyone who retained any degree of hearing to mistake a formation of weed whackers over their heads as a silent object.

- Fact: Ultralights cannot hover motionlessly in the air for five or ten minutes. In fact, the only completely motionless ultralight is one that has crashed to the ground because it tried to hover. Helicopters and vertical takeoff jets can hover; regular fixed wing aircraft cannot. (And FYI: neither helicopters nor vertical takeoff jets are totally silent, either. In fact, they are extremely loud, and I have yet to see one the size of two football fields.)

- Fact: It is illegal to fly ultralights at night. In addition to being illegal, it is also stupid and dangerous, not only to the lives of

66

the irresponsible pilots, but to the people on the ground they could potentially crash into. The last time I checked, when the police knew that someone was doing something illegal, they arrested him. If the police were aware that a group of stupid and dangerous ultralight pilots were flying illegally at night, why didn't they stop and arrest them? And where was the FAA in all this? They didn't mind that a group of ultralight pilots were thumbing their noses at the rules and regulations and putting people on the ground at risk to perpetrate a silly UFO hoax?

- Fact: Many people saw the formations of ultralights and small planes, as well as the unidentified flying objects, and no one I spoke to had any trouble distinguishing one from the other. These eyewitnesses all agreed the ultralights and other small planes were very loud and never stopped moving. They also could not hold a steady, tight formation, as the lights on the individual planes could clearly be seen moving position relative to the others. Many also reported that they could clearly see the field of stars between the planes, further indicating it was not a solid object. Noisy, constantly moving aircraft that shifted positions, and were easily identifiable as separate objects because you could see stars between them, are not the same as silent, motionless, solid objects that blocked the field of stars.

- In addition to hovering silently for as long as 20 minutes directly overhead at treetop height, some UFOs exhibited tremendous speed and acceleration, often racing off and disappearing in the blink of an eye. Many eyewitnesses described these objects as being faster than any jet. At a top speed of around 60 mph in a good tailwind, ultralights are not faster than any jet. They are not even faster than any car!

So, what can we conclude from all of this? If these pilots came up with the idea of perpetrating the hoax on their own, then shame on them. It isn't funny to frighten men, women, and children, cause traffic to stop on major highways risking accidents, and flying dangerous and illegal stunts that could have resulted in injuries in both the air and on the ground. The worst transgression of all, however, is that these reckless and thoughtless pilots muddied the waters of what could just be the most incredible discovery in the history of mankind—that we are truly not alone.

If these pilots were paid to perpetrate this hoax, then shame on them and shame on whoever paid them. The fact that no one was ever apprehended or prosecuted speaks to at least a tacit consent by authorities as to these night flying activities. Depending upon how conspiratorial are your leanings, it may also point to the fact that officials actually *appreciated* these pilots' attempts at faking UFOs, as it served to spread disinformation to cover up something the government doesn't want us to know.

This leads us to two suppositions: 1) These unidentified craft are experimental military vehicles, or 2) These unidentified craft are not of terrestrial origin.

If the first supposition is correct, then bravo to our military to be able to invent such extraordinary aircraft. However, in the same breath I must also say shame on our military for testing them over populated areas, scaring the crap out of a lot of people, and risking civilian lives as motorists screeched to a halt on crowded highways and roads.

If the second supposition is correct, then we have an entirely different ball of alien wax. If our government is aware of these vehicles—and obviously they are—then why are they so interested in spreading disinformation?

I am reminded of the allied troops during World War II, prior to the invasion of Normandy. In order to misdirect the Nazis toward Calais, or anywhere else but Normandy, they had inflatable tanks, trucks, and aircraft, which from German reconnaissance planes would appear to be the real thing. The deception was so convincing that a quarter of a million Nazi troops were shifted to Calais, as that is where the dummy allied forces appeared poised to attack. The allies also dropped small rubber dummies with parachutes behind enemy lines, making the Germans waste valuable time and troops hunting down the fake paratroopers.

Continuing this train of thought, it is clearly a brilliant and necessary tactic to create disinformation for your enemies in time of war. So what are the implications, then, of the official approval of those pilots who perpetrated the hoax, spreading their own brand of disinformation? Are we:

A) Involved in some kind of a war?

B) Does our own government consider its tax-paying citizens to be enemies who must be fooled?

And no, I don't want to hear that if our government is keeping something from us it's for our own good. Try telling that to all the people who have been traumatized by their UFO experiences. I also don't want to hear that if the truth came out there would be panic and people would do stupid things. People do stupid things anyway, so give the general public a break, and trust that they would be able to handle the truth.

In 2008, the Vatican even put out an official statement that it was acceptable for Catholics to believe that there was life on other planets. If the Vatican—a place not historically known for embracing free thinking and new ideas—felt comfortable opening this alien can of worms, shouldn't our great democracy of the people and for the people be given the same courtesy of the truth?

There is no doubt that there are unusual aircraft in the skies over the Hudson Valley, craft that are technological wonders. Regardless of their origin, they cannot all be explained away as formations of ultralights. We should once and for all stick that ridiculous excuse on the Wall of Shame and be done with it.

Don Alan Smith

5
Discs

Ever since the term "flying saucer" was coined in 1947, whenever people think of UFOs, they usually think of these disc-shaped vehicles. While all manner of shapes have been seen over the skies of the Hudson Valley, the classic flying saucer is among the oldest and most prevalent types witnessed. (There are unconfirmed reports that discs were seen over Pine Bush as early as the 1920s.)

Throughout this project, people have asked me what the different shapes of craft represent. Unlike some people who actually ascribe the names of different alien races to each craft design, I have no problem admitting that I haven't a clue! I can only postulate that because so many discs have been spotted over such a long period of time, it must be a great form for its function…whatever that may be.

A Family Affair

When Leon Royster was a child growing up in Central Nyack, he was out one night walking his dog. He saw a large white light in the sky moving in a straight line. The next day, he told his first grade teacher, Mr. Goldstein, that he saw Sputnik. His teacher explained that "Sputnik doesn't fly around here." After questioning his young student, trying to determine what he could have seen, he finally concluded that it was "unidentified."

One such event in a person's life is exciting, but imagine having your siblings, parents, children, and aunts and uncles, also having numerous sightings over the span of almost 50 years! Can it all be a coincidence? It's difficult enough for someone to believe you have had a UFO sighting, and if you try to tell them about multiple sightings you are instantly labeled a liar, crazy, or both. I will present some of the other things Leon told me about the family sightings and let you decide whether they are plausible or impossible.

In 1965, Leon's parents were driving one night along Route 59 in Nanuet near the E. J. Korvette's department store, which was on the south side of Rt. 59 by the Smith Street intersection. (Pathmark and other stores are in this shopping center today.) They were with two other couples, and the three cars all had two-way radios. Suddenly, a disc-shaped object swooped down close to their cars. The men all got on their radios to talk to one another about what they were seeing, and the women were screaming as the disc repeatedly came low over their cars before finally taking off.

In 1966, the famous Wanaque, New Jersey reservoir sightings occurred. A silent disc was seen beaming light onto the frozen reservoir, a light which actually burned holes through the 2-inch-thick ice. The list of witnesses included Mayor Harry Wolfe, three Councilmen, Civil Defense Administrators, Chief of Police Floyd Elson and numerous policemen, and the Mother Superior of a nearby convent— hardly the type of people who would

This photo is alleged to be that of the Wanaque UFO. The photographer has not been identified, and the authenticity cannot be confirmed. However, witnesses have verified that what they saw that night over the reservoir looked similar.

72

have the motive or inclination to make up such stories. Also among those witnesses that night were Leon's aunt and uncle.

However, his aunt did more than just witness this disc, which the mayor said was something "terribly strange"—she photographed it over her Pompton Lakes home. She showed the picture of the disc to her neighbors, and then something equally strange began to happen.

A black Lincoln Continental kept driving back and forth in front of her house. Then the occupants, two men in black suits, black fedoras, and dark sunglasses, got out of the car and just stood there and stared at the house for a while, and then left. This went on for a couple of weeks, and the woman was so terrified, she gave the photo to her sister to hide, as she wanted it out of the house. Even Leon's uncle, who was a big, tough man, admitted to getting "the heebie jeebies" at the sight of these mysterious men staring at their house day after day.

Leon said this incident was never spoken about to him when he was a child. Instead, he had eavesdropped when his parents and aunt and uncle whispered about what was happening. (And what kid doesn't snoop when his parents start whispering?) While his aunt has since passed away, Leon's cousin may still have that photo and negative, so hopefully it can be located. Also, while reading up on the Wanaque sightings, I found many references to men in uniforms who spoke with many of the witnesses telling them to remain silent about what they saw. Yet, official military sources flatly deny that it was any of their personnel, and referred to these men as "military imposters."

Oh, and do I even have to mention the offered excuses? Sure, why not, just for a laugh:

McGuire Air Force Base suggested it was a weather balloon. The Pentagon said it could have been an alignment of Venus and Jupiter. Stewart Air Force Base said it could have been a helicopter with a search light. And last, and certainly least, professional skeptic Philip Klass said it was ball lightning.

UFOs burning holes in the ice in front of scores of credible witnesses. Men in Black and military imposters intimidating those witnesses. Conspiracies and cover-ups. Does it get any better or stranger than that in the world of ufology?

For the Royster family, that strangeness would continue through the years and generations. In 1985, Leon's brother called him about 7pm one night. His brother was "all excited" and told Leon that as he was driving in his Datsun 280ZX, he looked up through the T-bar roof and saw an object above him which filled his entire field of view. He told Leon to go outside and look for it.

Running out of his house on Depew Avenue in Nyack, Leon didn't see anything a first. But just as he was about to give up, he spotted a silent, black triangle "at least 75-feet or bigger, hanging low in the air" near the Westgate Inn (now the Best Western on Polhemus Street). It had white lights underneath, "and 8 blood-red lights along the back."

Soon, the entire neighborhood came out onto the street to watch this object, including four Clarkstown police officers. One of the officers told the crowd that he saw the same object hovering over Bear Mountain two weeks earlier. When asked what he did when he saw it, the policeman replied, "The same thing I'm doing now, I just stood and watched it!"

After about ten minutes, the triangle slowly started to move north. Leon and his girlfriend jumped in the car to try to follow it, and headed north on Route 9W. They came within 75 yards of the craft as it passed over Rockland Lake, and the white lights reflected brightly in the water beneath it. As they passed by Tilcon (formerly Trap Rock, the site of many sightings by Gary and his family, Chapter 11), the triangle passed directly over their car. Then it "shot up" and rapidly headed east.

There have been several other sightings, as recently as 2011 and 2012, by Leon and his mother in Washingtonville, NY where they now live. Leon's brother, wife, and children in Ohio saw a bizarre meteor-like object with a tail that separated into five bright lights that hovered in formation. His brother's wife is a robotics engineer and she insisted that there must be a rational explanation, even though she had no idea what that explanation could be.

Leon's daughter saw a strange object at Sam's Point in Cragsmoor, NY, and she, too, is now a believer. And knowing how fascinated her father is with all of this, she has now made him promise her something—if Leon ever gets really close to a UFO that has landed, he is not to get out of the car!

So, how has a lifetime of personal and family experiences shaped Leon's life?

"It's made it a lot better," he says without hesitation. "I know we are not alone. I think they have always been here. I've never had any fear whatsoever. I've thoroughly enjoyed everything, and I hope someday they get close enough for me to say hello."

And what if that UFO does land next to his car someday?

"I'll tell them to come and get me and let me drive!"

Vincent Perna: Lake Tiorati, 1966

On December 18, 1966, Vincent Perna, his brother, and friend were fishing in Harriman State Park at Lake Tiorati when they witnessed a copper-colored disk approximately 15-18 feet in diameter hovering over the treetops. Perna had a Brownie camera in his tackle box, and was able to snap four pictures before the object silently accelerated to a lightning-fast speed and disappeared. Park police suggested that Perna tell his story to officials at Stewart Air Force Base. Air Force personnel then proceeded to interrogate Perna, after giving him a shot of sodium pentothal, otherwise known as "truth serum"!

While Perna appeared to be telling the truth, the Air Force nonetheless discounted the entire incident and concluded that the object was nothing more than "a blob of developing fluid" on the negatives. Members of Blue Book also examined the photos and negatives, and their experts concluded that the object was much smaller and closer to the camera, and labeled it a hoax—despite a written protest by Dr. J. Allen Hynek.

On the other hand, NICAP (National Investigations Committee on Aerial Phenomena) researchers examined the negatives and found no evidence of a hoax. It was also clear to them, and the staff of a local newspaper, that what had been photographed was something real and solid, not a blob of developing fluid. They concluded that the disc-shaped object had sharply defined edges, curved, sloping sides like the silhouette of a volcano, and reflected light as if it was made of metal.

Scott Webber: Harriman State Park, 1979

In 1979, *Rockland Journal News* reporter Scott Webber was on his way to work, driving south on the Palisades Parkway at about 5am. When passing by the Anthony Wayne recreation area, he saw a round, disc-shaped object sitting in the parking lot. It was about 25 to 30 feet in diameter, and there were lights flashing around its edge.

As Scott watched in fascination, the object lifted straight up, shot into the sky, and disappeared. He was certain the sighting was not his imagination, as at this time, many people had CB radios in their cars, and suddenly everyone in the area was talking about this strange round object with the flashing lights.

Melody Swanson: Nyack, 1983

Melody Swanson wasn't supposed to be in Nyack on March 18, 1983. She was supposed to be skiing in Vermont, but missed her flight the night before. Instead, Melody, her husband, and some family members decided to go on a hike from Nyack Beach State Park to Rockland Lake.

When they reached the top of a hill that had a sweeping view of the Hudson River below, someone yelled, "Oh my God, what is that in the sky!? *What is it!?*"

Looking up, they all saw a silver, metallic disc about 35 feet in diameter, hovering silently over the river at an altitude of approximately a thousand feet. Melody thought it was beautiful and said she hoped it landed. A family member was not of the same opinion, and ran down the mountain in fear.

After watching in amazement for several minutes, the disc tilted to about a 15-degree angle and "shot away in a burst of light." Melody was disappointed the object left, and sat waiting for it to return, even after everyone else headed back to the car. She said the disc-shaped craft didn't return—although she was gone so long that her family "wondered if they had taken" her "away."

Melody's husband, who was in the military, was previously skeptical about the idea of UFOs, but when she asked him what he thought the object was, he could only stammer the stunned reply, "I, I, I don't know!" He had to admit he never saw anything else like it.

At no point did Melody feel afraid. In fact, she was hoping for closer contact with the craft and what she believes were the alien occupants. Today, she is "looking forward to the day of disclosure" when the truth about UFOs is finally revealed. She believes that the extraterrestrials are here to help us, and is also certain the government is keeping us in the dark.

It is interesting to note that March 18 was the day after Dennis Sant and hundreds of other people in the Hudson Valley witnessed a massive V-shaped or triangular craft, and there were even more sightings on the 24th. There's no way to tell if these other UFOs are related to this disc-shaped object appearing over the river that day, but it does reaffirm that something strange was in the air in March of 1983.

Rose: Hurley, 1983

In September, I exchanged emails with Rose, who said she would send me a letter detailing her experiences, as well as a photo, and copies of newspaper articles reporting the sightings in the area.

Hi Linda!

I'm enclosing a newspaper article that appeared in the *Freeman* the following days. I also made a copy of my photo—where the craft was hovering above.

- Date- March 31, 1983
- Location- Between Cottekill and Hurley on Lucas Ave.
- Size- large
- Distance…maybe 40-50 ft. above/overhead
- Duration of sighting- maybe 5-10 min?!
- I was the only witness @ this site.
- How I felt? In awe!
- Did sighting chg. my view- Yes, I'm a believer!
- Sightings before/after- unfortunately…no!

Now to elaborate…I was driving home toward Hurley, on Lucas Ave. All of a sudden, there it was—awesome! I pulled over and this craft was hovering above the tree. I got out and shut the engine off. There was no sound to be heard !!! It was dusk and there was mist/fog around the craft, so I couldn't really see the UFO clearly. However, it was circular, because I could see windows that were lit.

Unfortunately, no beings were visible from the lighted windows. How long it had been there before I arrived, I don't know. I stayed a few minutes, then it silently and slowly

The tree that the craft was hovering abo

moved toward the east. (This is when the patient I once had, must have seen it!) [Note: In one of Rose's emails, she explained that one of her former patients saw the same craft that night.]

Anyway, I was in a bad marriage at the time. As the craft moved away, I say aloud, "Wait, take me with you!" (I guess they didn't hear, or thought, "Hey, Mike, step on it, there's a crazy earthling down there!")

Anyway, did time stop during this viewing? No! Was there any radio interference, no. I did note, however, that this tree which is still standing had no leaves for years. I've been watching the skies ever since. Even went to Pine Bush a couple of times, but no other sightings.

It was an awesome experience. Did I feel frightened–no! So anyway, there's my tale. Use my first name if you want. Thanks for considering this story. Good luck with your project!

This article from the *Daily Freeman* states that "a possible answer to the puzzle surfaced today—with Federal Aviation Administration reporting that a precision team of night-flying, single-engine prop planes was believed to have been in the area that night. Both an FAA controller and a spokeswoman at the Dutchess County Airport said they believed the sightings were probably the precision flyers operating out of Stormville Airport about 40 miles south of Kingston. Stormville Airport officials could not be reached for further details today. Yet the reports of most observers who have contacted the Freeman do not seem to conclusively fit that explanation. "

By **KENT ALLEN**
Freeman staff

KINGSTON — This is no belated April Fool's joke.

Thirteen youngsters from the Circle Drive area of Hurley said they recently saw an unidentified flying blimp-like object that hovered over and flew near their homes for several minutes.

"I never believed in UFOs until this," said David Bloch, 13, who with twelve other neighborhood friends said he watched the UFO about 9 p.m. Thursday.

The kids described the object as having a grayish-white color and being the shape and size of a blimp or space capsule. They said the craft had many lights of different colors.

When they called the Federal Aviation Administration after the incident, they were told the sighting may have been just three planes traveling in tandem.

But they dispute that possibility.

"It couldn't have been airplanes," said 12-year-old Tommy Schmidt, his friends nodding emphatically in agreement. He said the object, which was several hundred feet up in the air, could not have been more than one craft.

The youngsters also telephoned state police, who said they had had three other reports that night of a UFO. Radio station WKNY thought they were up to some premature April Fool's pranks when told of the sighting, said the kids.

At least one adult also saw the UFO, although only for a few seconds. Mimi Pagliaro said she was out on her porch when she spotted it, but then the UFO flew behind a tree that obscured the view. She said the strangest aspect of the object was its absolute silence.

Todd Hotaling, 12, and Tony Antonelli, 14, said they noticed no fuel exhaust emanating from the craft as it zipped east towards Kingston after staying in their sight for about 10 minutes.

"I wish some more adults would see it," said Todd, realizing that not everyone is apt to believe what kids say.

Besides those mentioned above, other eyewitnesses included Jennifer Pagliaro, 11; Ryan Hotaling and Kevin Kapila, both 12; Tad Cranfield, Karin Schmitt, John Heins, Jennifer Hartman and Nora Polinsky, all 13; and Neeta Kapila, 14.

Although some were skeptical before, all said they now definitely believe in UFOs.

ET phones Hurley? Area kids spot UFO

Drawing by Todd Hotaling

Some of the West Hurleyites who saw Thursday's UFO try to recreate the sight. Clockwise from the top, they are Todd Hotaling, 12, Jennifer Pagliaro, 11, Dave Bloch 13, Tony Antonelli, 14, and Tommy Schmidt, 12. Todd Hotaling's sketch appears top left.

80

Sandy Denicker

Just a day after meeting with the three teachers, Doris called me to tell me about someone she knew who had a fascinating story to tell. Over the years, "no one would listen" to what he had to say, and he really wanted someone to finally pay attention to his experiences.

The first part of his story didn't technically take place in the Hudson Valley, but in Queens, just 10 miles from the Hudson River. His second encounter took place down in Wildwood, New Jersey, nowhere near the Hudson Valley, but when you read this, I think you'll agree the story was too good to pass up.

On the evening of August 6, 2012, I spoke with Sandy Denicker, president of a construction company on Long Island. He was, at all times, forthright and open in his statements, and right off the bat he admitted that the second encounter really "messed" him up emotionally, and he has never fully gotten over the experience. But, first things first.

In 1993 or '94, his wife, Carol, went out onto the deck of their College Point, NY home one summer evening to check on the weather. She had to drive somewhere that night and wanted to see if it was raining. She was pleased to find that it was just overcast, but not pleased at what was right over their house.

"It was the strangest thing," Carol began. "There was a huge circle of pulsating lights just above the clouds."

She yelled for Sandy to come and look.

"At first I thought it might be a blimp, but it wasn't like any blimp I had ever seen. It filled the sky," he explained.

Living in College Point, they had seen many blimps covering the U.S. Open and Mets games nearby, but the Open was over and the Mets were on the road. And the circle of lights was enormous, far bigger than any blimp. Also, living so close to LaGuardia Airport, they were used to seeing all kinds of aircraft—and this wasn't like any airplane or jet they had ever seen, either.

"The lights were rapidly pulsating around this circle and it took only about a second to go completely around the circle. As far as I could tell, the lights were all white, no color," Sandy said, responding to one of my questions.

"We ran to our neighbor's house and knocked on the door so they could see it, too," Carol explained, "but they weren't home. Then we ran to the next neighbor, and the next, but no one was home."

If they couldn't get other witnesses to see this strange, massive ring of lights over their house, they would try to get photographic evidence. Unfortunately, of the many photos they took, not a single one captured the lights.

Long minutes passed as they stared at the pulsating lights. Finally, Carol had to leave, but even while driving on the Cross Island Parkway, she was able to look back and see the circle of lights over her home. All in all, the sighting must have lasted at least half an hour.

"I was afraid, and curious," Carol admitted, "and to this day I still look up in the sky. I'm still afraid at night."

While this was a long and unnerving experience, these inexplicable lights actually paled in comparison with what Sandy would witness in September of 2008. He was in a softball tournament in Cape May, New Jersey, and as it was a nasty, rainy weekend, there was doubt that the games would even be played. Fortunately, they were able to play their Saturday game which ended about 5pm. Afterward, the team went back to their hotel on Atlantic Avenue in Wildwood.

"It was a two-story hotel and on the top floor there was a big deck that stretched over the sidewalk below, and looked towards the ocean, which was just a block and a half away," Sandy began. "I was the first one to shower, so while I waited for the rest of the team to get ready for dinner, I grabbed a beach chair and sat out on the deck because it looked like the sun might come out. Suddenly, the sky opened up and there were three flying saucers in a military position."

I asked him to explain what he meant by "military position," and he said that one saucer was in front and the other two were slightly lower on either side, forming an equilateral triangle.

"They were huge, each one was bigger than a 747. They were less than a thousand feet over the water, maybe as low as 500 feet. They were so close I could see there weren't any windows, and they were smooth as silk, no differentiation on the surface. They were like porcelain, unglazed porcelain and a light grayish color. There was absolutely no sound or movement—it was like they were propped up on sticks perfectly still and silent. There was no illumination and they just sat there like pictures. I was only a block and a half from the ocean and they were right there over the water.

"*What the hell am I looking at?* I thought. I started to get an anxiety attack, which I never get, but I was so shocked!

"I stared so hard at them my eyes started to hurt. I mean, my eyes were really killing me looking at them, but I couldn't look away. And I didn't dare move a muscle because I thought maybe they hadn't seen me yet. It was like I was seeing something I shouldn't.

"They just hung there for the longest time, maybe 20 minutes? I don't know. I was straining to see every detail, and they were perfectly smooth, no corners or seams. I couldn't see the bottoms of them because they were pitched at an angle, downward toward the water.

"My eyes hurt like hell and I tried to rub them. Finally, I couldn't stand the pain and bent down for a second just to get my eyes off of them. When I sat up they were gone! I have no idea how they left or where they went. But they were gone and my eyes didn't hurt anymore.

"I was really shaken and upset. I called my wife to tell her what happened, but I didn't dare tell anyone on the team, and I'm usually a big mouth! I was just so upset, and it was so tough to deal with. I was really messed up by it."

Finally, six months later he told his team what he saw, but most of them thought he "was nuts or hallucinating." A few believed him, but for the most part they thought it was "nonsense."

"It was tough to admit what happened, but I know what I saw!"

Lake Oscawana

It has long been suspected that there's a correlation between UFOs and water. In the Hudson Valley, that apparent attraction goes beyond the river to its many lakes and reservoirs. Several witnesses related stories of seeing craft hovering directly over water, and this chapter contains accounts that involve Lake Oscawana in Putnam Valley.

Christine and Carol

After the *The Examiner News* article in June 2012, I received the following email from Christine Leonard:

Hi Linda!
I couldn't believe you had this article in the paper. I am now 46 years old and I live in Putnam Valley, New York. I have lived here for 40 years!

Back in the early 1980s my girlfriends and I would spend lots of time on Lake Oscawana. We had lake rights to a beach down the road from our home.

To this day, I have been trying to find out if there has been anyone who has witnessed what we did on that early evening night. I was about 14 years old and we had been hanging out at the beach, it was not yet dark. I was with a friend in a canoe by our raft and not out far, while my other friend was on the sand. Out of nowhere right overhead off to the right a bit, was this tremendous stainless steel, round object, with windows all around and tons of lights encircling the object. The two friends on the beach were yelling, "Oh my God" as we rowed back as fast as we could.

The UFO was exactly what you would see in a science fiction movie. It was TREMENDOUS!! I always described it as big as my house or maybe bigger!! And it was so close. Hovering over the lake about the distance up I would say about the top of a tree top. It came out of nowhere with NO SOUND and slowly turned. As it turned all the lights lit up around. They were white and bright. As it continued to slowly spin, more lights came on. You could see all the windows, but not inside. It was too far above our heads. But you could see the long rectangular windows going all around the outside.

We were in such shock that we knew nobody would believe it so we screamed for the woman who lived to the right of our beach to come out, Mrs. Glickman. Don't know where she was or why she didn't hear us. Our docks were connected, so she lived on the lake. Maybe she wasn't home. (She was about 65 or so back then.)

This all lasted about 5 minutes, I think. It was so fast. But it slowly moved away and then in the blink of an eye disappeared! Still without sound. It seemed to be moving towards the North end of the lake which is where the state park is.

We all ran home and never forgot this! Told our stories throughout the years. Don't know who believed, but I'm sure not many. It's a hard story to believe!

My mom grew up in the Bronx and she had also seen a UFO in the early 1960s when she was in her early teens. She saw it above the rooftop of her 5-story apartment house.

One cool thing happened back then when we told our story to a friend of a friend who had a summer home on Lake Oscawana. She had told her friend that while playing a board game that night, her whole summer bungalow lit up as if somebody was shining a spot light into her home. It was exactly where we saw that UFO hovering and it did light up pretty bright!

I always wondered if anyone else from the Lake Oscawana area ever saw what we saw.

Unless you've encountered anything ever like this, you would never believe. I do believe and hoped I would see it again. But never did.

I also saw those boomerang-shaped objects in the 80s, but they didn't look anything like what we saw.

Please let me know your thoughts.

Thank you,
Christine Leonard

My thoughts were to interview Christine, her mother, and her friends who were with her that night. Her one friend, Cathy, did contact me soon after, but as she now lives in Paris, I would have to content myself with a phone interview. (Although I was more than willing to fly to Paris to give that interview a personal touch!)

We arranged to interview Christine at the lake, and first met at her house early on the morning of July 2. As we spoke, I mentioned that it would be great if her mother could join us, and were pleased to find out that she would meet us at the lake.

Carol and Christine with their sketches of the UFOs they saw when they were each about 14 years old.

Lake Oscawana is beautiful, and we had a picture perfect day. And the moment I stepped onto the tiny sandy beach at the south end of the lake and looked to the tree line to my right, I fully appreciated just how incredible this sighting must have been at such a close distance. I've probably said this before, but I strongly urge anyone interested in UFOs (or any other subject, for that matter) to get up out of your chairs and actually go to the locations where these sightings occurred. As good as photos, video, and big screen TVs may be, nothing beats being there.

The lake looking north, where they first spotted the UFO.

Once Sarah and Felix got the audio and video rolling, Christine's mom, Carol Hughes Demarco, began to tell her story:

Carol: My first sighting, I was probably about 14, was around 1960. I believe, I was 14 or 15 years old. I was living in the Bronx at the time, and we lived in a 5-story walk-up apartment. We spent a lot of time on the roof, we called it Tar Beach at the time, and I was probably taking a line of clothes down for my mom, and it was dusk, and I spotted a metallic object with windows all around.

What drew my attention to it was that there was almost a beacon inside the windows that kept rotating, so that you would see the lights circulating inside this object that was disk-shaped on the top and on the bottom. It

87

was a silver metallic object, and it hovered. It stood there for quite a while hovering over—I can't say how far away it was, maybe ten blocks from where I was located in the city. And it just hovered over this Parkchester portion of the Bronx.

I watched, and I wanted to run down and get a pair of binoculars so I could get a view of this thing because it took me by such surprise, but I was afraid I would miss it and it would scoot away. And sure enough, within a few minutes it just scooted off and disappeared. It was not a plane, it was not a helicopter, it moved much too quickly.

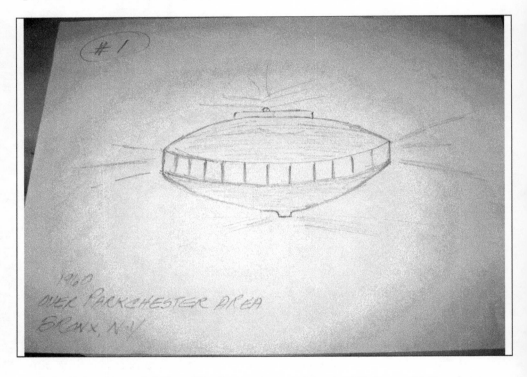

And the next sighting I had was as a resident of Putnam Valley later on in life, the V-shaped formations that were passing over the Hudson Valley at the time in the 1980s. I could see them clearly. I saw them several times. They were not ultralights; you could not see through the V, they were solid. On clear nights you could actually see that it was a solid object with lights all around it. There weren't many lights, but enough to indicate it was a V-shaped object. They were also silent, never any noise. They were close enough that you would have heard even an ultralight engine overhead.

And they were huge! They were the size of Shea Stadium when they did fly over.

And that's about it.

Zim: Could you just speak to how this has influenced your life at all?

Carol: Well, I'm a believer. After seeing both of them, they were very different the two objects I saw from one as a young teenager and one as an adult, but I certainly believe that there is another form of life. Why they're not contacting us is beyond me, but I certainly believe. I can say that much. I'm very open to anything else I might see.

Zim: So there was no fear involved?

Carol: No, no, I was fascinated. I was not fearful at all. I was really fascinated by the whole thing. I would like to see them again if they would like to come over!

Christine then recounted her sighting, which happened to take place at about the same age as her mother's first sighting. As interesting as it had been to read her email account, it was many times more powerful to stand "on the actual spot" and see exactly how and where the sighting unfolded.

She provided more details about how she and one of her friends paddled out in a rubber boat to get a better look at the three red lights that were approaching from the north. When they realized it was "a big object, we were getting scared and we came in as quick as we can. By that time, two of the lights took off from the one light—there were three altogether—and two of them darted out away from each other, and then red and green lights started encircling around and blinking and all of a sudden turned into this big craft right over this beach here, at the height of that tallest tree." (At this point, she indicated the area just to our right.)

"It hovered with no sound, I'd say for about at least a minute, or so. And these big white lights lit up as it slowly began to turn, all around the outside of the craft. They lit up so bright that it lit up one of the summer bungalows on the lake, and we could see a picture frame and a picture hanging on the wall.

The shoreline of the cove where the UFO hovered and lit up a house.

"And then it just slowly started drifting away. We couldn't actually see in the windows, but it was so bright we could see through the windows, because it was so high. Had it been a little lower we could probably have seen inside the craft, but it wasn't that low. And then it just slowly hovered over the beach right over here, and then without a sound it just disappeared, right in front of our eyes. And that was about it."

I asked what the size of this craft was, and she wasn't quite sure, but definitely "as big as a house, probably bigger." Christine also recalled the people farther out in the lake in a canoe that were illuminated "by spotlights" on the craft as it headed south. She also later met the girl whose house had been lit up that night. (See her friend Cathy's account

90

below.) They were playing a board game inside the house at the time, and thought perhaps a cop car was shining lights into their home. They literally didn't know what hit them!

I would love to track down that woman, as well as those two people in the canoe that night!

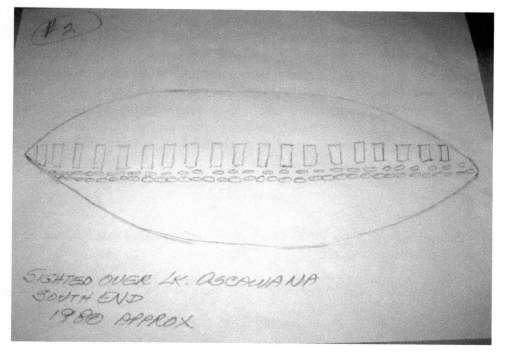

Christine's sketch.

For Christine, this experience inspired her "to do research about other people seeing sightings, and if anybody else saw what we saw that night, because nobody ever seemed to believe me." The sighting brought on a fascination with UFOs and she tried to learn everything she could about them.

I interrupted her at this point to say, "Well, hopefully your mom believed you."

"I did!" Carol said with a laugh. "I never doubted it."

As Christine and Carol were both 14 when they had their sightings, I had to ask if any of Christine's three daughters—ages 17, 15, and 11—had seen anything. Christine replied that none of them had, but "they are looking forward" to seeing something, and they are "always looking."

I thanked both of them and again remarked how interesting it was to have a mother and daughter see a similar type of craft—or was it the same one?—twenty years apart, both at the same age. And it was even more special when they both showed the sketches they had done of the two disk-shaped objects they saw. Christine admitted that her mom is a better artist, and that her sketch more closely resembles what she saw, but both sketches are clearly beyond the boundaries of coincidence. And I must point out that they made these sketches independently—Christine drew hers at her house, Carol drew hers at her home—so there wouldn't be any influencing one another. Before this, neither had ever drawn what they had seen, and were also surprised at the similarities.

Cathy

The following is the transcript of my conversation with Christine's friend, Cathy, who was one of the witnesses on the beach that night:

Zim: Can we start by you stating your name and where you are calling from?

Cathy: My name is Cathy, and I'm calling from Paris, France.

Z: Christine Leonard had given me your name and said you were present at the Lake Oscawana sighting, and I would love to hear your side of it.

C: Okay. So I remember it was the summer of 1981. I don't remember what month it was, whether it was June, July, or August. My friends Christine Leonard and Kim were down at the lake. It was not too late, maybe 8:30 at night. And the only reason I know that is after the event I went back to my parents' house where I lived on Cedar Ledges and it was around 9:30, so it had to be somewhere around there.

Z: It wasn't dark yet?

C: It was dusk, it wasn't dark. You could still see people on the lake. There wasn't a lot of action on the lake. There were no water skiers, no power boats. There was a canoe on the lake. There's a little peninsula where Babe Ruth used to have a house years ago, and I forget the name of the peninsula now, but there's a really nice old house right on the little peninsula that comes out into the lake, on the right side of the lake if you're looking from the south to the north. Cedar Ledges Beach is on the south end of the lake, and everything was from the north coming towards us.

So two people were in a canoe about the middle of the lake. We were standing on the docks looking out to the north end of the lake and we saw three red lights all the way at the north end of the lake. They were together and they just came over the mountain range, and then two red lights on the outside just quickly went out, one to the right and the other to the left and there was only one red light then, coming towards us. As it started coming towards us, it started circling red and green lights, circulating around. It was low in the sky. It was only right above the tree line. Maybe a little bit above the tree line, but it wasn't very high at all.

And it came right over these people on the canoe. And at that point, my friends Christine and Kim took a rubber raft out onto the lake. And they only went out maybe a couple of hundred feet or so from the docks, just, you know, to try to get a better look. And these red and green lights going around in a circle hovered right above the people in the canoe. We didn't hear them screaming or yelling or anything, and it stayed over them for what seemed like forever, but it was probably only 20 or 30 seconds, which is a long time when you're waiting. And then it started moving closer. There's another beach, the Columbus Avenue beach on the right side of the lake, and it shone these two huge searchlights. And it was so bright, there was a little house on the lake, like right up off the beach, and you could actually see that there was a framed picture on the wall of the porch. That's how bright it was.

We didn't see any people inside the house, I didn't see any people, but then it came close to us, really close to us. There's a beach closer to us on the right, it's called Lookout Beach, and right when it got to that point, the red and green lights were still going around in a circle, and it was humongous. But you didn't know at the time. You couldn't see that it was so big until it turned on all these white lights, hundreds of white lights, little white lights.

And you could actually see the frame of it and it almost looked like a pewter-type of metal, the color of pewter. And there was a long pole in the center, round, long, like a cylinder, and there were two poles jutting out from the left side off the cylinder that were longer than the ones that were coming out…so there were two poles jutting out the back of the cylinder, and then two jutting out off this main cylinder to the right. But they were a little bit shorter and the ones to the left were a little bit longer.

But you could see the sky, you could see the frame of this craft, but you could see the sky and the stars in between where there was no craft, were there were no cylinders. So you could actually see the stars that were behind it.

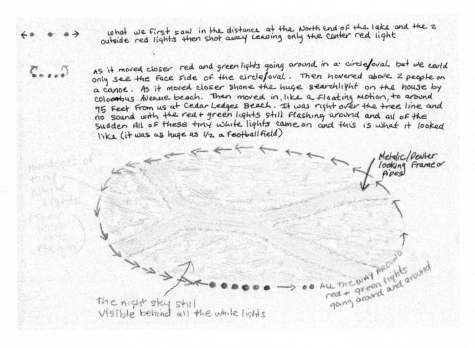

Cathy's sketch.

94

Zim: Okay, so this wasn't one solid--

Cathy: It didn't look solid to me. And there were these kind of windows that were underneath these red and green lights. And it was at least the size of half a football field. It was huge. It was low in the sky. And at this point, Christine and Kim had rowed the rubber raft back in, and Christine was yelling and freaking out, and I was hoping that it was going to land.

It didn't make a sound, it had no noise whatsoever to it. And then it just floated off over to the mountain range to the right. So it was just floating away from the lake. And at that point there were some other lights from way over the north end of the lake that were probably just regular aircraft that were following it, chasing it, trying to chase it down.

Zim: Oh really?

Cathy: Yes, and that was it. That's all we saw. I was hoping it would land, they were hoping it wouldn't land.

Zim: Why were you hoping it would land? I'm just curious.

Cathy: Because I always had a fascination with UFOs since I was young. I had a bunch of dreams about UFOs. I've had many UFO dreams in my life.

Zim: Before this sighting?

Cathy: Yes, before the sighting.

We discussed these dreams, and one recurring dream she had when she was young involved her standing in the driveway at night. She would look up and see a dark, unlit UFO above her. Then a beam of light would come down and try to lift her, and then she would wake up. Another dream she had several times had her standing on the back deck of the house. There would be several UFOs in the sky above her. These dreams were always accompanied by "a certain feeling that's hard to explain." These were feelings of nervousness, anxiety, and the distinct impression "that something wasn't right." Cathy does not believe she was abducted, however, and thinks that these were simply dreams.

We then discussed an odd light she saw over Paris, but couldn't say for sure it was a UFO. She also told me about Gloria LaPolla and her story of a similar sighting over the lake. (Cathy actually lived in Gloria's house for a time, which may or may not be another of these pesky little coincidences.)

Getting back to the Lake Oscawana sighting, Cathy told me that the next day she was at the Putnam Valley Market, which at the time was probably called Townsend's, and she was telling a friend about the sighting. Another girl overheard the conversation, and when Cathy mentioned the part about the UFO illuminating the house, the girl spoke up and said, "Oh my God, that was my house! All of a sudden our house lit up as bright as day!"

We spoke for a while more about the various experiences in her life, and I mentioned something about the huge triangle-shaped craft witnessed in Putnam County in the 1980s. With a casualness approaching talking about the weather, Cathy said, "Oh yeah, I saw them too. But *everybody* did." In fact, she had seen the V-shaped lights two or three times, but after her very close encounter at the lake, these lights did not make the same impression on her. I found it remarkable and kind of funny that she hadn't thought to mention these sightings previously, as they were just run-of-the-mill UFOs…

Finally, I asked Cathy how all of this influenced her life, and she said she was so excited when she saw the UFO, and she wished it had landed. She hopes she will see something again. In fact, she said she "would be lucky" to see something again. And Cathy is always looking up at the sky. Always.

Gloria

One thing does often lead to another, and Cathy did indeed get me in touch with Gloria LaPolla, who witnessed a similar craft in 1984. Gloria and I spoke on the phone on June 18, 2012, and after that conversation we arranged to film at her house on July 2. Gloria was very open and candid throughout, and a genuine pleasure to interview.

During the phone interview, we first established that she lived "near Fahnestock State Park on the north end of Lake Oscawana," and that the sighting occurred during the summer of 1984.

"I was in my kitchen, and I was ironing on the countertop," Gloria began.

She then described how the kitchen was actually on a raised, second level of the house. From her position at the countertop, she had an excellent view through a pair of large, sliding glass doors that lead to a deck which stood above the lawn, and looked out to the tree line. When she looked up from her ironing, she saw an object "that was not high, it was just above the treetops." The object was "floating and it was big."

Gloria "got very excited" and ran to the top floor to tell her parents, and they went out to the upper deck, which is about treetop height. She then ran downstairs to try to find a camera, but couldn't locate it so she went back out onto the deck off the kitchen. Despite the time that had elapsed, the object "was still there and had just moved not far, maybe about 100 feet or so, because it was so slow. It was very, very slow and there wasn't a sound. And I just watched it go over the treetops, and it headed, I guess, north."

I asked how big the object was, and explained that many people compare what they have seen to the football fields.

"Um…it was big, but I can't really picture a football field flying! I don't go to football games," Gloria replied, which made me laugh.

I then suggested something more familiar to her, like comparing it to the size of a house. She said it was at least as big as her house, and she then described the object in more detail.

"It had small lights, and a very, very thin light going from one light to the other light. And it was circular. And the rest of it was dark. It was dusk when I saw it."

Once the circular craft had floated out of sight, Gloria called the police department. She asked what had just flown over Putnam Valley and received this wonderfully honest response, "I'll be damned if we know, lady!"

I asked a few more questions just to clarify some points, and found that the lights were all white and that nothing on the craft appeared to be moving or spinning. It was definitely "not round like a balloon, it was elongated." She couldn't tell if the object was metallic, or if there were any windows. It was moving so slowly that she "could walk faster" than it was going.

"The main thing that caught my eye was those lights. And it wasn't a triangle. You know they were trying to tell people it was planes flying in formation. It didn't look like that *at all*."

Gloria reiterated that it was completely silent, and added that the entire sighting "took quite a few minutes." During the entire sighting, she never felt afraid, she only felt "excitement. Because at the beginning, you don't know what you're looking at."

I asked how this incident influenced her life, and she replied without hesitation, "Oh, I'm very curious about UFOs!"

Gloria's drawing.

Gloria on the deck of her house. The UFO appeared over the trees behind her.

In the following days, Gloria discovered that other people had seen the same thing as articles appeared in the local *Pennysaver* newspaper. She also found out that there was going to be a UFO conference in Brewster, NY. Gloria attended that conference and was amazed at how many witnesses showed up to share their stories. To this day, she still has the big, blue button which reads "I Saw It" that was given out to conference attendees. The button mentions the conference date and location, and the UFO hotline phone number to contact the people who were researching the sightings.

We wrapped up our conversation by agreeing that what Gloria saw was neither planes, nor the planet Venus, nor swamp gas, and I told her I would be in touch about setting a date to come to the house for the film interview.

It worked out that after interviewing Christine Leonard and her mother on the south end of the lake, we drove to the north end to Gloria's house. Everything she had told me just snapped into focus when I saw the house, the tall decks, and the tree line which was much closer to the house than I imagined. At that distance, this house-sized UFO must have been a spectacular sight!

Gloria and her family, and their little dogs, were all quite welcoming. While Sarah and Felix set up the cameras and sound equipment, I sat down at the counter where Gloria had first spotted the object, and it gave me some sense of that exciting moment. It also helped that Gloria is a very talented artist, and she drew a sketch of what the object looked like and how it was positioned in a gap along the tree line. (And yes, I was just a bit envious that I never saw anything like that!)

When the cameras were rolling, Gloria recounted the story she had told me, only it was like hearing it for the first time, because now I could see the excitement in her expression and more clearly visualize the events as I was right where it happened. We next went out to the deck, and she pointed to the gap in the tree line and traced the path the slow-moving craft took as it was so very close to the house. If only she had found her camera that day!

Gloria and I were to meet again, when she came to my July 24th presentation at the Josephine-Louise Library in Walden. I didn't know she was coming, and I also didn't know she had drawn a special color picture of the UFO for me. I told her, it was my first piece of UFO artwork!

On the 27th of July, I went up to the BGM studio for a production meeting, and we discussed the various interviews that had already taken place. And we all unanimously agreed that Gloria's account was one of the clearest and most credible, and we were most grateful that she took the time to share her story and artistic talent for the project!

7
Congers

The location of the following sightings are just half a mile from one another (and may have occurred on the same night), and within a mile of the house where Gary and his mother had their sightings and close encounters in the 1950s and 60s (see Chapter 11).

What is it about Congers that seems to have attracted UFOs for at least 60 years? Is it the Lake DeForest reservoir, the Trap Rock (now Tilcon) quarry at the north end of the lake, or the proximity to the Hudson River?

Big UFOs, Small World

In July of 2012, the *In the Night Sky* Facebook page received a message from Scott DiLalla, mentioning two sightings he had in Rockland County, NY. As I wanted more Rockland stories, I messaged him back asking for some details. His response is below, but first here's one of those "small world" incidents.

Scott lives in Los Angeles, but his sightings took place at his parents' house in Congers, NY. I mentioned that my husband, Bob Strong, grew up in Congers. Scott replied that his parents live right across the street from Bob's mother, and that Bob's father, who used to own a television repair shop, used to fix the family's TVs. (Scott also mentioned that Bob's dad caught him in one of the most embarrassing moments of his life, but I'll let Scott tell that story!) What are the chances that someone living in Los Angeles contacts us about a UFO project, and he grew up next to my husband's family!

Anyway, here's Scott's response:

I could remember this as if it was yesterday. The first account happened on a summer night in 1986 at dusk in Congers, NY. I was with my good friend working on a motorcycle in my garage and my father was outside finishing up some yard work. It was only minutes away before the sky would have been totally dark. At that moment, my sister comes pulling into the driveway yelling, "Look up into the sky," over and over.

My friend and I ran out to see what was going on. My father, sister, friend and myself clearly witnessed the most extraordinary UFO sighting. There was this huge, silent and very low flying object moving, what appeared to be a little above tree level, northbound along Congers Lake. We couldn't figure out what we were looking at. It seemed long, maybe about a football field in length. There was a cluster of lights that seemed to be in a circle in the front and one small light in the tail.

It eventually went out of sight, but after a few minutes it reappeared moving southbound. This time it started to move towards us and seemed to have completely stopped in between my house and our neighbors. Out of excitement I started to flick our patio light on and off to try and attract it, but after a few seconds of doing that my father yelled for me to stop. The second that I noticed my father's serious and worried expression I stopped immediately. That was also the moment I started to feel a little nervous. My father told me when I was turning the light on and off the object actually turned towards it and began to move in my direction. When I stopped it stopped.

After about a minute it began to move again and continued southbound. At that point, we noticed something shoot out of the bottom. To this day, we are not sure what that was, but it seemed to be an orb of light shot out of the bottom of the object. My father got on the phone and called the police. The police had told him that they knew about it and also told him that he was already the 200th caller about this object. It eventually went out of sight. My sister actually saw this object again driving with her boyfriend. They followed it for a while until it eventually went out of their reach.

This was the object we saw. I just grabbed this off youtube:
http://www.youtube.com/watch?v=o5kIbcT4E1g&feature=results_main&
playnext=1&list=PL682F4A5F2704615D

The second object I saw happened a couple months after. It was a quick, but very exciting encounter. I happened to be with my same friend, the one in the first story. We were walking around the block, at night, when we noticed this very low, silent, tree level, object fly over us. It had a triangle shape with a large bright light in each corner. It moved slow enough that we kept up with it at a running pace. We knew we would lose

102

it soon so we decided to run to my friend's car and try and follow it. We didn't have much luck finding it again, but it was another mind blowing experience.

My father and sister also so had another experience. Something flew over them when they were at my neighbor's house. It was so low, that they saw structure and the outline of it. They said it was octagon in shape.

I came across your site through my research on this topic. I am also a filmmaker and I am currently writing a script about the Hudson Valley UFO. Feel free to call or write if you need more info on my experience. I'm currently in Rockland County visiting my parents for a few weeks, but I normally live in Los Angeles.

After reading Scott's account—especially the part about the UFO responding to the patio light going on and off!—his offer of more information was definitely one I couldn't refuse! We arranged to interview Scott and his family at the house where the sighting occurred.

We all met at Scott's parents' house on August 8. After speaking for a while with Scott and his parents in the cool air of their kitchen, it was unfortunately time to stand out in the back yard in that hot summer sun again. Couldn't we catch a break of a single mild or cloudy day to film? It was clear it was going to be another interview where you just hoped the cameras didn't pick up on us all sweating profusely.

Scott and his father, Art, were real troopers as we all roasted while they recounted their experiences. Art confirmed that the object had been long, "with a cluster of lights" in the middle "and one at the end." He pointed out where the "floating" object stopped between his and his neighbor's house. And despite the heat, I got a chill as Art told of how the object "responded" and actually turned and headed towards them as Scott turned the patio light on and off.

"What Scott didn't see, or doesn't remember," Art added, "was that it stopped over there around that pine tree area, between the pine tree and the lake, let's say, and it stopped dead. No sound. It was quivering though. It was sort of shaking slightly when it was stationary. And then it started to proceed south. As it proceeded south—it was kind of following the railroad tracks—maybe about 500 feet in the air, when it got like beyond my neighbor's house, we saw something shoot out the back down to the ground, like a light. It wasn't a beam, it was a white ball of light."

While Sarah and Felix get ready for filming, Scott and I pose for a photo.

Scott said he was running all around the neighborhood trying to get the best view of the craft, and remembers coming across a man walking down the street. He was "young and drunk" and when Scott pointed to the sky and asked, "What is that?" the drunk man looked astonished and simply said, "Whoa!"

The sighting from their home lasted about 10 minutes. After the craft headed south, it must have turned west at some point, as Scott's sister later spotted it again over Lake Deforest.

Scott then talked about his second sighting of a large triangle a few months later, just two blocks from his house. This one was moving much faster in comparison to the first craft, but it was also silent.

Art spoke about the sighting he and his daughter had while sitting on the deck of his neighbor's house one night around the same time period as the other two sightings.

Art and Scott Dilalla—father and son UFO witnesses.

"It was either an octagon or a hexagon, I don't remember, but it was that type of shape," Art said. "And again, lights at each corner, I guess you would say. And it just flew right overhead with no noise whatsoever. And that was it. We just saw it for a few seconds. It wasn't going that fast, but a pretty good clip."

The wires run along the railroad, which borders Congers Lake.
The UFO the Dilallas saw was directly over this spot.

Three different types of UFOs in the span of just a few months, coupled with all the other sightings of saucers and egg-shaped craft in the Congers and Lake Deforest area over the decades, make this town something of an Extraterrestrial Highway of the East!

I asked if these sightings had influenced or affected them in some way and Art was the first to speak.

"Well, I always believed in UFOs since the '50s, when it was a hot issue. And I'm always looking in the sky. Especially now that we saw something, you know I keep looking."

Next, Scott spoke.

"Yeah, it influenced me a lot. First, just like my dad, I was just so excited, I felt privileged to actually witness something that was so unbelievable. It wasn't just a little flicker in the sky, it was something you could almost reach out and grab it. So, I would tell people to keep looking up, because there are things up there you can't explain.

"I'm also a film maker, so it inspired me to do some of the projects that I'm into, now. I'm writing a film about the Hudson Valley experience, not my experience, but just this area is so interesting when it comes to paranormal and UFO, that it plays right into the stuff that I'm writing about.

"I just keep looking up. And I think it's harder for everyone to notice today, because they are always on their texts, computers. I would just tell people to look up and text less.

"For people who live in the Hudson Valley, there's something going on here, something extraordinary. People who live around here are lucky to be here, and have a chance to really explore it. And I wouldn't miss it if I were them."

Can't Help Being a Detective

On August 26th, I got an email from Peter Milo, a retired New York City Detective and Vietnam vet. I had met him several months earlier when I had spoken about publishing at the Suffern library. Now *he* had something to tell *me*, and it involved a UFO sighting. I didn't hesitate to set up an interview with this decorated detective, whose credibility was beyond reproach.

In June of 1986, Peter and his wife, Susan, were visiting his sister at her house on Pine Street. The three of them were in the yard, along with his 5-year-old nephew. In the distance, they spotted a "brilliant green light." It was exactly at 9:07pm. He knows exactly what time it was,

Susan and Peter in 1976.

because he instinctively looked at his watch. "I can't help being a detective," he explained.

"Oh look, it's a UFO!" he joked, but as the intense green light drew closer, they began to realize this was no laughing matter.

They watched the light for three minutes, during which time it had "come right over the neighbor's house and was just above the treetops."

"What is it?" his sister asked, starting to get nervous.

They all stood there "dumbfounded" as the craft slowly moved toward them, "at about 7 or 8 miles per hour." The object was completely silent and about 80 feet long. It was "wedge-shaped, like a slice of pizza, with a circular light at the point. It was solid and dark, with no visible texture, and we were just amazed that there was no noise."

Peter asked his sister to run in the house and get her binoculars. When the craft was directly overhead, they heard a slight humming sound, but Peter observed that the trees were perfectly still beneath it and around it, with no signs of turbulence being generated by whatever type of propulsion this vehicle was using.

"Should I go in for the baby?" his sister asked, fearful of what this craft might do.

"If they were going to do something, they would have done it by now," Peter replied, trying to reassure his sister. Still, he was glad he was wearing his gun...

The craft continued to move away ever so slowly, "perfectly straight and smoothly, as if it was on tracks." Down the street, the object suddenly turned left toward Congers Lake, and eventually went out of sight. They had been able to watch this object for eleven long minutes!

"I was tempted to get in my car and try to follow it, but I knew I should immediately try to document it." Realizing that there would be "all

108

kinds of naysayers," he tried to cover all the bases before skeptics could tell him that he didn't see what he knows he saw. Peter quickly called Westchester Airport, explained that he was a detective, and posed a series of questions to someone who was very cooperative.

"Are you seeing anything strange on radar over Congers, New York," he asked. The man responded, "No."

"Are there any small plane flying clubs in the air tonight over Rockland County?" The response was that there were no clubs flying that night.

"Are there any blimps in the area for the Westchester Classic?" Peter asked, knowing that the golf tournament was going to begin in a week. Again, the answer was negative, there were no blimps in the area.

Finally, the man at the airport couldn't resist asking what was going on, so Peter explained exactly what they had witnessed. Prepared for ridicule, the man surprised him by saying, "You should have called me right away so I could get a radar fix on it!" However, when Peter mentioned that it was only at treetop height, the man realized it was too low for their radar.

Peter's next call was to the sheriff's department. After introducing himself again, he asked, "Are you getting any crazy calls?"

"You mean that goddamned thing over the lake?" the deputy replied.

Apparently, the sheriff's department was inundated by calls and was well aware of the object, although they clearly had no clue what it was.

Peter then added a few more important details about the sighting. (Oh, how I wish more detectives were witnesses!) First, as they were able to see the object from several perspectives—coming, going, sideways, beneath it, and at eye level as it moved away—he was able to determine that the object was relatively thin and flat, not round and thick like conventional blimps. This led to his astute observation that if this had been some type of lighter-than-air craft, it didn't appear to have enough volume for helium or hydrogen to keep it aloft.

Also, the brilliant green light they first spotted was coming from some sort of "cockpit" at the tip of the wedge. Peter even concluded that this cockpit had to have had some sort of shaped or angled glass like a jet windshield, "as the green light appeared bent" by whatever it was shining through.

Peter recreated his first view of the brilliant green light at treetop level.

Path of the UFO down Pine Avenue in Congers, NY. The craft came from the north and then turned sharply east.

Finally, he mentioned that his young nephew described the object as being "like a Christmas tree," as it was an elongated triangle with lights. With this boy's limited frame of reference, it's a very good comparison!

The next day, Peter started telling people what he saw, and immediately was doubted and scoffed at, to the point that it was tantamount to calling him a liar. He became very aggravated by the unwarranted response—having his integrity challenged just because he happened to witness an object in the sky that hundreds of other people also saw! It was then that he was able to sympathize with all of the other witnesses who tried to speak out; witnesses Peter admits he used to think must be crazy.

Friends who were knowledgeable about science, all told him that what he saw was impossible, and they asked how he could explain it. His response came from years of experience as a detective.

On tough cases, he was often asked how someone was able to commit a particular crime. Peter would simply reply, "He did it." And then he "would go about proving how." It is simple logic that seems to escape most people, even very educated and normally logical people. Something is observed, but due to bias and preconceived ideas, people refuse to believe the witnesses.

Just because you can't understand how something happened, doesn't negate the fact that it happened!

I often feel like telling such skeptics to get over themselves, that just because there are things beyond *their* comprehension, it doesn't mean that they doesn't exist. The history of science is replete with people who let their egos and ignorance keep them and others from pursuing potentially valuable research. But let me get off my soapbox now and continue with Peter's story.

He also mentioned an incident that occurred in Manhattan. Some officers were observing an unidentified flying object, and all of the police radios went dead for a full fifteen minutes! When communications were restored, "everyone went about their business as if nothing happened, and no reports were filed." If you had any hope of career advancement, you obviously didn't talk about flying saucers!

I really can't emphasize enough the importance of this account by such a seasoned, trained observer. As much as I have appreciated the information of every witness I've interviewed, Peter's cool, calm attention to detail under potentially stressful circumstances, was like a breath of fresh air. And it was really a smart move to quickly call the airport and sheriff's department to rule out anything conventional—even though for Peter, his wife, sister, and nephew, there was clearly no doubt.

Over the years, Peter has put a lot of thought into what he saw. He has spoken to other UFO witnesses and read a lot on the subject. From his research, he has also noticed that these craft tend to be seen near lakes and reservoirs in the area. In fact, another police officer witnessed a UFO rising out of the Croton Reservoir. Is this where these craft reside during daylight, under the surfaces of these bodies of water? Numerous observations may yet build a convincing case for this.

And I know of at least one detective who would like to solve that case.

8
Ulster County

Hank Vanderbeck: Saugerties, 1953

It was a beautiful, cloudless June day in 1953 when young Hank Vanderbeck was outside playing with his older brother, Bob, and several other neighborhood kids on Canoe Hill Road, near Cantine Field in Saugerties. It was after lunch, about 1pm, when one of the kids pointed to the sky to the northeast, in the direction of the Hudson River, and excitedly told everybody to, "Look!"

There was a dark brown, cigar-shaped object about 300-350 feet long, about 50 feet wide, which hovered motionless at an altitude of approximately 1000-1500 feet. In addition, there was a series of four red and green lights spaced evenly down the craft "like hula hoops around it. The first was red, then green, then red, and green. They must have been 100 feet in diameter." They appeared to be solid rings of very bright light (and they must have been bright to show up so clearly on a sunny day), but Hank can't be certain—they may have been individual lights spinning so fast they gave the appearance of being solid.

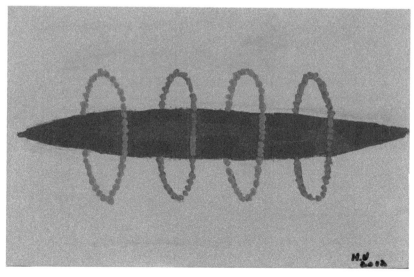

Hank Vanderbeck's painting of the object.

Han Vanderbeck stands on the spot where he watched
the cigar-shaped craft for 20 minutes.

Word spread through the neighborhood and more than a dozen concerned housewives (yes, there were housewives in 1953!) came out into the street to see the cigar-shaped object. The women were frightened, as this was the era of the Cold War, when the threat of a nuclear attack from the Soviet Union had everyone stockpiling survival supplies and building bomb shelters. This certainly wasn't any type of American aircraft they had ever seen, so could it be a Soviet weapon?

After ten long, agonizing minutes, one of the women called the police. The police never arrived, but ten minutes later something even better did—three fighter jets! They came from the south, so today, Hank assumes they came from Stewart Air Force Base in Newburgh.

Instead of approaching the craft head on, the three fighters went northwest toward the mountains. When they reached the mountain ridge, they swung around due east right toward the side of the long, cigar-shaped object. Everyone was breathless at the impending confrontation of the U.S. military vs. the UFO!

However, as the fighters headed straight for it, the UFO slowly started to rise for a few seconds, then, "Zip! It rose up vertically so fast it was just a dot in the sky and then was gone completely!" A few seconds later when the jets arrived at the spot where the UFO had hovered for 20 minutes, there was nothing but air.

Would the fighter jets have fired on the UFO if it hadn't sped away? We will never know, and we will probably never get the Air Force to admit the truth, even though there were at least 20 witnesses. The newspaper the next day said that jets had been scrambled from Stewart AFB, but it had simply been a weather balloon!

While the addition of the military jets makes this an even more fascinating case, what stands out for me are the "hula hoops" of light that circled the cigar-shaped body of the craft. Is it some clue as to the type of propulsion? Were they sensors, shielding, or some type of communication device? Who knows, but this is a very intriguing case worth remembering whenever officials deny the existence of UFOs.

Oh, and FYI, it wasn't a weather balloon!

Ray Sowa: Phoenicia, c.1960

In late September, John Bendetti phoned to say he had a friend, Ray Sowa, who had an interesting sighting about 50 years ago while camping. I called Ray and left a message. The next day Ray called to get more details about the project and set up a time for an interview. He didn't really give me any information about his sighting at the time, but he did say, "They didn't take me away or anything." I then heard a female voice in the background, and Ray laughed and told me, "My wife said that's too bad!"

I assumed it would be an interesting interview, but I had no idea just how fascinating Ray's story would be.

I gave him a call at 9am on October 3, which was yet another rainy, dreary day—a good day for a UFO story. I first found that Ray is now retired from AT&T, and prior to working for them, he was in the Navy. He served in Naval Air Crash and Rescue, had top secret clearance as he dealt with atomic bombs in B-52s, personally saw SR-71 Blackbirds take off and fly, and could tell what kind of aircraft was approaching just by the sound of the engines. So it became clear right off the bat that if this man said a flying object was unidentified, it was unidentifiable!

It was May or June of 1960 or '61, and Ray had five days of liberty. He planned a camping trip on the privately owned land of a friend at the end of Pantherkill Road in Phoenicia. The almost 200 acres bordered vast tracts of state land, so there would be nothing but peace and quiet, or so he thought.

Ray arrived on a Friday, as he recalls, and two of his buddies would be joining him the next day. He set up camp in sight of Giant Ledge to the right and Roamer Mountain to the left, and the "saddle," which was the low, V-shaped area between the mountains. Once camp was set up, he did his "Marlboro Man stuff" and cooked dinner over an open fire, and then relaxed with a cup of coffee as sunset approached.

(And just a side note here: Although Ray jokes about his "Marlboro Man stuff," he was quite the outdoorsman—once taking a 16-day trek alone through the woods just to prove he could survive and follow a course!)

As he gazed in the direction of the saddle, he caught a glimpse of what he assumed "was an early evening star." Upon closer look, he realized "it was not only too early to be a star, it was green!" He got his binoculars out of the tent and saw that the object was an intense green color, similar to today's laser pointers. It was difficult to judge the size of the object as he didn't know the distance, but it was most likely around a mile away, and there was no sound. When it grew a lot brighter, Ray assumed it was because the object was getting closer, but still there wasn't any sound.

He watched the object maintain its general position for several minutes, trying to figure out what it could be, when it suddenly began to move rapidly. It made "sharp, angular turns" at an incredible speed. The object also made series of 90-degree turns "like Pac Man" suddenly moving up and to the left, down and to the right, but always in sharp angles, "never any circular or elliptical turns." Then the light faded and disappeared, and Ray assumed it had moved away.

However, "about three to five minutes later, a streak of green light came from Roamer Mountain and moved to the same spot" where he had first seen the object. Again, the brightness intensified, it shot straight up and then "dropped straight down into the saddle and out of sight." Altogether, Ray had been watching this object flying for about ten minutes, but now that it had apparently landed, not more than a mile from his campsite, he admits to becoming "a little alarmed."

Loading his shotgun, he got into his 1958 Volkswagen and headed into town to a friend's restaurant. He needed two things there—a drink, and the payphone. Calling information, he got the number for the National Weather Service in Albany. He called and gave them the coordinates of the object he had observed, and they told him to hold on. After about "ten minutes of dropping dimes" into the payphone, Ray said he wasn't going to hold any longer, so they asked for the number of the payphone.

Sure enough, the phone rang several minutes later, and a man identified himself as a member of a government agency Ray never heard of, located at Fort Belvoir in Virginia. The call must have been on speaker phone, as "several men" began asking him a long series of questions. They had a "stern, no nonsense attitude" and kept him on the phone for at least half an hour.

I asked if he could try to recall the name of the agency, and he just couldn't remember what they told him. However, from their attitude and the way they asked questions, Ray "got the impression that they were CIA."

Once the interview was over, Ray braced himself with another drink, and headed back to his camp. Only he didn't drive right up to the campsite, as he "didn't know what" he would find there. Instead, he parked about a quarter of a mile away, grabbed his gun, and actually did a "military crawl" through the woods until he was in sight of his campfire, which had since been reduced to embers. Moving closer, he sat against a tree with his gun at the ready and continued to watch for any signs of movement or any sounds.

When he was satisfied that "no little green men" had entered his camp, he went into his tent, kept his shotgun by his side, and finally fell asleep. Then just before dawn, the flap of his tent was yanked open and there was a roaring sound like a bear. Grabbing his gun, he "almost shot" his two friends! They had just arrived and thought they would play a joke on him.

When he told them his story, his friends just laughed and said he must have "had a drunken nightmare." But Ray knew what he saw, and between that night's events, and his friends scaring the hell out of him, his nerves were rattled, and he was on edge the rest of the trip. However, the story didn't end there.

When he got back to the Naval Air Station, at what is now known as Floyd Bennett Field, he was summoned by none other than the Operations Officer. He couldn't imagine what it could be about, and was stunned when the officer revealed that he had been briefed about Ray's sighting, and knew all the details!

The officer then showed him maps, coordinates, and documents, and told him that this same object had first been reported that night by a Navy ship in the Philippine Sea! From there, the object was tracked and repeatedly spotted across the ocean to California, through Utah, etc., in a straight line all the way to the Catskills, just a mile from where Ray had been camping, and the object had been moving two to three times faster than an SR-71 Blackbird, which had a top speed of about 2,200mph!

At the end of this meeting, Ray was told, "You will not discuss this with anyone!" That put him in a bit of a bind when his commanding officer asked why Ray had been to see the Operations Officer.

"And my boss didn't appreciate it when I said I couldn't tell him," Ray said, and then explained that he finally had to tell his boss what it was all about. "His response was that we were all crazy and that was the end of it."

Many years later during the Putnam County sightings of the 1980s, Ray was reading a newspaper article about the recent UFO activity, and the article actually mentioned the object he had seen, and how it had been tracked across the country! So apparently, someone had talked at some point. Even so, I made sure to ask Ray if he was breaking some sort of confidentiality agreement by telling me his story.

"I don't remember signing anything," he replied. "And frankly, at this point, I don't care!"

That night over 50 years ago left quite an impression on Ray. He still looks up at the sky, and still wonders what it was he saw. He never had any sightings before that night, and he hasn't had another one since. And no, he didn't see aliens or get abducted.

"And thank God for that," he said laughing. "I have enough to deal with!"

Author's Note: I mentioned to Ray about RG's sighting (see below) in Woodstock in 1988, and how what RG saw exhibited the same sharp, angular turns. Ray said that Woodstock was "about 10-12 air miles" from Phoenicia. So, although these two sightings were almost three decades apart, they were in the same area and displayed the same unique flight characteristics.

The "Almost" Sighting: August, 1968

The following is a letter I received from a woman in West Shokan. If you have ever just missed something by a few minutes or even seconds, you can sympathize with her. (And if you've ever had a husband who sleeps through everything, you can also sympathize with her!)

Dear Ms. Zimmermann,

I was very happy to read about your interest in UFOs in the *Freeman* (Kingston, NY).

My husband and I built our home in a remote part of West Shokan in 1960. We loved the peace and quiet and at night our view of the sky was spectacular. We saw many things that were "unexplainable" and after a while we just took them for granted.

But one <u>very</u> still, <u>very</u> dark night in late August, 1968, I was awakened by a sound. A <u>strange</u> sound, sort of like a motor, but <u>not</u> a motor, <u>and</u> there was a flickering light overhead (which shone through the closed drapes). I woke my husband to listen. He turned over and fell back to sleep. I nudged him again to get up and look out the window. He mumbled something and was sleeping again!

So I got up (hesitantly), tiptoed to the closest window and tried to see outside by moving that drape slightly. I couldn't see anything and the light was no longer flickering. But I could still hear that sound.

I moved the drape a little more and as I did that sound was louder, and then it was quiet! And dark! I looked up at the sky, but didn't see anything out of the ordinary. I went to the front door and stepped out on the landing, nothing! No sound and no light.

The next day I saw in the newspaper that there were sightings along the east coast down to Georgia! I showed my husband the paper. He shrugged and said, "Hmm."

Thought you'd like to hear about this "almost" sighting

RG: Woodstock, 1988

It was November of 1988, and RG had just moved to his new home in Woodstock. The house was on a mountain and "had a great view of the Hudson Valley and the sky." Due to all the excitement and activity of the day, he couldn't sleep, so he got up about 2am. He went into the empty living room to look out the window and saw "a very bright white light about three times the size of Venus."

The light was not moving, and as he stood there for a minute or two trying to figure out what it could be, "it suddenly shot up to the right at a 45-degree angle at an amazing speed." At that same high rate of speed, the silent light "zipped" back and forth across the sky, "zigzagging at sharp angles." RG was clear that the object did not make rounded turns, it made sudden, sharp, changes in direction that no craft he knows of could possibly duplicate. After watching "a little breathless" for a couple of minutes as this incredible object performed seemingly impossible maneuvers, it sped over to the horizon, "zipped straight up and was gone."

He told his wife what he saw, and she knew him well enough "to know when I was not joking." Although he didn't need to convince his wife he was telling the truth, he was nonetheless glad to hear on the radio the next day that "many people in the Woodstock area had called in to report" this strange light.

RG was never scared during this sighting, as the object never appeared to be threatening in any way. However, he admits if it had been much closer, his fascination may have turned to fear.

As he worked his entire career in a creative field, RG "had to be open to" all kinds of possibilities, so the concept of other life in the universe wasn't anything new, and the sighting "didn't change his views."

And what did the people in town think about the UFO sightings?

"In Woodstock, everyone believes, because it's Woodstock!"

Terri: Kingston, mid-1980s

From: Terri
Sent: Thursday, September 20, 2012 8:02 AM
To: 'lindazim@optonline.net'
Subject: UFO Sightings in Ulster County

I came across the story printed in the Daily Freeman today in regards to UFO sightings in Ulster County. I know in the story it states you are really looking for residents that have had this experience along 32 just south of Saugerties but my experience was in Kingston near the strand area in downtown Kingston.

My family & I, (my parents and my brother), experienced a UFO sighting when I was a young child. I don't remember all of the details but I do remember we were driving back from my Nanny & Poppy's house (on Hunter Street in Kingston), seeing something in the sky and my father stopped driving, looked up and he turned the car around and followed it back down to my Nanny & Poppy's house. I remember getting out of the car, looking up and seeing this strange shaped object hovering above my Nanny & Poppy's house. There was a lot of people outside watching this. I think there may have been more than one but that isn't clear in my memory. I got so scared, (be it I was probably 7-8 years old as my brother was just a baby at that time – so it was most likely mid 1980s), I ran inside my Nanny & Poppy's house and hid behind a recliner.

William Marchetti: Ulster, c.1987

On September 20, I received the following email from William Marchetti:

My whole family and friends saw a strange sighting several times above the town of Ulster/Kingston. It was a RING of lights slowly hovering and moving across the sky with a weird motor sound. Always happened in the early eve when it just got dark. It lasted a half hour or so until it disappeared from view off in the distance. I called my Air Force "know-it-all" skeptical friend during a sighting and told him to go outside and look up. I asked him what he thought it was and he said I HAVE NO IDEA!!! These sightings lasted for several weeks somewhere in the late 80s. I believe it was summer time, and they did a report of it on Unsolved Mysteries. No way it was ultralights or whatever. No airport in the area could verify any aircraft to justify these sightings...

122

We arranged to speak a few days later so I could get more details. The sightings took place in a development just to the north of the Wiltwyck Country Club, which is just east of the NYS Thruway. The circle of lights always came from the east, but never went any farther west than this development, essentially always stopping short of crossing the Thruway, and would then head back the way it came.

The circle of lights may have been more accurately described as being shaped like a stop sign, with about a dozen clusters of three white, unblinking lights evenly spaced around the object's symmetrical perimeter. The clusters of lights appeared to remain equidistant from one another, and gave every appearance that they were attached to a single, solid object.

However, unlike the majority of UFO sightings in the Hudson Valley over the years, this object had a clear engine sound, "like a buzzing hum." In fact, William and his family knew when to go outside to look, because they could hear the object approaching. Also, this ring of lights appeared about the same time, and only on Thursday nights, for four or five weeks.

"That sure sounds like it would be some sort of flying club," William admitted, clearly allowing doubt to creep in.

During our conversation, he wavered between absolute certainty that what he saw *could not possibly* have been planes flying in formation, to uncertainty due to the engine sound and the regularity of the Thursday night sightings. There was even more doubt when I mentioned that on the *Unsolved Mysteries* segment, Robert Stack said that they spoke to some of the pilots who admitted flying in formation to fool people, and that they had done this on Thursday nights.

Was the object the Marchetti family saw a true UFO, something that cannot be explained, or was it a formation of planes low enough to hear the engine noise, but high enough that they appeared as one solid object?

Thanks to the hoaxers, we may never know.

"Sally": Mohonk Mountain, 1990s

The following are excerpts of a letter I received after "Sally" read the *Daily Freeman* article:

I am, I believe, a fairly "normal" person, or at least I try to be. I've never seen things that aren't there. I am intrigued by your work, and that is why I am responding.

When my mother was still alive, she told me about a bright light, like a spot light, coming toward her from the direction of Mohonk Mountain. We live in [location removed] with a good view of Mohonk. She said the light seemed to be searching for something and aimed at her then went away. She asked me please not to mention this to anyone. "I don't want people thinking I'm crazy. I've got to keep my job."

In Feb, 1995 (or 6?) she was in the hospital having developed some aging problems. I was taking care of the house and dog while she was there. I stepped out on the back porch for a moment and saw what looked like a colossal, gigantic airplane outlined with lights at intervals, just giving the (illusion?) of the craft, moving slowly and silently south just above the horizon (trees)—again heading parallel or heading to Mohonk. I didn't know what to think, it was strange, as an airplane could never be that big. I thought maybe it was smaller planes flying in formation, but there was no sound. You can always hear sound from airplanes if they are near enough to be seen.

A prank, perhaps, I thought, but what for? Who would have the time and money for that? I told my mother about it when she came home and her reply was, "Just don't mention it to anyone. You don't want people thinking you're crazy. Life is hard enough as it is."

Then 2 nights later, Fox 5 had a special on UFOs. They showed a clip of the huge "airplane" saying several people saw this and no one knew what it was. (OMG—that's what I saw the other night!)

After my mother passed on, the next Dec or January (winter) I was walking the dog and looked up to see a bright light in the sky. Again, no sound. It was quite high up, toward the southern horizon. The light flashed toward me, then it seemed there were other lights, like search lights, moving about as though seeking something. A police helicopter? Central Hudson? [The power company.] At 10:30pm? Then it disappeared silently and in the blink of an eye toward Mohonk. Seems it must have been a helicopter, but aren't they noisy?

So that is my story. I hope it will be helpful to you. There is definitely something going on, but what?

Ray: Rosendale, c. 1990s

Ray has seen more in this world than most people can imagine. He was with the Marines on Okinawa in 1945—a battle that cost him most of his hearing. He spent decades in law enforcement, and worked on special dignitary security teams with the FBI. However, for all of his experiences, nothing compared to the sighting of a metallic disk off of Route 32 in Rosendale.

Sometime prior to that night, Ray saw an odd, yellowish light in the sky on the right side of the road near his house. He had a high-powered light and decided to flash it a few times. The yellow light flashed back the same number of times. Coincidence? Ray then flashed his light five times, and then the yellow light flashed exactly five times. He continued flashing his light in different sequences, and each time he got an exact response! Then the light just moved away.

Not too many days later, Ray and his wife were in the house when "three perfect circles of light" appeared. These circles moved through the house "as if they were scanning the rooms" looking for something—or someone.

Then one moonlit night, Ray and his wife were driving home. As they approached their driveway, they saw a metallic disk on the side of the road, just across the street from their house. In the moonlight they could see it was silvery, and about 35-40 feet in diameter. It was sitting silently, just a few yards from the road.

"It was like two saucers together, with a ridge around the center. There was a reddish glow inside."

Ray parked the car and he and his wife just stared in amazement. He was tempted to get out of the car, but his wife warned him to not get any closer. They watched it for a least a minute, and then the craft silently rose up and took off. Ray admits he "doesn't know what would have happened if he had gotten out of the car" and approached it.

Sometime later, his wife noticed an odd mark on her upper leg, and it's a spot to this day that doesn't seem to ever heal completely.

Ray's wife had another sighting years later, when they lived in Stone Ridge. Ray was out responding to a fire one night, where he rescued a burned baby raccoon and brought him to the vet (the raccoon survived),

Don Alan Smith

and when he came home, his wife came running out telling him to hurry. She had just seen something strange, but unfortunately it had gone.

She described looking out her second story bedroom window and seeing a very bright light coming from the direction of the Mohonk tower. As it approached, it became so bright it was blinding. She couldn't make out any shape, until the craft went right by the window. Once the bright light had passed, she could see that it was a circular, saucer-shaped craft.

Ray had two more stories to share, but these were not sightings he had personally, they were told to him by friends. The first involved a farmer from Saugerties. He went out to a field to bring in the cattle for the night, and when he reached the crest of a hill he looked down and saw a saucer-shaped craft on the ground right below him. There were several figures nearby, and those figures must have seen him, as they hurried back inside the craft. The saucer then lifted up to tree height, but before taking off, the farmer saw what looked like an arm reaching out of an opening to pull something closed—as if they had taken off so quickly they had forgotten to close the hatch!

The other story was from a friend who was taking his boat from the Rondout Creek by Kingston into the Hudson River. At that point, he saw a bright circle of light under the water. He watched the lights for several minutes, and then they disappeared. Either the lights turned out, or whatever it was went deeper and out of sight, he couldn't tell.

So here we have some fascinating firsthand accounts, where attempting to communicate with a light in the sky led to a very close encounter, and a couple of other stories that illustrate that very strange things are going on *around* and *in* the Hudson River.

Ashley: Kingston, 2009-12

In 2009, Ashley went outside her East Chester Road home in Kingston to have a cigarette. It was a beautiful day, and "there wasn't a cloud in the sky." However, *something* was in the sky—three round, silver metallic objects were moving "from the direction of Saugerties" toward Kingston.

The three objects moved very slowly with absolutely no sound, and seemed to be going back and forth over the area. She observed them for 15 minutes, and while she really couldn't estimate the altitude, they were "higher than the birds" that flew by, but still rather low in the sky. Then they just disappeared. Ashley was quite clear on this point—they didn't move off into the distance and out of sight, they simply vanished.

A year or two later, Ashley was again outside on a pleasant afternoon, and another round metallic object appeared, only this time there was just one. This object also moved very slowly, and then just "disappeared before my eyes."

A third sighting occurred one night early in the summer of 2012. She saw what she thought was a star, but the previously motionless light started moving when a plane flew by. The light slowly started to move, then accelerated and followed the plane until they both traveled out of sight.

I asked how these things have influenced her life, and Ashley replied that they will "stay with me forever." She says that UFOs were never anything she really gave any thought to, but now she believes and is not afraid, just very curious and excited. She wouldn't even mind "saying hello" to them!

As I have found that people with sightings often have family members who have also experienced something unusual, I asked Ashley if any relatives had any stories. I was amazed when she relayed the following.

In 1967 when her mother was a little girl, the entire family was on the porch of their Kingston home. Her mother's parents, grandparents, and many other family members witnessed or encountered some sort of UFO, but that's all Ashley knows, because no one will speak about it! What could have happened that this group experience is now a closely guarded family secret?

In lieu of this tantalizing mystery, it may not be a coincidence that Ashley has now had a few sightings of her own. This would certainly not be the first case I dealt with that involved several generations of the same family, and I'm certain it won't be the last.

9
Pine Bush

The official kick-off of this project was a tale of two extremes, and they were both to be experienced at the Pine Bush UFO Fest on April 28, 2012. I began the day by attending the lectures at the local school, given by UFO researcher Robert Vanderclock, and Bill Wiand of the United Friends Observer Society.

It ended with the parade through the center of town, where people dressed like aliens, they dressed their dogs like aliens, and even dressed their cars as aliens. There were also games, prizes, food, and fun for all humanoids!

It was the perfect day to see the two sides of the UFO phenomenon—those who take it seriously and look for answers, and those who treat it as legends and nonsense, but aren't shy about making a buck on rubber aliens and plastic UFOs.

So how did this sleepy little town surrounded by farms get its own festival, and become the topic of books and videos? Because for many decades—possibly even as early as the 1920s—Pine Bush has been visited by things that no one can explain.

Dino Mavros, owner of the famous Cup and Saucer Diner,
leads the parade in his Pine Bush UFO Patrol Car.

Butch

All good UFO stories need a colorful character, and for Pine Bush, there's no doubt that character is Larry "Butch" Hunt, the local barber. He has lived in Pine Bush since 1944, and since 1968 when he had not one, but two sightings, he has never wavered about what he saw, and has never been shy about telling his stories.

Butch and four friends were driving home from an evening at the pool hall, and were crossing Red Mills bridge, a few miles north of town. There was a "huge, circular craft the size of the bank across the street." [The bank across the street from his barber shop in town.] There were three lights beaming down, and the object made a "whishing sound" as it passed over the trees.

They stopped the car and got out, and had two pairs of binoculars to get an even closer look. "Around the rim were windows, and I could see figures looking at us, and we were looking at them." At one point, the circular vehicle was so close Butch "could have hit it with a slingshot."

As another car approached from behind them, the "craft tilted and went right out of sight. It was gone in three seconds." Butch often wonders "what would have happened if that other car hadn't come by."

Butch's interview with BGM.

It's hard to miss Butch's shop on the main street of Pine Bush.

Butch's second sighting occurred when he was coming back from Walden, and was passing through a rock cut near the Jewish cemetery. He saw a "silver craft going up Searsville road," below the tree line, and at first, "thought it was a dirigible." However, he thought about it for another moment and realized that "dirigibles are shaped like big watermelons, have the big cabin underneath, and the propeller [and this object had none of those feature], so I turned around and went back, but by that time it was gone."

So how did these sightings influence Butch? For starters, they made him a believer. Even one of his friends, who was with him during the first sighting, who was "a dopey guy who didn't believe anything," changed his opinion.

Butch has spent almost half a century cutting hair, telling his UFO stories, and listening to what others have to share—"everything from hybrids, to encounters, to abductee stories. Everybody and everything." He's heard it all, and "can spot a phony" when he hears one.

Many reporters, UFO groups, and famous personalities have passed through his door, including Bill Birnes from *UFO Hunters*. His shop has become *the* place to find out about the latest sightings, as well as hear about the long, strange history of Pine Bush.

Just about all the visitors are believers. And what does Butch think about skeptics who ridicule witnesses? He says their motto should be, "Aging is mandatory, intellect is optional."

He also has a sign at his shop which reads, "UFOs are real. The Air Force doesn't exist."

Who Else Can We Tell?

The end of May and early June were filled with writing press releases, conducting and giving interviews, speaking to reporters, scheduling, and all manner of research. On Monday, June 4, I thought about the monthly meetings which Bill Wiand had told me about at the Pine Bush UFO Festival. I thought I recalled that they held their meetings on the first Wednesday of every month. Realizing that was only two days away, I looked up their website and sent an email to confirm that their next meeting was June 6. I received a speedy response from Sue Wiand that there would indeed be a meeting, so I immediately circled the date with my black Sharpie, which is the modern equivalent of etching something in stone.

At the last minute, my husband Bob's plans changed, so he was able to go with me. We headed up to Pine Bush in a nasty little thunderstorm, but fortunately the skies quickly cleared and we had a pleasant 45 minute ride through rolling pastures and horse farms, with the stately Shawangunk Mountains framing the horizon.

The United Friends Observers Society, obviously so named to accommodate the acronym U.F.O.S., was founded in 1993 by the late Margaret Lay and her daughter Dawn. They had both witnessed UFOs in the Pine Bush area in the 1980s and wondered if other residents were having similar experiences. They placed a small ad in the local newspaper which simply read, "Have you seen a UFO?" That single line of newsprint generated over 300 calls from people from all walks of life—policemen, doctors, teachers, and just ordinary people looking for some answers to something extraordinary they had witnessed.

The number of attendees at these meetings grew steadily and by the fall of 1993 they moved to the spacious VFW hall in town. Over the years, the meetings were held in many different locations and the number of attendees ebbed and flowed. However, one thing never changed—this was finally a place where people could go to be heard, where they were able to speak out without fear of ridicule, to find some small haven in a skeptical and critical world, where they could finally find the support and understanding that they needed.

I wasn't quite sure what to expect at the meeting or how it would be conducted. I also didn't expect a crowd of about 30 people, most of whom knew each other, although there were a few newcomers like us. Bill Wiand, the group facilitator, opened the meeting with a brief statement and then yielded the floor to those of us in the audience to introduce ourselves and to share any recent experiences, or just to say what was on our minds.

For the most part, people had nothing new to report since their last meeting, but there were certainly a few surprises. For example, a couple of weeks earlier, one woman felt compelled to take a drive into Pine Bush one night. She saw a very bright light and began to follow it. She suddenly felt quite ill, and sometime later, she found herself in a completely different part of town, and was "completely disoriented." She repeatedly mentioned being disoriented, and also described the feeling that compelled her to go for that drive as being "like a rope around me that someone was pulling."

Another woman was there for the first time, and with some hesitation and trepidation, she said that she had come because of an experience she had over 40 years ago. She seemed content to leave it at that, but several people gently coaxed her to say more. She slowly began to tell her story, and with each passing word she seemed to become a little more comfortable about speaking out in public for the first time in her life.

Her story was a remarkable one—while spending some time on her grandmother's farm in Pine Island, New York, she saw what she thought was a bright street light behind some trees every night. Later that night the light came up to the house and started to shine in every window as if it was searching for something—or someone. What ensued were two nights of terror, and many hours of missing time. (See Abduction Alley chapter.)

After the woman divulged her story to the group, there was an odd mixture of emotions on her face. In some ways, she was obviously relieved to unburden herself in a room full of people who had similar encounters and understood what it was like to undergo such a traumatic experience. On the other hand, she was visibly shaken and admitted that recalling the episode brought back a lot of feelings and rekindled that fear she had experienced more than four decades ago. For her, the memory and emotions are as fresh and raw as if it just happened yesterday.

I showed a first draft of this chapter to my friend, Detective Michael Worden, and he made a very interested observation and comparison: "It has to be terrifying—and I know from talking to crime victims who have said that the helplessness and lack of control over the crime compounded their emotional situation."

Indeed, comparing what was happening to these people to crimes, literally *crimes against humanity*, seemed to be very appropriate.

This woman's story made quite an impression on me. Even being in the early stages the project, I could already see that there were some common themes coming to light. First, regardless of whether someone had an encounter or a sighting last week or 40, 50, or even 60 years ago, the memory of that experience stays as sharp, vivid, and clear as if it just occurred. Also, for whatever reason, it seemed that *now* was the time that many people had decided to speak out. It was far more than a simple coincidence. It was almost spooky how many people had already told me that for the first time in years or decades they wanted to talk; they wanted to finally tell their stories.

The other recurring theme, and one which is far more disturbing, is that many people—often as innocent and defenseless children—have been subjected to things beyond their control, things they could not explain, and things that have terrified them for the remainder of their lives. Of course, there are those courageous few who claim to have never been afraid of their encounters, but I have to believe that given the choice, they would not have consented to be subjected to these experiences, and they are glad that there are many details they can't recall about their "missing time."

After the meeting, I spoke individually with many of the people. A lot of critics say that it's impossible to believe stories of UFO sightings and encounters, but when you look into the eyes of a person who has seen something that has changed their lives, you have no doubt that it is completely real to them. Of course, one could still argue that these people are simply delusional and suffering under a fabricated alternate reality—and I admit there are certainly such people—but the vast majority of eyewitnesses I have spoken to are very credible people who simply want answers as to what they have experienced.

I told Bill that I thought these meetings were very important for people to have a chance to unburden themselves and for once have the opportunity to speak freely. His response perfectly summed up the value of having access to such group.

"Who else can you tell?"

Gene DeJong: Summer, 1984

Sarah, Felix, and I had a meeting with Dino at his Cup and Saucer Diner in Pine Bush in June of 2012. Dino is definitely the "go-to guy" in town as he seems to know everyone. When I mentioned that I wanted to interview some witnesses to the UFOs in the area, he immediately dialed the phone number of Gene DeJong of Nashville, TN, formerly of Pine

Bush. Dino then handed me the phone and I conducted the interview right then and there.

For many years, Dino's Cup & Saucer Diner has been *the* place for UFO enthusiasts to meet, and it became our "Pine Bush Headquarters" during the making of the documentary.

It was the summer of 1984, and Gene was driving east on County Road 48 toward his parents' dairy farm on Bullville Road. He was driving a convertible, and he stopped the car at the stop sign by the church in Thompson Ridge at the intersection of Route 302. Looking up, he saw a "giant triangle right over the trees, no more than a hundred feet off the ground." It was "the size of a football field and I heard a very low hum. It was moving very slowly and I started to follow it, but it sped up and moved quickly away toward Montgomery." As it moved away, Gene could see blinking lights on the back of the craft, and the lights made the metal of the ship appear to be like stainless steel.

At 3:30am the next morning, Gene had to get up to take care of the cows, and he put on the radio while he worked. He was amazed to hear news reports of countless eyewitnesses to the same triangle he had seen the night before. Reports had come in from Orange and Rockland Counties, and all the way down to the George Washington Bridge. The newscasters said the State Police had requested that anyone who saw the object should call them and file a report, which he did.

He said that the next day, he also heard reports of "red balls of fire" coming down in the town of Beacon, NY. He also said that the "five planes in formation" excuse was being offered in the news, an idea to which Gene responded with an unquestionable, "No!" What he witnessed was solid and almost silent.

Gene was a pleasure to talk to, as he was clear, concise, and absolutely certain of what he saw. He had no problem with his real name being used, nor of speaking about his sighting, as he quickly came to realize that thousands of other people saw the same thing.

The Pine Bush Archive

Half of the battle in any project is to track down reliable information. In the case of UFO research, it's about 90% of the battle. If only there was one central location for every town where every eyewitness account was collected in a database...

Well, if C. Burns has anything to say about it, one day Pine Bush, NY will have a comprehensive, searchable database of every local UFO report ever made. Sounds like an overwhelming project? Of course, but for historians and researchers, this is what we refer to as a gold mine of information.

On July 18, 2012, I spoke to C. Burns to mine a few of those gold nuggets, to try to give me a sense of the big picture of the Pine Bush UFO story. He began by recommending I read Vincent Polise's book, *The Pine Bush UFO Phenomenon*, to understand the nature of the sightings in the last couple of decades. My obvious first question was how many decades back does this phenomenon go?

I was surprised to hear that the first known sighting was in the early 1920s, although no details of the case appear to have been written down. Certainly by the 1950s, the Pine Bush area was already something of a UFO hot spot, and at least one group was formed to investigate the many sightings. These were the days of the "classic saucers," the shiny metal disks that were seen to land in fields and fly through the night sky with their ring of lights.

The 1970s brought another wave of sightings. According to Mr. Burns, many of these involved seeing green lights in the woods and lights close to the ground in fields. Another group of "UFO Chasers" was formed at that time, but no one from that group has yet to come forward to tell their stories. It was also during the 1970s that Harry Lebelson of OMNI magazine began investigating the numerous reports of disc-shaped objects and photographing the lights that he personally witnessed.

In 1980, Lebelson brought Ellen Crystall to Pine Bush, and she eventually authored *Silent Invasion* (published in 1991) about her years of sightings, many of which then involved triangular or chevron-shaped craft, alleged underground UFO bases, and bizarre glowing and flashing lights. Personally, I found that the book stretched the limits of credibility, but regardless of my opinion, by all accounts Crystall was a tenacious ufologist who dedicated her life to the pursuit of the Pine Bush phenomenon. Many people accompanied Crystall to the fields of Pine Bush during the 1980s and 90s, and they also had numerous sightings of the triangles and lights.

Crystall's book sparked a "sky watching" craze, as UFO enthusiasts began lining West Searsville Road every night. On a good night, as many as 100 cars would be parked along the road, much to the eventual dismay of developers who were eyeing the land for houses. Local officials passed a law that any parked cars had to have all four tires off the road, which essentially eliminated the ability to park on West Searsville and many other streets.

In 1997, the number of sightings began to dwindle, and by 1998, it is rumored that some developers put the final nails in the sky watching coffin, as it were, by resorting to putting tacks in the road to flatten the tires of the UFO chasers. A few sightings still occur today, but the old sky watching grounds are now housing developments, and the UFO heyday of Pine Bush appears to be in the rear view mirror at this point in time.

During our conversation, Mr. Burns made two particularly interesting observations about the history of the Pine Bush sightings. First, the sightings of the 1980s and 90s were very much "ground based and treetop level," as opposed to the more traditional sightings of lights or craft in the sky. Also, over time, the phenomenon appeared to shift from solid craft with defined shapes to simply lights.

What all this means, neither of us was willing to speculate. What is important, is that these decades-worth of eyewitness accounts are being gathered and preserved, and hopefully eventually made available to the general public. And hopefully, someday, all of the saucers, triangles, and lights will make sense to a future generation.

Nancy: August, 2012

I gave my first UFO presentation at the Walden Library on July 24, and afterwards, Ginny D. from the library mentioned that she had a friend in Walden who had some interesting experiences many years ago. Fast forward to September, and Ginny emails me that her friend, Nancy, is willing to be interviewed, so we set up a time for the 17th, and planned to meet at Nancy's house.

I programmed my Garmin with Nancy's address and headed out late that afternoon, and was surprised that the GPS was not taking me on the usual way I go to get to Walden. After a few minutes, I hit the route tab and found that I would actually be going a way I often travel—when I go to Pine Bush. Not only that, but the last part of the route was on Albany

Post Road and Hill Avenue, crossing the intersection with West Searsville Road—all of which are well-known local UFO hot spot viewing streets!

Of course I knew that Walden was the next to Pine Bush, but until I was on my way I had no idea that Nancy lived in the hot spot zone. And I was also in for another surprise when I arrived.

After greeting Nancy and her lovable dog, Chewy, we sat down at the kitchen table to talk and wait for Ginny, who arrived shortly after. When I got down to the questions, Nancy started recounting a sighting that had just occurred a couple of weeks ago. It was a fascinating story, but I thought I must be confusing all of the interviewees, and assumed that this was not the woman Ginny had originally told me about. But allow me to let the story speak for itself.

It was the end of August during the week of the second full moon of the month. It was about 10:30pm when Nancy was letting Chewy out in the backyard. She stepped out onto the deck, and there, clearly visible in the bright moonlight, was a large craft, about "the width of three cars," hovering silently at treetop height just at her property line, only about 100 feet away.

It was "shaped like an ice cream cone," pointed at one end and rounded on the other. At the curved end she could see round lights, but they were not on. Nancy said that the curved section also gave her the impression that it could turn or rotate. Another unusual feature was the rectangular section that extended out of one side, also unlit. I asked her to sketch the shape so I could better understand, and the following is what she drew, with my notes scribbled in.

The craft "just seemed to be stalled there" as it didn't move. It looked to be made of metal, but other than the rounded lights she couldn't make out any other structural features.

"What the hell is that!?" she repeated over and over as she stared in amazement at the silent vehicle. Then after "at least 60 seconds" of watching this object that was so very close, "it took off fast to the left" (the south) and was gone. Even the rapid acceleration produced no sound.

"I came inside and sat down, and just kept saying, 'What the hell did I just see?' I was trying to comprehend what just happened."

Nancy said she had wanted to go get her neighbors or come in and grab a camera, but she was afraid the vehicle might take off and she would

Nancy points to the spot in the sky where she observed the odd-shaped craft. I inserted her sketch at the height she indicated it was hovering.

miss it. Also, she admits the sighting "really scared" her, and she couldn't sleep that night.

"I was afraid, thinking if they saw me, you know, are they going to come? I really had a very bad night, I couldn't sleep. And I still think about it all the time now when I go to sleep."

I was quite pleased with the interview, as not only was Nancy very credible, but this was a very "fresh" sighting. Clearly, the Pine Bush area sightings were not just a thing of the past! This brought the history of the Hudson Valley UFO experience up to "here and now," and gave me hope that on our proposed "stake out" we might have a chance of seeing something incredible.

I asked Nancy if she had ever had any other UFO sightings, or if any other family members had seen anything, and she said that it was the only sighting she had, and no one in the family had any that she knew about. As I was wrapping up my questions, Nancy then mentioned in passing something about the times she saw "the figures" in her bedroom. I think I sat straight up with an expression as if someone had just slapped me in the face, and said something to the effect of, "Say what!?"

It turned out that this *was* the same woman that Ginny had told me about, the same woman who had a couple of very close encounters decades ago, but hadn't thought to mention them since the recent sighting seemed to be far more important. I suggested she start from the beginning and tell the other part of her story.

It was about 1988, five years after moving into their new house. It was late at night and Nancy suddenly "woke up with an excruciating pain" in her left side. There at the foot of their tall, 4-poster bed, were two, short, hooded figures. She could only see their heads, as they were so short and the bed was so high.

"I wanted to scream and wake up my husband, but I couldn't move and I couldn't make a sound," she recalled. "Then one of them lifted his arm and out of the sleeve it pointed a long finger," and then the two figures in the dark cloaks were gone and she could once again move and speak. She screamed and shook her husband, telling him what just happened. He told it was just a bad dream and to go back to sleep.

Of course, nightmares and sleep paralysis are perfectly good explanations for such alleged encounters—certainly far more rational than aliens in hooded robes in your bedroom! However, nightmares and sleep paralysis don't cause round, bloody, burn marks on your left side.

"It was about the size of a pencil eraser," Nancy explained. "It was like something had burned me, and there was some blood around it."

The mysterious spot hurt for days, and left a circle of scar tissue. I asked if she smoked, and could have burned herself with a cigarette in bed, but she wasn't a smoker. Her husband said she must have scratched herself, but it was a perfectly circular burn, not a scratch.

And how did this encounter make her feel?

"I was petrified!" she confessed.

As bad as this encounter had been, it wasn't the last. About a year later, Nancy again awoke to see two hooded figures in her bedroom, and once again, she was unable to move or speak. Only this time, the figures "were very tall" and they were facing one another. When they left, she regained the ability to move and speak, and her husband told her it was just another nightmare. Fortunately, this time, however, she wasn't hurt in any way.

Over the next twenty-three years, nothing else happened that she can recall, until the end of August. It made a lot more sense now that Nancy had been so frightened by the sighting, and had wondered if they were coming for her. It also turned this incident from a random sighting to something more—perhaps much more. I suggested she keep a camera and strong flashlight by the back door, just in case something else appears over the yard. I also told her to call me ASAP if anything more happens.

It's doubtful that it was a coincidence that this odd-shaped ship chose to hover just 100 feet away from Nancy that night. The question is, did these encounters begin only after she moved into the Pine Bush area, or had things been occurring for much longer, things she can no longer remember? Of course it's all speculation, but I won't be too surprised if some night I get a call…

The Stake Out: November 3, 2012

Undoubtedly due to the fact that I whined and complained about the extreme heat all summer, the night of our Pine Bush stake out was "unseasonably cold" and windy. I dressed in a couple of layers and brought out "Big Pink"—my long, LL Bean down coat rated to -50 degrees. I such cases I am always willing to sacrifice fashion for comfort.

When discussing where we would hold our UFO vigil, Sarah, Felix and I had to consider things such as avoiding trespassing, safety from passing cars, noise, lights, etc. We needed a place that was safe, quiet, had a good view of the prime UFO hotspots, and wouldn't involve having the police make us leave, or worse.

In September, the offer of the perfect location was presented by Ginny D. (see previous story) when we met at Nancy's house. Ginny suggested a field she owned where we would have plenty of room, and wouldn't be bothered by the police. It was a wonderful offer, but I would have to see what the view was like, of course. I followed her to the field after Nancy's interview, and was blown away by what I saw.

One of the most popular UFO viewing locations over the years has been the Jewish cemetery on Route 52, as the fields behind it and across the street from it have generated a lot of reported sightings. Ginny's field *overlooked that entire area*, and more! We set a date of Saturday, November 3, and I anxiously awaited the chance for a real Pine Bush UFO experience.

We were fortunate to have C. Burns join us, as well as Nancy. Sarah, her cousin, Jackson Kellogg, Felix, and I arrived about 4pm, with the others arriving around nightfall. Before we officially started, Ginny went above and beyond the role of UFO Stake Out Hostess by providing us with pizza and hot beverages, and we were fortified for our hours sitting out in the cold.

We set up lounge chairs and snuggled under blankets as we searched the mysterious skies of Pine Bush. I brought two pairs of binoculars— 7x50 with a nice wide field to quickly locate moving objects, and the big 15x70 to get a close view of whatever might pass by.

The first thing I noticed was that a lot of things were passing by— Pine Bush appeared to be in the direct path of at least two airline routes. A steady flow of air traffic passed throughout our time there, all easily recognizable by the sounds and running lights. We did have one exciting moment, however, as Felix said, "What's that?"

I turned to see a classic Hollywood, *Close Encounters*-type of scene—low clouds eerily illuminated by flashing lights. My heart skipped a beat, but only for one beat, as jet airliner noise rumbled through the sky. A large passenger jet emerged from the clouds, apparently preparing to land at nearby Stewart Airport. It was disappointing it wasn't the Mother Ship, after all, but the night was still young, and C. Burns reminded us that much of the activity in Pine Bush does not take place in the air, but on the ground and in the trees.

He related some of his many experiences, and we tried to keep our eyes on both the sky and the fields below. At one point, a very bright light did appear in some trees in the distance. It actually grew in intensity, but went out after just several seconds. While it was much brighter that any street light, we couldn't rule out that a local farm or house had just turned on a spotlight to let out their dog.

Ginny, Nancy, me, and C. Burns look more like Eskimos than UFO hunters on our Pine Bush stake out.   Photo courtesy of BGM

The highlight of the night was when I passed around the big binoculars so everyone could see Jupiter and its moons, as well as our big, beautiful moon, which made an impressive ascent over the horizon. But that was about it for objects from beyond Earth, and when I couldn't feel my fingers or face any longer, it was time to call it a night. It would have been nice to see a triangular ship, the strobing lights, or a mysterious pulsating glow in the woods, but maybe next time.

I encourage anyone interested in UFOs to go to the Cup 'n Saucer diner for a good meal, visit Butch the barber and listen to his stories, attend a meeting of the United Friends Observers Society, and even dress like an alien and go to the next UFO Fest. But most importantly, try to find a dark, quiet spot overlooking one of the fields and just look and listen.

Something inexplicable is still visiting Pine Bush, and maybe you will be the next person to see it.

10
The Skeptic

In order to present a fair and balanced approach to the subject of UFOs, we needed to find someone who was skeptical, yet knowledgeable about the night sky, and who better for that than an astronomer? We were fortunate to get astronomer and author Bob Berman to agree to be interviewed for the book and documentary, and the following is the transcript of that interview, which took place in his home outside of Woodstock.

Bob: Public knowledge about the sky is so low, that almost anything can be misconstrued. People can't spot the brightest planets, like Venus and Jupiter. People have no idea that the North Star isn't the brightest thing in the sky, and this is simple astronomy. This is something the ancients would have known, that every village idiot would have known 500 years ago—that one star is stationary, and all the other stars go around it. What's more basic than that? I don't think one person in 50 knows that today.

So of course when people go out and whenever they see anything—and I don't think it's necessarily even something unusual—I think when they see anything they are noticing for the first time, they may be as apt to attribute something dramatic to it as something ordinary. And a lot of people like drama.

The poles are shifting is a good example of this. And the poles have always shifted. But you ask people what poles they are talking about, because there are two sets of poles. The world has geographic poles around which we pivot, and magnetic poles where compasses point. But if you ask people, "Which poles are you concerned about?" you'll get a blank look. They don't even know which poles worry them.

The magnetic poles have been moving rapidly—37 miles per year— the geographic poles never move more than 50 feet in a year. So, one moves and one doesn't, and the magnetic poles, it doesn't matter where they are or whether they shift. They've always been shifting. Compasses point to the new spot wherever it is. And yet a lot of people are worried about this, the poles are shifting!

So, my only point is that drama, and a threat to all life on life, and Armageddon, is something that a lot of people are attuned to. And I think when they look up in the sky there's a tendency among some people to go for the dramatic rather than seek a commoner cause.

In science we have something called Occam's Razor—you know what that is. Occam's Razor is the simplest explanation is usually the right one. For example, if your car doesn't start in the morning, Occam's Razor would say well, maybe the battery died, maybe I left a light on, maybe it's out of fuel. You would never think that maybe a meteorite hit the car overnight and destroyed its electronic ignition system. It's possible, but it's not the simplest, most likely explanation.

So Occam's Razor says you go to the simplest explanation, then you go to the next simplest, and that's the way science works if you really want to find answers. But a lot of people don't do that. They'll start with the most unlikely thing. If they see a light in the sky they'll say, "Aliens from another galaxy!" or worse, "Aliens from another galaxy trying to find me!" Rather than something more likely like maybe that's a star that I've never noticed before, or maybe it's a military plane, or maybe that's

148

an airplane landing light, maybe that's a bright planet. They start from the unlikely and they work from there. A lot of people do that.

So I think once you've eliminated that, you've eliminated a lot of the UFO reports.

I am also wary of people seeking publicity. Just like those pilots of Stormville—I know you've heard of them—years ago, that loved to fly at night in formation, so that they could read about the UFOs that were spotted in the paper, the *Kingston Freeman* and some others. The *Poughkeepsie Journal* used to report on UFO reports and these people loved that. Like that guy in Seattle who used to launch pie pans with a little electronic battery light in them, a translucent pie pan, and the wind would carry it over a stadium at night so that thousands of people would see this UFO slowly going over the stadium. And some people enjoy that. So I don't know, once you eliminate the hoaxes, and the pranks, and the misidentification of the military aircraft, and the mentally ill people, I don't know how much you have left that are genuine, that you really have to explain.

My experience is that there are some. There is a residual of some that are rational, and that you can't just easily dismiss, but there are not a lot.

Zim: Could you discuss your experience, introduce yourself, and talk about your background?

Bob: I'm Bob Berman, I'm an astronomer, I was astronomy professor at Marymount College for years, author of a number of books. I've been for many years *Discover* magazine's astronomy columnist every month for 17 years. I've been *Astronomy* magazine's editor and columnist it must 15, or 18 years now. I'm also the astronomy editor for the *Old Farmer's Almanac*. I also ran the astronomy program at Yellowstone Park for the National Park Service for 15 years.

And what else—popularization—I have a radio show on Northeast Public Radio. I've been on the Letterman show, done a fair amount of television shows in popularizing astronomy. So essentially, I let other people—the researchers—do the hard work, and my easy job is to translate that for public and try to make that clearer.

I tend to be a skeptic, because in science that's the way you get at the truth. If you believe everything everybody says, you're not going to get anywhere, because people are often wrong, or they have motives. But when it comes to UFOs there's an additional thing, and that is, as an observatory director here in the Hudson Valley, for now, well, since '82, that's, many years, we get phone calls from people who claim to have seen UFOs. People think that observatories are UFO reporting centers. I guess people think, "Where am I going to report this?" and it would either be a police station or an observatory. So we get calls I would say, maybe one every month or two.

Zim: Can you give an example of a call?

Bob: An example is someone who called the station and reported a bright light that went up and down. And he and his wife were both seeing it and it changed color from green to red and back to green again, something that couldn't have been a star, but it couldn't have been anything natural. But the fact that he was seeing it in the same direction night after night made me give him my private phone number and told him to call me the next time he saw it, and he did.

And we both faced the same direction. I told him to face the way the sun set and then tell me which way it was, and he said to the left, so I looked to the left toward Orion. I asked him if he could see three stars in a straight line, he did, Orion's belt. And then just to make sure it was Orion's belt I said, "Do those stars point down and to the left to a bright star?" and he said, "Yes! Yes!"

And that's the Dog Star, Sirius. I even asked him what color that star looked, and he said, "It looks a little blue." Correct. So I knew we were looking at the right thing.

And so we pinpointed it to, of all things, the star Betelgeuse in Orion's shoulder. Why he and his wife picked this one bright, but not particularly bright star as the UFO, as the one that was moving up and down, as the one that was changing color, I don't know. But it is naturally and orange color, it does change color thanks to the scintillation that the atmosphere often does, twinkling, makes it change to green and back to orange again. And imperceptible eye muscle movements often seem to make objects move.

For example, when we look at Earth satellites in the night sky, they'll never appear to move in a laser-straight line, even though they're moving in a straight line, they'll always seem to zigzag. And that's because of imperceptible eye muscle movements that produce this illusion. I see it myself, and even though I know it's an illusion, I still see it.

So, many times we are able to trace it to an obvious source, many times I don't even have to look. People are describing an obvious meteor, or a bolide—an exploding meteor. And very often it's Venus, by far the brightest thing in the sky. People can't believe that something can be so much brighter than other stars. When Venus is out that accounts for a lot of them [UFO reports].

But there is a—honestly speaking—there is a residual small amount of reports that we get that I can't explain.

Zim: And that's okay to say that you don't know what it is. You mentioned that in addition to being an astronomer, you're also a private pilot.

Bob: Yes. I've had a four-seater plane for the last 20 years. Been a private pilot for 27 years now, and I do a fair amount of flying at night.

So I would like nothing better than to see a flying saucer, a genuine UFO, at night. It would be very exciting. Because as an astronomer I already believe that the universe is probably teeming with life. How could it not?

Zim: Could you discuss that a little, the size of our galaxy and its place in the universe?

Bob: Oh yeah, yeah. Starting with that source of all life, the sun, which we've just learned more about thanks to my new book, *The Sun's Heartbeat*—my publisher tells me I must mention it at every possible opportunity—but we knew very little about the sun until very recently. But here's a book about the sun written, oh, it must be 50 years ago, and back then, what did we know about it back then.

[At this point, Bob opened the book and flames erupted from the center of the gag book.]

151

Chapter One says that the sun is hot. All we knew was that there were flames in the sun, we knew nothing…[He closes the book and the flames go out.] All right never mind. The sun is the center…[We both start laughing.]

Zim: You got me on that one, too.

Bob: I did that for Katie Couric on NBC once, and I told the producer I had a little gimicky book, and they hadn't told her and she jumped in the air like a cat.

Zim: I'm not as jumpy as Katie Couric.

Bob Berman with flames shooting out of his book.

Bob: So what I would say is, you look at what nature does here and you extrapolate it elsewhere. Here on Earth we have more life forms than we've even been able to catalog obviously, from zebras and giraffes to amoebae. And that's just on one planet. So if we have this kind of diversity here, could the rest of the universe really be barren? It doesn't make sense for that.

Plus, we have started discovering the amino acids elsewhere. All the amino acids, the building blocks of life have now been discovered amongst the nebulae, toward Sagittarius, beyond the constellation of Cygnus. We found some of the simpler amino acids like glycine in meteorites, in comet debris, and these are the building blocks of life.

So this suggests maybe that panspermia idea, that at least the building blocks of life, if not simple life itself, like viruses, may be transported and live in a kind of dormant state for millions of years and land here and there and seed incipient planets. You know this [once] sounded like wacky, science fiction stuff, and now it doesn't sound so wacky anymore.

So if this is true, then life would probably be plentiful. We don't seem to see any in our own solar system, although on one of the moons of Jupiter, Europa, with its ice sheets, we have water—warm water, salt water, oceans. Life started on the oceans of Earth, and here are oceans that have lasted as long as Earth's. Life may have been seeded here by the impacts of comets and asteroids. They've been getting more comets and asteroids impacting them.

If I had to bet that if you could drill or burn your way through that mile of ice and see what—if anything—is swimming or floating in those oceans on Europa, I bet that there's life there.

And that's just our own solar system. I mean once you get far away you get to the unfortunate interstellar distances where any aliens had better have lots of coffee makers. That's probably what all that gleaming equipment is inside those UFOs, those flying saucers. You know you look in and they're probably just big coffee pots and coffee makers to keep them up.

Zim: For their 50,000-year journey.

153

Bob: It's a long way. Just staying awake would be tough.

So that argues in favor of it, plus, you know our minds are still in their little narrow infancy in figuring these things out. In *Biocentrism*, Bob Lanza and I argue that the whole universe may be a form of life, that consciousness and the universe are correlative. In supporting quantum theory since the 20s, saying nothing is a real event unless it is an observed event.

We've had John Wheeler, a Nobel Laureate in physics saying the same thing. In fact, that was his quote. And that objects only exist in a probabilistic state, and only upon observation do they collapse and become actual objects with actual positions.

So that in other words the universe, nature, and us as observers go together. That's all we're saying, it's correlative. And the old view, that there's a dead universe out there, even if we're not around to observe it, has no validity.

Now if this is the case, then life is everywhere, because life, consciousness, the observer, we all go together. And so, nothing is not life. So it may not be limited to creatures crawling on the surfaces of planets.

Plus, we have a surface bias. You know we have found life hundreds of feet under the ground, so most of any object's mass is below the surface, so maybe that's more common than cities on the surfaces.

So another words, we've been limited by the science fiction movies that we see and by the limitations of our past experiences. We're all prisoners of our background and experience and this has biased us in terms of what we think is possible in terms of life.

Zim: So then you could see when somebody does see something they cannot explain, how it would blow their mind and really change their life?

Bob: Absolutely! And the only reason I'm skeptical about life having visited us here—now that's a separate issue—now if I had to bet the farm on whether life is actually here, circling Earth, visiting us, being spotted by this person or that person, in the Hudson Valley, there I would say no.

First, because I see so many false reports that people have. Secondly, because I'm skeptical about the incompetence of any aliens to have made it all the way here, to have generally kept themselves hidden—they don't want to come out of the closet, they're not landing on the White House lawn, they aren't landing in London or any place like that, so they want to keep themselves hidden, yet they're spotted. This guy spots them, this farmer sees one—so they're incompetent! They want to keep themselves hidden but they can't. They're like cat burglars that keep getting caught and arrested. And to me, I would think that if they are aliens they would do better than that. They wouldn't just be caught here and there.

Plus, for me as a pilot, flying hundreds of hours over the Hudson Valley, I never seem to see them. Astronomers never seem to see them. So why are they avoiding us? It doesn't seem fair that they're avoiding us astronomers, the one group of people who could identify them instead of the planet Venus or some of these other things.

So, putting it all together on balance I'd say...but you know, I don't know about specific reports, some seemingly rational people who say they've seen this or that. I don't know, it's not for me to say they're mentally ill or they're looking for publicity, or what it is. I just wish I could be out with them and see what they say that they've seen.

Zim: Would you give an example of what you would think would be a rational observer giving you a report that can't be explained?

Bob: The best one that I've gotten, again, as a columnist for *Astronomy* magazine, and my column tends to be about cutting edge and far out things, so people I think feel comfortable writing to me and that I won't just dismiss them out of hand. And I don't.

And I got one letter years ago by a fellow who said he was a physicist, and who began the letter in just the right way, saying, "This is going to sound crazy, but I just want to share it with you." And he reported something he saw when he was young. He reported a formation of objects that zoomed across the sky, and then stopped, and then the formation broke up and each moved in a different direction.

And from what I know about military aircraft, although I'm no expert on it, this sounds like a military formation could do that, but maybe I'm wrong. It certainly couldn't have been a planet or anything celestial. And because the reporter of this seemed so rational, this leaves the door open just a little crack for me. Not anything close so that would say I'm a believer. As I say, if I had to bet it I wouldn't hesitate to say that there's a rational explanation for all of these so-called reports here.

Zim: You mentioned an incident of seeing military craft, possibly on maneuvers in this area. Could you speak about that?

Bob: This was something that I've never seen before. It happened this past May, we're talking about May of 2012. And a friend from Arizona and I were in the village of Willow on Jessup Road, watching the sky, using laser pointers to look at the constellations, a beautiful, clear night, and we heard a roar coming from the west—a loud roar as if it was a jet engine.

And then zooming overhead was an enormous, unlit, no windows, no marking lights, no port and starboard green and red light craft at low altitude, 500 or 1,000 feet, certainly below the mountain tops, that zoomed at very high speed directly over us. And here's the stranger thing, right behind it, a smaller craft with a single green light in the front, trailing it, almost as if it was on a tether, but it was a little bit too far away to be a cable or a tether. I think it was an independent, separate craft that was deliberately keeping pace with the first one.

Now, if I had been anyone else but me, I might have thought alien spacecraft there. Enough people have seen these, and this wasn't the first time this May, in the spring, that this happened, but the sheriff was notified, the sheriff called Stewart Airport and the other air bases. The newspapers interviewed the sheriff on this, and so that this was well documented and seen over and over again.

It appears as if perhaps in preparation for, or in training for, flying in Afghanistan, and flying in valleys at night with no lights, they were using the Catskills. It's kind of foolish, this is an inhabited area, and there are military operations areas in the Adirondacks that such planes could use. I don't know why they would chose to bother us here.

Clearly military, but people could definitely say alien spacecraft to that.

Sarah: Since you are a pilot, could you talk about the different airports that are in the Hudson Valley, and the capacities that they have?

Bob: Capacities in what way?

Sarah: Well, obviously like Stewart is a big airport, relatively speaking, but then there are all the small airports. What kinds of planes can land in those?

Bob: In the Hudson Valley we have an assortment of airports that range from controlled airports, that is Dutchess, Albany, and Stewart Airports. Controlled means there's a tower, there is radar at all three to help planes come in and track them. And there are also a number of uncontrolled airports where nobody is even required to speak, although it's always good practice to radio in to tell your position. Those include Millbrook, which is called Sky Acres, and Kingston, South Albany, Columbia County Airport, and these have only small planes, singe engine and two engine planes with typical two to eight seats. And there's no proscription about flying at night.

Whenever I have to do a lecture in Binghamton or elsewhere I cross the Catskills at night, and it's beautiful. You see the stars beautifully and sometimes we see the aurora from the plane. And you can see other aircraft from incredible distances. Occasionally, I've had a passenger that's been worried about a bright light that's slowly moving in one direction and it looked bright and close. And I've occasionally asked air traffic control, "What's that at 2 o'clock that I'm seeing?" And almost every time they've all but laughed at me and said, "Oh, that's a Delta jet and it's 45 miles away."

So you see tremendous distances at night. And if an aircraft has landing lights on, even if it's far away and low on the horizon, but has landing lights on, it's going to look like an almost stationary UFO. And I think a number of the UFO reports are probably based on that, probably based on aircraft. And I wouldn't blame them.

Zim: Hypothetical: If a large flying saucer just landed in your backyard right now, how would that change your life? Or would it?

Bob: Well, of course it would change my belief in whether they are possible or not. If I saw a metallic saucer-like thing land, again, being a skeptic, I would probably wonder if it was some homebuilt thing, if somebody has found a way to make something like that happen, for fun. Whether it's a military craft, because I wouldn't first think aliens. Because

157

again, you use Occam's Razor: we are people, we live on Earth, there is a technology for flying objects. That's known, so first you investigate that before you get to the Zanthams of the Andromeda Galaxy or something like that. That's the way you would proceed.

But what if a ramp opened and there were things in there that were non-human?

By the way, why always a ramp? I always wondered about that. You know, all of our planes have stairs that come down. You know, when you charter a plane it's a staircase, never a ramp. I wonder whether they have laws about disabilities and things like that on other worlds? Where it's required that they have to have ramps, which we don't.

Anyway, if a ramp opened and there were clearly extraterrestrials, well of course, I would instantly change. When you see it with your own eyes, that's the proof. It's one thing to hear a rumor about your boyfriend or girlfriend going out with someone else, it's another thing to come home and catch them. So you know, you catch these things in the act and that will change your mind. You would be a fool not to have your mind changed.

And then what? Where would you go with that? Well, I don't know about personal life being changed, now that you know there are creatures in the universe, which we already assumed was the case. I don't know if that changes that.

If there motives were evil? You know in sci fi circles some say cow experiments or some crazy stuff like that. You know, if they gave evidence that they were wacky, meaning that humans are not the only wacky ones in the universe, that would be kind of interesting. If there's some kind of sadomasochistic or weird creatures out there that might change your philosophy.

We would like to believe that they are benign, and just have the best motives. That's why that famous *Twilight Zone, To Serve Man*, you know the cookbook thing, was such a hit, because that may have been the first one that suggested that aliens might not have benign motives.

But to see one? I wouldn't blame anyone for having their life changed in terms of their philosophy. Personal life though? You know, barring being taken aboard and having horrible things happen to you…I don't know, do you think your personal life would change if you saw one?

Zim: No, I don't. But we are interviewing quite a few people who it has. But possibly, they don't have your depth of understanding of the universe and your already accepted idea that there is life out there. As you were saying, a lot of people have such limited understanding of the cosmos here, that anything new is a surprise.

When we first spoke a month or two ago, you were mentioning your skepticism about the ineptness of the aliens and I had made a comment at the time that maybe they aren't as intelligent as we think. And the more I thought about that, why would they come here, and I was wondering, maybe humans are unique in their intelligence, in the depth of their creativity. Perhaps we have something they don't?

Bob: We might also be unique in terms of loving technology. For a moment, what if there are no aliens. What if the SETI Project, which has been negative during the decades it has been running, searching for sounds, radio waves, what do we make of this, that we've now gotten to millions, tens of millions, of stars and there's no trace of radio waves, either spontaneous from them or in answer to ours.

But again, we look around Earth and we don't see any other mammals who show this interest in technology, even intelligent ones like whales, that may be more intelligent than us in some ways. They show no interest in computer chips and silicon wafers, and creating metal spaceships and hurling themselves away from their native place.

Since we are the only ones who do so, I think it's more logical that that's the paradigm, that's the normal thing in the universe is not to do it. So even though we're doing it, why do we assume that people are coming out in metal spaceships to visit us?

Zim: So we may be unique in that way and we are trying to judge the rest of the universe based upon ourselves.

Bob: Exactly, yes. In that case, it would not in any way indicate the SETI negative results, or any lack of actually being visited means nothing, so far as indicating no life anywhere else in the universe. It just means that they don't have the restlessness that we do, or the technological part of the brain that we do.

159

Sarah: On a similar note, there's this description we keep coming up against of the classic alien, white, kind of large heads, small bodies, thin limbs, huge almond-shaped eyes, you know what I'm talking about. Is there any science that would make sense of that kind of physiology, or does that just seem like a ridiculous form?

B: It seems like personification—that's what we look like, and even in the best science fiction, even in that big movie two years ago...help me out...

Zim: *Avatar*?

B: Thank you. In *Avatar*, you can't just have either a friend or an enemy in an alien and have it look like an amoeba. You can't have it just look like a sponge. It can't just be squirmy, it has to look humanoid, either as friend or enemy—preferably like Ricardo Montalban as Khan. There's nothing like a handsome guy who is evil. Everybody's going to hate this guy. Like the heavy in *Titanic*. He was a good looking guy and everybody loved to hate him.

So with our aliens, of course they have to have two eyes, and change it around a little bit making the head a little bigger or smaller, the eyes bigger, because making them smaller, that kind of doesn't work. So that's just what you need to have an alien that we can relate to.

In fact, the fact that everyone reports that would be one check mark for me in the "Let's Ignore This Person" category. You know, the fact that they're seeing humanoids, I'd say okay, it's is a good sign that they're making this up, or imagining this. Because what are the chances that aliens...look at the life on Earth. How many humanoid life forms do we have with more genera than we can even categorize? We can't even catalog all the life forms on Earth, and how many of them look like us?

So you're going to tell me on a world with a different gravitational field, a different radiation flux, a different atmospheric composition, that creatures are going to evolve to look like us in some way? Of course not.

If it was me doing your job, and I was secretly, quietly saying to myself, "All right, this guy's a nut, this person is looking for publicity. Okay, here's one that seems rational," as soon as a person said they saw a humanoid they wouldn't get the rational checkmark. If someone is seeing

160

a metal craft or a light or something like that I would keep them in the "Okay, Maybe" category.

[At this point there is conversation about his telescope and observatory, his current projects, and other general topics. As we were wrapping up, I had one more thing to ask.]

Zim: I have just one final question. If you do see a UFO, will you call me?

Bob: Yes, I will call you! In fact, you'll be the first person I call.

11
Abduction Alley?

The first interview we filmed was with a man named Gary, who came to my house and blew my mind with his stories. He not only had some incredible sightings of discs, triangles, and egg-shaped craft, he had missing time, strange scoop marks on body, and a bloody nose. It all began when he was a child, and continued for decades.

This interview immediately placed this project in a much wider arena—people didn't just *see* things in the Hudson Valley, they *had contact*, which is a polite way of saying they were abducted. Some people don't like the term abductee, (preferring contactee) but how can you sugar coat believing you were pulled out of your home or car and subjected to tests against your will?

Of course, skeptics, such as Bob Berman, state that anyone who claims to have had any form of alien contact is either mentally ill or looking for publicity. Granted, there are such people, but there are many others who appear to be sane, rational individuals, who have no idea what happened to them—only that something happened that can't be explained.

Judge for yourself from the following accounts, whether abductions are fact or fiction. And if even a fraction of them are indeed true, than the Hudson Valley should also be known as Abduction Alley.

Where Does the Time Go?

In 1960 when "Marge" was three, she and her brother, "Bill," entered foster care with a family that lived in Rifton, New York. They lived in a big house on Route 213, across from Central Hudson Recreation Road. Strange things began to happen soon after moving in.

"For as long as I can recall, I had very vivid dreams about flying out my window and being taken up into ships," Marge said.

When I asked if she ever had any kinds of physical marks after these dreams, she replied that she couldn't recall any, "But my brother and I were always getting bloody noses."

And does she recall seeing any types of beings on the ships?

"Yes, many different kinds," she replied.

Fast forward to 1973, when Marge was 16. Her parents were away on a camping trip, and her brother was with friends.

"It was summer and I was sitting on the deck by the pool. My friend and her boyfriend were in the pool, and they went underwater to kiss.

"Suddenly, the woods lit up with an intense flash of white light that lasted several seconds. The young couple under the water saw the flash and jumped up. They were so scared they hurried out of the pool and left. I was scared, too, and now I was alone. I called my boyfriend and told him what happened. He said he could come by later and he would tap on my bedroom window."

Marge's room "was on the ground floor and it was tiny, with a big window." She remembers going to bed, but then doesn't remember anything else until morning, even though her boyfriend did tap on the window.

"When I didn't respond, he tapped harder. Then he got concerned and started to bang on the window and shout. I never responded, and as my room was dark, he couldn't see if I was actually in bed."

Marge can't understand how she could have slept through such a racket right by her bed, and suggests, "Maybe I was taken?"

Of course, a child's dreams, nose bleeds, and flashes of lights in the woods don't necessarily add up to alien abductions, and I might not have even included this story if the activity didn't continue.

Fast forward again to 1984, and Marge is married and had just moved to a home on a mountain in Saugerties to the west of town. She and her husband had a daughter, who also happens to be "a vivid dreamer who sees beings."

Marge, who loves horses, decided to join a group of about 20 on an overnight ride from Palenville to a camping area by North and South Lakes. It was a steep, narrow trail, but the view at the top was worth the ride. Their campsite was near a ledge that had an incredible view of the Hudson Valley below. Unfortunately, all of the other riders were much younger and were more interested in partying than the view. Marge didn't join the party, and so was the only one who was not drunk when they finally climbed into their tents.

She had trouble sleeping because the horses kept making noise, and she was concerned for two of the more rambunctious horses who kept managing to untie their ropes and start to wander off. With the treacherous drop-off from the ledge so close, Marge was forced to get up two or three times in the night to retrieve the horses and tie them up again. Then about 3:30am, everything fell silent.

"You could hear a pin drop," Marge explained. "Then the tent lit up with light."

Lifting the tent flap, Marge saw "six or seven bright white lights hovering over the edge of the ledge. There was no sound."

She woke up her tentmate and told her to look at the lights. The drunk woman became frightened, said she had no idea what those lights were, and buried her head under the covers. Marge continued to look at the lights "for I don't know how long. Then the next thing I knew, it was morning." Marge has no recollection of what happened during those missing hours. One moment she was staring at the lights over the ledge, and then it was daylight. She has no idea what happened to the lights, or to her.

One night when she was sleeping at home, she felt compelled to get out of bed in the early, predawn hours. She went into the living room, which "has big, tall windows." She saw a bright light in the sky "that startled to tumble down. Then it broke into 7-9 pieces that streaked off into all different directions. It gave me chills from the tip of my head to my toes. I kept asking myself, what made me get up so I could see this?"

On another occasion in the 1980s, Marge's family was out with her husband's family at a popular Italian restaurant on Route 28. They had all met at the restaurant, so when they were leaving, Marge and her daughter took one car and got on Sawkill Road, but her husband started to take a different route home. As the two women were driving alone on the dark road about 9pm, they saw some lights off to the right. There were far fewer houses along the road at that time, and Marge wondered if there was some brand new construction taking place.

"Then I realized the lights were over a swamp, and no one would build there."

She also realized the lights were moving, and they slowed down when she slowed down, and sped up when she accelerated. Stopping the car, the row of about ten white lights with colored lights in between, also stopped. Her daughter opened the window to see if they could hear anything, but there was only silence. Even though they were just a couple of hundred

164

feet from the lights, they couldn't make out any shape or surface features, but it was "very long."

Then she saw other lights; the headlights of her husband's car pulling up behind them. She frantically waved and gestured for him to look over to the lights. "There was no way" she and her daughter were going to get out of the car with that thing so close, and after a few minutes they had "had enough" and pulled away. Her husband later claimed that he never saw the lights!

However, the next day he told his parents what Marge and his daughter had seen, and his parents said they had both seen the same lights very low in the sky and assumed "it was a dirigible." Marge's sister-in-law also witnessed the elongated craft with lights in Kingston, and said there was a story in the local paper the next day and many people had witnessed it.

Marge and her daughter had a few other sightings over the years, most recently several years ago when her daughter looked out the back door at dusk and saw a craft in the sky. I asked if Marge thought she would have more sightings, and she said she thinks she will, and isn't afraid of these beings or any future encounters. She is convinced that the government must know what is happening, but continues to try to cover up everything.

Marge describes herself now as being "very spiritual." She and her husband are retired, and she has the time to pursue her interests in studying various spiritual topics such as healing energies. If Marge is a lifelong abductee, her experiences have not made her fearful or reclusive. She views these beings as "our brothers and sisters from the stars" and hopes the day will come when the truth will be revealed to everyone.

"Florence Madison": Big Indian, 1963

Twelve-year-old "Florence" and her three brothers were coming back from the movies in Phoenicia, where, along with their mother, they had just seen, *It's a Mad, Mad, Mad, Mad World*. Her mother was driving the family's Country Squire station wagon along Route 28 toward Big Indian, and it was around 10pm. When they were about five miles from home, her mother suddenly pulled the car over onto the side of the road and shouted, "Get down!"

"My brothers and I had all been standing up, because no one used seat belts back then. We all got down immediately, because of the sound of fear in my mother's voice," Florence said.

That fear was particularly startling, as her mother "was a strong-willed woman" who sold real estate in Scarsdale, and nothing usually rattled her.

As Florence got down on all fours, she could see that there was a massive ship in the sky. It was below the level of the trees and seemed to take up the entire sky. Because it was so large it was hard to tell the shape, but she would say it was either oval, or had straight sides and rounded ends.

There weren't any individual lights she could see, but the whole ship "seemed to glow" and brightly illuminated everything, including the interior of the car. She remembered "thinking how odd it was that there was this bright light, but it didn't cast a shadow of my head on the floor."

There was something else she distinctly remembers while looking at the floor of the car.

"The fibers of the carpet were all standing straight up and vibrating."

At that moment of terror, she "heard" a male voice in her head, saying, "Don't be afraid."

It was "a calming, soothing voice" that instantly put her at ease, and she "was no longer afraid."

"The next thing I knew, we were all walking in the house, chattering away about the movie. My father and grandmother were very upset, because we were at least 45 minutes late. They were very concerned, and we couldn't understand because none of us remembered a thing. It wasn't until we were all together for a big family dinner in the 1980s when it all suddenly came back to us. I asked if anyone else remembered that night on the way back from the movies, and everybody who was in the car that night suddenly remembered the same things.

"It was like we all woke up from a memory coma twenty years later. It was like all memory of that night had immediately been erased, and then we all remembered at once."

Still, even though they could recall the huge ship and the bright light filling the car, no one was able to fill in the gap between the first few seconds of the sighting and then walking into their house. That was five miles and 45 minutes that were still missing. One of Florence's brothers decided to see John Mack, the Harvard psychiatrist who studied abduction phenomena. Mack used hypnosis on her brother, who claimed that just the two of them were taken into the ship and subjected to tests. Florence has no recollection of any of that, and is skeptical of any results obtained through hypnosis.

In any event, something extraordinary happened to Florence and her family that night. When I asked if there had been any physical signs of the event, she first replied, "No," but then thought for a moment. She couldn't say if this was related, but she had a mysterious scar "at the top of my leg, in the crease." It was about half an inch, straight, and she has no idea how she got it, but she got it around that time of the sighting.

"Now that I think of it, the scar is kind of in a weird place, and I never knew how I got it."

Will Florence or her brothers ever recall more details that night their station wagon came under siege from the massive craft? Perhaps. I'll bet that if they do, they will all remember at once.

Pine Island 1973

In 1973, "Debbie" went to stay with her grandmother after the old woman had a stroke. Her grandmother's house was in Pine Island, in the "black dirt" region in southern Orange County, NY, known for its onion farms. Debbie was 15 years old, and she wanted to do whatever she could to help her grandmother.

The house was quite isolated out in the fields, and there was just one small stand of trees nearby. The first night there, Debbie—who was supposed to be sleeping on the couch in the living room—found herself restless and awake most of the night. She finally got up and started walking around the house. Through a large picture window in the living room, she noticed a bright light behind the stand of trees. She assumed it must be a street light, even though there weren't any other street lights anywhere else in the area. The fourth or fifth time she looked out, the light was gone.

167

As she stood by the window wondering what had happened, to her "surprise and fear" she saw a bright ball of light "hovering about a foot or two off the ground." The light appeared "as if it was looking into the downstairs windows of the house." Sensing that the light was going to come up to the picture window, Debbie became "really scared" and "tried to hide, crouching on the floor against the couch." She then "started praying to God" to help her and she clenched her eyes shut.

Tense moments passed, and when she dared to look, "sure enough, there was the light in the window. It was about the size between a grapefruit and a cantaloupe, and it was a beautiful, brilliant, blinding, white." Up to this point, the light had been steady, but now "it flashed. I remember it flashing three times. And you could feel the vibrations in the air, and this energy surging with each flash. You could hear it and you could feel it, and it was just like a *ffffffft* sound."

"I was just shaking with fear, saying, 'God, get me out of this! Get me through this! I don't want to know this.' Then the next thing I remember it was several hours later. It was morning and I was waiting for my grandmother to wake up."

Debbie told her what had happened, and the woman said, "No, no, no, you were just dreaming."

Debbie told her it was real, but her grandmother insisted she had only been dreaming. She then called her mother and told her about the strange light, but her mother also said it was either a dream or she was making it up. The two women simply refused to believe her, and they convinced her to stay another night.

Debbie went to a circus that evening and tried to forget about what had happened. She got home about 11pm and her grandmother was already in bed. Shortly after arriving back at the house, she became "frantically scared" as the light had returned behind the trees. Again, she prayed that whatever it was would go away, because "I didn't want to see anything, and I didn't want to know anything." Debbie has no more recollections of the rest of the night, as the next thing she knew it was morning. "The whole night" had become missing time.

This time when she called home, she insisted that her mother "come and get me, because I don't want to be here anymore!"

Her mother did come and brought her back home to Middletown, but the story doesn't end there. As Debbie was changing her clothes, she

168

noticed she had three strange marks on her abdomen, below and to the left of her navel.

"They were sort of circular and sort of oval, but not perfectly circular or oval. But they were perfectly spaced between one another, and the outer image...there was no flaw," Debbie said, describing the smooth outlines of the reddish marks that were positioned in a perfect equilateral triangle, as if they had been made by some instrument or machine. She showed the marks to her mother and a few of her friends, and the bizarre triangle lasted about three weeks until it finally faded away.

I first heard Debbie's account when I went to the June meeting of the United Friends Observer Society in Pine Bush. It was her first meeting, as she had finally decided after all these years to tell her story. She was hesitant at first to speak, but realized she was in the right place to mention the marks on her abdomen. Before she could describe them, some of the other female attendees asked if the marks had been below her navel on the left side, and if there had been three of them in the shape of a triangle! These women who posed the questions had personal experiences similar to Debbie's and had received the same marks in the same location!

After the meeting, I gave Debbie my card and told her about my project. I hoped that she would let me use her story in the book and film, but after a week when I didn't hear from her, I had pretty much given up hope. Then I received the following email:

"You and I met at the last Pine Bush UFO meeting in the Walker Valley Schoolhouse. I told my story of my experience with a UFO abduction when I was 15 at my grandmother's house in Pine Island. You were intrigued and asked if I would be interested in telling my story for a documentary you are putting together. I have given it some thought and have decided to do it with the understanding that I would like to be kept anonymous."

A few weeks later, Sarah, Felix, and I met at Debbie's house to film the interview. She was understandably a little nervous, but I assured her that the beauty of video was that everything could be edited, and if she felt something wasn't quite right, we could do it again.

And thank god this wasn't a live broadcast, because just as the cameras started rolling, Debbie told me "there was a large gap" in my blouse along the button line. It was a new shirt and I thought the bright blue colors would look great on camera, but didn't realize that when I sat down the spaces between the buttons kind of opened outward. Sarah came to the rescue to remedy this "wardrobe malfunction" with bright yellow duct tape! I carefully placed pieces of tape on the inside of my shirt and between the buttons, and hoped that it would not show, and would hold together long enough to finish the interview.

As Felix put it, "It was all footage for the blooper reel."

Once I had battened down my hatches, we began. Debbie told her story with true feeling and emotions, and I wished the audience would have the opportunity to see her eyes and expressions as she spoke, but we were honoring her request to have her image concealed. When she finished recounting the Pine Island experiences, I asked if she had ever had any other unusual things happen before that.

"I always thought it was my first experience, but then after going to the meeting, it made me realize there were more things that happened earlier in my life. I had to have been younger than ten, because it was in a certain house that we lived in, and I remember this family of 'ghosts' visiting me. There were two adults and two children.

"Every night I would sleep with my bedroom door open and this family of ghosts would literally stand along the door entranceway. And they would just stand there peacefully and quietly, and I remember that after they were visiting me for a couple of weeks or longer, that it became a nuisance to me. I was never afraid of them, but they became a nuisance to me."

"Why did you refer to them as ghosts," I asked. "What did they look like?"

"They were again, perfection, a beautiful white, not a brilliant, bright white, but they were a beautiful, perfectly formed white. And the reason I say two adults and two children is that two were taller and two were shorter. And they just stood there peacefully. But when it became a nuisance and it was interfering with me trying to fall asleep, I closed the bedroom door and they never bothered me again."

I then asked Debbie if anything had happened prior to these white beings at her bedroom door. She replied that when she was very young she "had a lot of nightmares." Having had children of her own, she realizes that children often do have nightmares, but hers were almost every night and always with a similar theme.

170

"I'm not going into the details," she said, "but they always had to do with being kidnapped...the process of being kidnapped."

I asked if she had any dreams since she told her story at the meeting.

"Actually, yes, I have been noticing I have been having dreams. They're...they're...like an intrusion of my privacy," she replied, choosing her words carefully. "Just things that I'm trying to get away from...things that I can't escape."

"Do you think the fact that you're speaking about this, that more memories are coming back up?" I suggested.

"It's possible, or I'm just becoming more aware of things that have been," Debbie replied thoughtfully.

"Any of your children or grandchildren ever have any experiences?"

"Not that I know of, no."

"Have your parents or other family members ever mentioned anything unusual?" I asked, continuing this line of questioning, as experience had taught me that these people often have relatives who have also had some type of encounter.

"Actually..." Debbie began slowly, as a light seemed to be dawning in her mind, "my mother had an experience when I was, again, probably under the age of ten, when we were in that one house. She had this experience where she kept seeing a light, but it wasn't a bright light. And she wanted to tell us, but nobody believed her. And she was like, 'Really, really, this really happened.'

"And I remember she woke us up one night, and looking out the front door of the house, and this light that looked like a moon—that type of light—it was in the sky, and it came forward and got larger, but I don't remember the size, it was so many years ago. But I remember this moon-like light coming closer, like zooming in, and then zooming out. But that's the only other thing."

"Okay, well, that's important," I replied, not at all surprised that these sightings extended over many years and to different family members. Even with only a few months of research and interviews, I knew a pattern when I saw one.

"You know, you don't start thinking about these things until you start thinking!" Debbie stated, a point which emphasized the importance of examining the big picture of any suspected UFO case. Things that at first

171

seemed completely unrelated could be important pieces of the whole puzzle.

"Have you ever been under hypnosis, or plan to be?" I asked

"No."

"Okay. The incident that occurred when you were fifteen definitely frightened you. How have you felt in the decades since then?"

"Uh…Mostly I just push it aside as a life experience. But at the same time, it kind of irks me."

"In what way?"

"It makes me curious as to what it all means, or what it *could* mean later on. I think that's why I went to the meeting at Pine Bush, because I thought maybe I would learn something more, or become more aware of what's happening. And sure enough, I did. I was surprised to see all of those people—there were a lot more people than I expected. And they knew stuff that I didn't even know was occurring."

Debbie then "got chills" recalling how the women at the meeting had described the three marks on their abdomens, and she thought, "My God, this is something that's happened to other people!"

I admit having goose bumps, too, as she recalled that moment. I remember at the time I was thinking, *How do they know where the marks were?*

"Did this meeting, then, give you a kind of a comfort," I asked, "knowing that there are other people?"

"Yes, I'm anxious to go to the next meeting," Debbie replied smiling, with a sense of relief that she didn't have to remain silent any longer, and that there were other people out there who would not only listen to her, but *understand* what she has experienced.

"So how would you categorize all of your experiences? Positive, negative, a mixture?"

"I feel like I'm in the loop," she replied with a laugh. "You know, I feel like something inevitable, something eventual is going to occur for everyone to understand. And I'm like, two steps ahead of them!"

While Debbie admits she "still has a little fear in me," she is open and curious about the field of UFO research and wants to learn more. She doesn't know if she will have any more personal encounters, but at this point in her life she has "more curiosity than fear."

I concluded the interview by asking Debbie what advice she had for other people who may have had a similar experience.

"Don't…take it personally…in the sense that you ridicule yourself, or allow others to ridicule you. Understand that there are thousands upon thousands of other people that have experienced similar things, and just have an open mind. Try not to be afraid of it, but be wise."

Audrey Garay: Millerton, June 1972

It was June of 1972, and Audrey Garay was driving home from Sharon, CT where she worked the second shift at a hospital. Her mother had watched her five-month-old son that night, and she was driving both of them back to her house in Millerton, NY. It was about 11:50pm, and they were on Coleman Station Road heading towards Route 22. The sky was clear and the stars were shining.

Suddenly, the two women noticed a star-like light high in the sky that was twinkling blue, red, and green. At the same time, both of them said, "Look at that plane." They had no sooner spoken those words, when this small light descended so rapidly it looked as though it was falling out of the sky. They both put their hands over their ears, because they didn't want to hear that terrible sound of the plane that was obviously about to crash into the ground.

"In the blink of an eye," however, the bright object came to a "complete, dead stop" right in front of them, and it "absolutely wasn't a plane." It was a disc-shaped object that hovered about 50 feet in front of the car at an altitude of about 50 to 75 feet. "It was it least the size of two houses. It had a dome on top, a silvery, metallic color, and just beneath the dome were a bank of rectangular windows. The bottom edge was ringed with bright, multicolored lights that appeared to rotate. The only sound they heard was a hum, "a very soothing, soft hum." But that's where the soothing part ended.

The craft was brightly lit on the inside, and Audrey and her mother could clearly see the occupants through the windows. Although Audrey remembers there being about six figures, her mother adamantly maintained that she counted seven. However, that wasn't really the most important observation. There was something they both agreed upon, and it is arguably the most unsettling aspect of this case.

"*They were definitely non-human*, and I will take that to the grave! We could see them from about mid-chest up, their faces were pear-shaped, and they had *huge* black eyes that were almond-shaped. Their chests were concave and their shoulders and arms very thin and very spindly. They had grayish skin, no clothes, and the interior was so brightly lit we could see what looked like computers or control panels."

I asked what these figures were doing, and Audrey replied, "They were all looking right at us!"

The location on Coleman Station Road where
the UFO hovered over Audrey's car.

The six or seven strange figures and the two terrified women stared at one another for about 45 seconds, then a brilliant blue-white light came out at an angle from underneath the craft and "lit up the car like lightning." The blinding light hurt their eyes and they raised their hands to shield their faces. Then just as suddenly the light and the craft were gone, but as their eyes were readjusting to the darkness, they could still hear that distinctive humming sound.

"Mom, where is it?" Audrey asked, straining to see where the huge craft could have gone so quickly.

"Audrey, it's over the car!" her mother shouted. "It's right above the car!"

That was the moment Audrey experienced the most terror—not for herself, but for her baby. She had no idea what was happening, but her primary concern was to get her son to safety. They waited breathlessly as the seconds ticked by, then one minute, then another. Finally, the edge of the craft inched over the windshield and came into sight. Maintaining the same low altitude, the large disk slowly moved ahead of the car, following every bend in the road. She waited until the craft was about 100 feet ahead of her before she eased the car forward. Audrey didn't want to catch up with the craft and its bizarre occupants, but she had to take that road if they were to get home.

At the creeping rate of about 5 mph, Audrey drove the rest of the way on that road—a distance of 1.6 miles she later measured—with the frightening craft just five or six car lengths ahead. She reached the intersection of Route 22, where they saw another car that had pulled over so the driver could watch the slow moving disc. The craft continued to remain directly in front of them on Route 22, but when Audrey turned down her street, MacGhee Hill Road, they finally lost sight of the craft, but not before noting that it was heading in the direction of Albany.

Audrey told her husband what they had witnessed, and he thought they were "just crazy." As they had no camera, there was no way to prove what they had seen, or so they thought. The next day, Audrey's mother was watching television, and she yelled to her daughter to come and look. There was a newscast about two NY State Policemen who saw the same disc-shaped craft the night before around 2 am, in Albany! Unfortunately the newscasters were making fun of the report, and it was clear they all thought it was a big joke.

At that point, Audrey decided she had to report their sighting to someone, so she called the Civil Defense Department in Poughkeepsie. She expected that they would either hang up or laugh at her, but instead, they carefully took down all the details of her sighting, including the direction the craft took, the duration of the sighting, etc. When she was finished telling her story, she voiced her surprise that they were taking her seriously. The man replied, "Ma'am we have had hundreds and hundreds

175

of reports coming in all night long." Audrey was even further surprised when he admitted, "We have been tracking the object."

So what was done about this mysterious craft seen by hundreds of witnesses, including the State Police, in 1972, a craft being "tracked" by Civil Defense? Apparently nothing, as no word about the incident was heard on the news again.

About seven months later, Audrey was just getting into bed when she heard her dog—and all the other dogs in the neighborhood—start barking frantically. As she was wondering what could be going on, she heard that distinctive and unmistakable humming sound again, directly over her house! She tried to wake her husband, but found she couldn't move or speak. Once again, she was afraid for her child in the next room, but she was powerless to help him.

Audrey is certain she was not asleep, as she had just gotten into bed. The paralysis lasted about three or four hours, and then just at sunrise the humming ceased, and she was suddenly released. She jumped out of bed and ran to her son's room. She checked him all over for any kind of injuries, but he appeared unharmed. When her husband awoke she told him the story, but he hadn't heard a thing. Later that day, she asked the neighbors what they thought about all the dogs barking all night, but they hadn't heard anything either.

There were no more encounters over the next six years, and despite her fear for her son's safety, Audrey's attitude toward the strange visitors changed.

"I think they chose me to talk about them because they somehow knew that I'm not one to be intimidated. I don't care if I'm ridiculed for speaking about UFOs, because I'm confident in what I saw. And I haven't stopped talking about it!"

Audrey actually grew to feel that she had some sort of connection with the beings in the craft, and she was going to get the opportunity to prove it around 1978. Her husband and cousin were away on business, so she and her cousin's wife, Julia, decided to have "a girl's night out." They went to the Red Barn Tavern in Millerton, but as soon as the ladies entered, they realized it wasn't their kind of place. "It was a very rough crowd, filled with bikers," Audrey explained, so they left right away.

They decided to go to a nicer place in Amenia, the Tallyho, and took a back road toward the town. As they were driving south on Downey Road,

176

Audrey noticed an orange-amber light in the sky. The light was "diving, then shooting up—things a plane could never do."

"Look at that UFO!" she said to Julia.

"Every time you see a light you think it's a UFO!" Julia chided her. She then went on to make fun of Audrey and laugh at her belief in aliens and spacecraft from another world.

"How could you say it's not a UFO?" Audrey replied, incredulous that her friend wouldn't believe what she was seeing with her own eyes.

Despite the inexplicable movement of the light, Julie continued to mock Audrey.

"Then I thought to myself, I wish it would please come closer so I could prove it to Julia," Audrey explained. "No sooner had I thought that, when the light began rapidly dropping altitude and heading straight for us! Julia began screaming for me to get us out of there because the object was suddenly right over the car.

"I was just learning to drive a standard transmission, and I stalled the car several times, and each time Julia kept screaming for us to get away. Once I got going, the disc-shaped craft continued to follow right above the car for the next half mile, and Julia kept begging me to drive faster. We decided to head straight for my house, but the disc stayed with us. It wasn't until we turned down MacGhee Hill Road that it broke away and took off."

Julia was so traumatized, she wouldn't drive to her house alone, so Audrey's brother had to escort her. From that night, Julia was a firm believer in alien spacecraft. Also that night, Audrey became convinced she had some sort of telepathic connection with the beings.

There were to be several other sightings over the years, but none so close again. Audrey did see several other types of craft, including some in the 1980s that were so massive she described them as "flying cities."

I asked if anything unusual had happened to her when she was a child, and wasn't too surprised to find out that something had occurred in October of 1961 when she was eleven. She was outside with her twin brother and three friends, when they saw "a thing with multi-colored lights move very, very fast from horizon to horizon." Oddly, her brother has no recollection of the event, which at the time made quite an impression on everyone. Two of the friends have passed away, but the third witness is a man who has retired after a 35-year-long career with the Air Force. He still vividly recalls the sighting, and maintains that after a lifetime of dealing with all manner of aircraft, he still never saw anything like that multi-colored object in 1961.

Although her twin brother couldn't recall that sighting, another brother was to have a remarkable experience in 2009 when he spotted a huge, triangular craft. It silently passed directly over him while he was driving, and he jumped out of his truck and aimed a bright flashlight up at it. He described the underside as "rippling like liquid mercury." A very unique sighting, to say the least, and one that made him a firm believer, too!

So, have all these sightings had any lasting impact on Audrey? Yes, as that night in June of 1972 was nothing less than "life changing."

"All of my ideas about religion changed. I just can't buy into all that anymore. There's something so far beyond that. I feel honored that they chose me. I can stand the ridicule because I trust my own eyes, and I trust my own judgment. I feel that they are like family. It's cool!"

Addition: A couple of days after my interview with Audrey, she emailed me that she tracked down Julia, who is now living in North Carolina. I called and left a message, and the next day Julia and I spoke so I could get her side of the story of what happened that night in 1978.

"There are some details of that night I don't recall, but there are things that are still so clear I will never forget," Julia began.

She and Audrey had gone to a bar that night hoping to meet friends, but there wasn't anyone there that they knew so they left right away. Julia was letting Audrey drive her car, as she wanted to learn how to drive a standard transmission. As they were driving down a road that had big, flat fields on either side, Audrey pointed out a strange light in the sky that was making odd turns and drawing closer.

"All of a sudden it was right above us!" she said, the excitement still noticeable in her voice over 30 years later. "I was screaming for Audrey to drive faster. She kept stalling the car and I was yelling at her to let me drive. I was scared!"

Julia described the circular, metallic craft as having bright lights and "it wasn't flat, there were ridges on the bottom." She has no idea how long the craft was above them, and there very well could have been "missing time," but the light disappeared as suddenly as it had come. She was still

178

so frightened when she got back to Audrey's house that she asked Audrey's brother to follow her home. "Of course, now that I think about it, what could he have done?"

Julia was scared for quite a while after the event, but despite the fear, she "learned never to doubt that there are UFOs out there!"

About five or six years later, Julia had another sighting, but this one was different in a number of ways. First of all, this UFO was not circular, it was clearly triangular, and it didn't come nearly as close. Also, as Julia "didn't doubt" the existence of UFOs, she was "a little more prepared" so she "wasn't scared this time." Many others around the area saw the same triangle that night, including her husband, who saw it from another location, so she didn't have the burden of trying to get her family and friends to believe the story of what she saw.

So, how did that first sighting influence her life?

"I am much more open to things. I am glad I did see it, because then I knew something more is out there. I'm not afraid anymore...although, I sometimes wonder if we were abducted that night..."

Another Addition: On the hot and humid Friday, August 17, Sarah, Felix, and I met at Audrey's home in Sharon, CT. I was a little early, and Audrey and I sat in her kitchen talking about all kinds of things. Audrey has an amazing sense of humor and I was laughing my rear end off at her stories. When Sarah and Felix arrived, Felix made some preliminary sketches of the circular craft Audrey had seen.

Then I went in Audrey's car and Sarah and Felix followed us on the exact course Audrey, her mother, and son took that night in June of 1972. We stopped in the road right where she had stopped 40 years earlier. This is where we had chosen to conduct the on-camera interview, and while it was visually a great location, other aspects made it less than ideal.

For starters, the stench of fresh manure from the farm fields was so overpowering I had to repress a gag when the wind blew our direction. Then there were the flies and bees that kept landing on us after the cameras were rolling. We tried to surreptitiously swat them away, but when a fly lands on the tip of your nose, not once, but twice, there's just no way that it's going to look good on the big screen. I silently hoped Felix would do some creative editing!

179

Audrey points to the area where she and her mother saw the UFO hovering.

Despite the sickening odor and bugs, it was fascinating to hear Audrey's story at the exact location where her first sighting occurred. It was even more eye-opening when we drove the few miles to her old house, and I realized just how long this sighting actually took. All in all, she estimated that the ship was within 50-100 feet of her for a full half an hour!

Audrey also took me to the spot on Downey Street where she and Julia had the other close encounter. This little trip illustrated the importance of actually visiting these sites, because I realized it was less than two miles from her old home, and less than a mile—as the UFO flies—from her first encounter. The Downey Street location was essentially due north from the Coleman Station encounter, across an expanse of open farm fields. When you see how close together her old house and the sighting locations were, it's hard to believe it was all a coincidence!

John Rella: Yonkers, 1976

John Rella is a retired accountant living in White Plains, NY. He was "always good at math" and enjoyed the sciences, which led him and two friends to a very strange encounter. It was the night of August 21, 1976, and there was to be a meteor shower that night. As John and his friends were all amateur astronomers, they set up their telescopes on a field at the Dunwoodie Seminary in Yonkers, NY, and prepared for a night of observing. They didn't suspect that *they* would be the ones being observed.

The three men had their telescopes set up on different parts of the field, and they all kept logbooks of the times and descriptions of the meteors they saw. Suddenly, at 1:52am there was something in the sky that clearly was not a meteor, or anything else they had ever seen.

"It was bright red and moving quite fast," John wrote in his letter to me. It "seemed to be aiming toward us."

When I spoke to John on the phone, he said the object first appeared to be the relative size of a golf ball held at arms-length, and quickly grew to the "size of a beach ball." And that's where things got really strange.

"The next thing we knew, we were all standing together in the middle of the field."

They walked back to their respective telescopes and log books, and each found that *80 minutes had passed* since they all wrote their entries about their first glimpse of the red light.

"Almost an hour and a half was gone and we had no idea what happened. It was like our memories had been wiped clean!"

The next day John called the Hayden Planetarium to report their sighting. He said they were "very hesitant" to even talk to him, but then told him that he must have seen "the planet Mars coming out from behind a cloud." Really? That's the best they could do?

"I told them I was an amateur astronomer and knew the difference between a planet, a meteor, and a huge bright red light. I also told them it was a clear night and there were no clouds."

John also called one of the nearby airports to see if they had tracked anything on radar. He was told—now brace yourselves for this creative and original excuse—that he and his friends had seen a weather balloon!

181

So there we have it, case closed. The experts have confirmed that this fast moving, huge, bright red object that caused three amateur astronomers to find themselves in the center of a field 80 minutes later, was obviously a combination of the planet Mars, non-existent clouds, and a weather balloon! In all fairness, airports and observatories must get tons of calls from people who don't know a planet from their elbow, but when someone calls who is familiar with astronomy and the night sky, don't insult him with a ridiculous excuse. It's okay for scientists and officials to simply say, "We don't know what you saw."

I asked if there had been any physical effects of the encounter and missing time. John couldn't recall any pain or marks on his body, but he and one of his friends suddenly "noticed we were very sensitive to light, especially while driving at night." That light sensitivity still affects both men to this day. His friend, Tony, also started having headaches after that night, but John isn't sure how long those headaches lasted.

On a more positive note, John started craving more information on science, and tried to learn everything he could. He didn't realize how much he had absorbed until he and Tony were in Hawaii and had gone to visit a planetarium. While waiting for the program to begin, John started telling Tony about the stars and planets, and soon a crowd had gathered to listen to what he had to say!

After the program, John showed an astronomer a sketch he had drawn sometime after his sighting. It was a pattern of stars and he asked if they had any meaning. The astronomer replied, "Well, there's no way this could have been drawn from Earth. This had to be drawn from space." The man recognized the constellation, but the stars had been drawn as they would appear far out into space! (What we see as a "flat" pattern of stars in a constellation is actually a group of stars that are vast distances from one another. In other words, we have no depth perception of the field of stars.) John has no idea how he was able to make that drawing.

With their newfound curiosity in UFOs, the friends started "Operation Skywatch," to record and investigate UFO sightings. John said he even put signs in his car windows stating that he investigated UFOs and giving his phone number. At the time, for some reason NASA had begun sending him newsletters, even though he had made no such request, and they assigned him "a NASA number. So I included that on my signs so people would think I was more official!"

When people saw the signs, "a lot of them would tell me I was nuts," but he was certain of what he had seen. Years later, he was to get some additional confirmation from a very interesting source. He had an appointment with his chiropractor, and during the visit the subject of UFOs came up. The doctor then told him about a sighting he had late one night in August of 1976 near the Dunwoodie Seminary. He and his doctor had seen the same exact object on the same night!

After all of his experiences and studies, how does John view the possibility of life on other planets?

"There is life on other planets, definitely! How could we be the only ones in this vast universe?"

Overall, his encounter and research into UFOs has been a positive one. "It has opened me up to many more things"—things that weather balloons and the planet Mars could only dream of doing…

William Rundle: Cortlandt Manor, 1976

When the first article about the project appeared in the *Examiner* newspapers in Putnam and Westchester Counties in June of 2012, a lot of people responded by sending me their UFO stories. On June 14, I received an email from Bill Rundle. In Cortland Manor in 1976, he saw six shiny, metallic, round craft, with spinning lights.

Even though I had a lot of things I was working on, I just felt I should give Bill a call right away. One of the first things he said to me was that even though he knew I would get swamped with responses, he really hoped that I would call right away. He also said that it was great that the article appeared when it did, because he just recently had been feeling that he would finally like to talk about his experiences. (To be honest, I would have been surprised if he didn't say that, considering it now seemed to be the standard response!)

We spoke for quite a while, and I found him to be very well spoken, and he had an excellent ability to describe what he saw. I had a lot of questions, and the more Bill spoke about his sighting, the more subtle details he began to recall.

He also became noticeably more excited about his experience from 36 years ago, which I think was, in part, relief that he could finally openly express himself. However, I think that enthusiasm was predominantly the result of the vivid memories of arguably the most exciting event of his life, which were still "as fresh as if they were yesterday." In fact, in an email he sent about twenty minutes after our conversation, he remarked that he "was still shaking."

This was just one more piece of evidence that a genuine sighting is intense, emotional, and leaves an indelible impression that never fades. It also is usually a life-altering event, for better or for worse. This was the case of Bill's sighting, but I will let his own words speak for themselves.

Dear Linda,

In the summer of 1976, June I think, three friends and I along with several other people saw 6 UFOs on Buttonwood Ave. in Cortlandt Manor. They were disk shaped with three lights in a triangular configuration underneath. The ships were doing amazing acrobatics, going up and down, sideways, in circles, all the while staying in a group. Sometimes returning to formation as a rectangle, 3 on top and 3 on the bottom. Occasionally some would leave the formation and shoot out at amazing speed toward what we thought was a mother ship (a light far away). It was dark, I don't remember what time it was, but probably around 8 or 9 pm. One craft left the formation and my friends and I decided to follow it in my car. We followed it east on Rt. 6 to Baldwin Place where it turned around and headed west. When we got near where the Taconic Pky crosses Rt 6 it stopped in midair and hovered right over my car. It did not make any noise and lights were moving very fast around the circumference of the craft. It was hard to tell how far above us it was, because we didn't know how large it was but I estimate that it was larger than a car and maybe 20 feet above us. I could see that it was metallic and had small bumps like rivets on its underside. I was very frightened and closed my eyes thinking that it was going to do something to us. When I opened my eyes and looked up it was gone. I don't know how long it hovered over us but my friends and I thought that a long time had passed. Possibly an hour or more although it seemed like only seconds. Somehow our story got to a reporter for the *Reporter Dispatch* newspaper in Mt. Kisco. He called me and asked if I would meet him for an interview. The

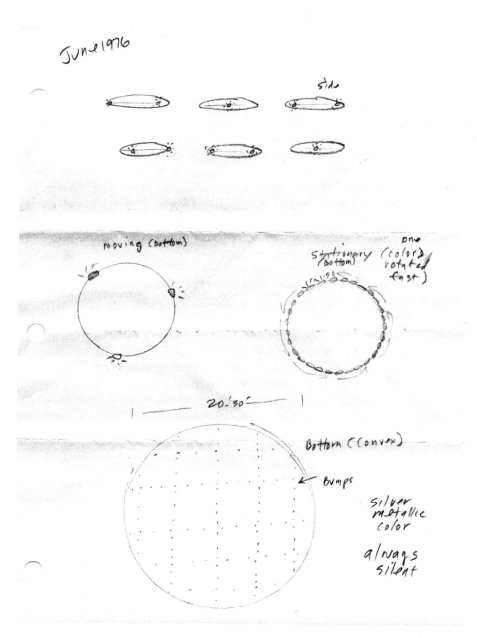

June 1976

side

moving (bottom)

Stationary (bottom)

one (color) rotated fast

20'-30'

Bottom (convex)

Bumps

silver metallic color

always silent

Bill sketched the objects he saw.

story made headlines in that paper. I don't know if it's related to what happened that night, but less than 2 years later I was diagnosed with a hyperactive thyroid and had it removed with radioactive iodine. I have not seen the three other people who were with me in many years but could find them easily. They all still live in the general area.

After hearing his amazing story, we talked about trying to track down the other three people who were in the car with Bill that night—most of whom he hadn't seen in decades. I sent one of the women a letter to ask if I might interview her, but she never responded. Bill contacted the other two, but they did not want to be interviewed.

He also said he would try to sketch what he had seen. At the time, he had made a painting of the objects, but assumed it had been thrown out at some point. He did draw (see above) the side and bottom views of the ships he saw, and also provided some additional details, which I will summarize.

Bill couldn't remember what color the lights were, but he does recall "thinking they were similar to airplane colors." As the six ships began their "acrobatics," the formation remained "so close to together" it was "like flies in a jar."

"When they stopped moving or 'hovered' the lights would go around the circumference very fast, not just the three mentioned, but many lights close together. I remember one color, different than the three mentioned (possibly white). Occasionally, one or two would leave the formation and go at a very fast speed toward what looked like a star or planet or 'mother ship.'

"After about ½ hour they all left. Then one came back and we decided to follow it. I drove. We followed it east on Rt 6. It must have known we were there because it kept weaving back and forth all the time staying on route all the way to Baldwin Place where it disappeared.

"So we turned around and headed back on Rt 6. When we got near the Taconic Pky overpass, I pulled the car over and stopped to look for it. I poked my head out of the window and looked up. It was hovering silently right above the car about 20 feet overhead.

"It was round, silver metallic color with bumps like rivets in crisscross lines all around the bottom. It was about 20'-30' in diameter. I remember yelling, 'It's right over us!' and pulling my head into the car and closing

186

my eyes, putting my head down. I was very frightened. When I looked up again it was gone. Driving home I remember discussing how late it was and that it seemed as if we had lost 1 or 2 hours."

The *Reporter Dispatch* subsequently ran a front page article on the UFOs, and "there were several other people on Buttonwood Ave. that night who also saw what I described."

Bill has never recalled what occurred during the hour or two of missing time, and this I not the first case where someone attempted to follow or signal a craft and ended up losing their memory for an extended period of time.

Mr. Science

On August 10, I received the following email from a doctor who clearly did not want to be identified, but just as clearly wanted to tell his story:

I hesitate to write you as I am a respected [doctor], but when I read the 3 accounts of people witnessing silent triangular shaped large ufos not high up, I got chills up and down my spine. I witnessed the exact same thing in 1980 over the golf course on New Hempstead Rd in Spring Valley, across from the ambulance corps, early at night. What struck me MOST was the absolute silence. I've told 4 people about this my whole life. If you want to talk to me but will keep my name private, feel free to email me back.

After checking his credentials to make sure he was legit, I emailed him back right away, and we spoke soon after. I found this doctor to be very intelligent and well-spoken, and, of course, highly educated. He was certain that he saw something real and solid, but this is where the certainty ends for a man who calls himself "Mr. Science." He has "a problem with religion" as it lacks empirical proof. He has based his life upon logic, reason, and "cold, hard facts." However, the facts of this case shook him to his very core and threw into question his entire set of beliefs.

It was a summer night in 1980 as the doctor was driving by the Spring Hill Community Ambulance building and the golf course on New Hempstead Road in Spring Valley. Today, the course is run by the New York Country Club, but in 1980 the golf course was not operational. It was dark, but not late.

The doctor pulled over because there was a strange object in the sky right above the golf course. It was huge and "solid and blotted out the sky." The silent, triangular-shaped object "was dark, and there were lights underneath it. I thought 'What the hell is that?' It was just like something out of a Spielberg movie!"

At first, Mr. Science felt that it must be "some government thing I wasn't supposed to see." Then the massive triangle "took off with no noise at a speed I never experienced," and he began to seriously doubt this was something made by Uncle Sam. However, it wasn't until he spoke to his brother and his friend, a physicist, that he shifted to the belief that it was possibly something otherworldly.

"At first they said I was nuts, but after I described the object and the way it took off, the physicist said there was no way we have the tech to do that, that it had to be something extraterrestrial."

As if one such experience wasn't enough, the doctor had an even more incredible encounter not too long after. It was the middle of the day, and he was sitting in the yard of his Spring Valley home, which was no more than two miles from his first sighting. All the details of this incident are firmly etched in his memory.

"I was working on some homework, I had on some music, and I was eating Yodels," he clearly recalls. "Suddenly, I saw this shiny, silver, metallic object high up in the sky. The sun was shining off of it and it was highly reflective. When I looked away, the object shifted position to right where I was now looking! I felt this paranoia and panic, was it tracking me!?"

He then closed his eyes and thought that when he opened them, he would be looking toward a small row of trees. And when he opened his eyes, the object was now above those trees! He tested the object a couple of more times, and each time he thought about where he would look next, the object somehow read his thoughts and instantly moved there!

"At this point I had a complete panic attack. This freaked me out more than anything else in my entire life. All I had to do was think about an area in the sky and the object would move there. It was reading my mind, there's no other explanation."

It was a "terrifying and almost mystical experience."

And how many years did this fear last? Has it affected his entire life?

"I was scared for a long, long time," the doctor confessed. "I'm not really afraid now, but I don't want to see anything again—unless someone like my wife was with me to share the experience so I could show her proof."

As with the first sighting, he told his brother about what he saw. His brother was fascinated, and wished he had seen it, too. But it wasn't until relatively recently that the doctor realized that there were some other experiences he shared with his brother.

"When I was a kid, the front door of our house had a square glass window. I had many dreams that I was looking out that window and there was something terrifying out there, but I didn't know what it was. Then just a few years ago I was talking to my brother and he told me had had the same exact dreams! We had both been dreaming about something terrifying out that front door."

Does the doctor now think there is something more to of all these experiences, something that goes beyond mere observation of an object to some sort of contact? It's a lot to ask of Mr. Science to get him to state that he may be an alien abductee, but he does admit that there is a possibility of something incredible that goes beyond what we know in science today.

For a man of logic and reason, what other conclusion could he draw?

Michael Barnecott: Saugerties Area, 1984-2006

Michael "Barnz" Barnecott was about ten years old in 1984 when he was living on Route 32 in Saugerties. He was in bed one night when he felt a shiver run the length of his entire body. He turned and saw "an illuminated being" at the foot of his bed. He couldn't make out any details, other than it was humanoid.

Thinking it must be his imagination or some trick of the streetlight or nightlight, he looked all around but could find no explanation for the figure with the greenish glow. Terrified, he tightly shut his eyes and "kept saying the Hail Mary." The next thing he knew it was morning, and his mother found him on the floor, facing in the opposite direction of the way he slept, so he hadn't simply rolled out of bed.

She asked what he was doing on the floor, and he replied that he had seen a ghost. In fact, Barnz went to school that day and told all his friends he had seen a ghost in his bedroom.

Fast forward seven years, and he and his friend, Patrick Chambers, were in the Barclay Heights area of Saugerties, in a fort they had built by the Esopus Creek. Some friends were going to get beer, and Barnz and Patrick built a fire and prepared for a night of partying. They waited over two hours and their friends never returned, so they put out the fire and headed back on the path through the woods.

A large tree had fallen in the path, so they went off to the left to get around it. As they did, they both stopped dead in their tracks, overwhelmed with an intense, seemingly "irrational fear." However, the "fear had a direction," and they both turned to look at the same place.

"Holy shit!" Patrick exclaimed. "Do you see that?"

There in the woods, about 30 feet away, were two small, "greenish, illuminated figures. One was standing up, the other hunched over, pushing back branches" to get a better look at them. Barnz remained relatively calm and didn't move, but Patrick was very excited and started to walk towards them. After going about 12-15 feet, Patrick's excitement began to turn to terror. Even though he thought that he was "twice their size" and "could break them in half," fear got the better of him and he took off running down the hill, leaving Barnz alone.

"I didn't want to get any closer to them, because I remembered that night when I was ten," Barnz explained. "I stood there as long as I could to watch them—maybe seconds, maybe minutes—then I turned and ran away."

Barnz found Patrick sitting by a fire hydrant on Sterley Avenue, and his friend was in a very agitated state. He was smoking a cigarette—in fact, he had the time to smoke two cigarettes while he waited anxiously—and he kept telling Barnz they had to get out of there right away. Clearly, Barnz had been gone much longer than he thought, although he doesn't remember anything else about the encounter other than just looking and then running. However, about a year later, he "had a dream where a tan-

190

colored face was very close" to his, and a voice asked him, "Do you want to remember this?" and he replied, "No."

Barnz is the first to admit that "the typical little green men" story is hard to believe, but he also staunchly maintains that he "will go to the grave" swearing it happened. Patrick can also attest to the details of what happened that night, and also believes that whoever they were, they were there for Barnz.

While two such encounters are enough excitement for one lifetime, Barnz has also had several UFO sightings. One night in 1992, he and a friend, Tim, were in Malden. In the sky to the east, they saw three objects with bright white lights that constantly maintained an equal distance from one another without wavering. They followed "an hourglass pattern" as they flew silently overhead for at least an hour!

Barnz estimates the altitude to be less than five thousand feet, and the objects were never more than a mile away at any given time. They called a radio station in Poughkeepsie to report it, "and the Air Force base" (most likely Stewart) to see if anything was on radar, but they were told nothing was there.

There were two other sightings in 1995, another in Malden and one in Saugerties. The one in Malden involved two of Barnz's cousins, and admittedly, some partying. Normally, I would discount any sightings while "under the influence," but the incident was in the newspaper the next day and witnessed by many people.

One of his cousins suddenly yelled, "Oh my God!" and pointed toward the river. Rising up and arcing across the sky was a bright green sphere of light with an intense yellow core. It was about 300 feet up, and looked to be about six feet in diameter. As the sphere raced upwards and off to the southeast, "it left a trail like a 4th of July sparkler." Several minutes later, "a military jet came in low and fast" as if it was pursuing the object. The following day, the newspaper had reports of people seeing "green balls of light in the sky."

Later that same year, Barnz and another friend, Nicholas, were on Churchland Lane in Saugerties. Barnz pointed out what looked like a star, and his friend asked why it was of interest. "Because I think it's going to move," he replied. Nicholas was skeptical, to say the least, until the "star" started moving. It drew closer, hovered, and went through a series of color changes from red, to green, to white. Then it moved over the Thruway and appeared to follow the highway north. When Barnz told other friends about the sighting "they belittled" him, until one friend said that he had seen the same object over the town of Catskill that night!

I asked if any other family members had ever seen anything unusual, and Barnz replied that in the 1980s, his mother and stepfather were in the front yard when "the Hudson Valley V" passed overhead. The large, V-shaped craft hovered silently, directly over their house for a while, before moving on. The next year, his mother also saw planes flying in a V-shaped formation, but she immediately knew they were planes and they didn't fool her for an instant.

The final odd occurrence was more recent, in 2006. Barnz and his girlfriend were living on Glasco Turnpike, and one night he had a dream that they were in the yard and a UFO was hovering close by. His girlfriend wanted to get closer, but he warned her to stay back. She didn't listen, and as she approached the "UFO fired a blue light" that struck her.

The next morning, Barnz wasn't even going to mention his dream, until his girlfriend said that she had a strange nightmare. She dreamed that she had been struck by lightning!

I asked Barnz what the impact was of all these experiences, and he feels that he learned "the simple message that we are not alone," and he wants to spread that message. He also said that he used to be very timid, but he has "been emboldened" by the close encounters with beings from another world, so "people don't scare me anymore."

Admittedly, though, he still does have some lingering fear of another encounter, which he feels will happen at some point, but he hopes he "will be better prepared to handle it" if they come for him again. As to the aliens' agenda, he can't begin to speculate. And he doesn't care if people are skeptical—it took years for his own family and friends to believe him—but he is determined to try to spread the message that we are not alone.

It was why he didn't mind having his real name in the book, so he could tell as many people as possible. "After all, that's what I'm here for."

Patrick Chambers: Saugerties, c.1990

Several weeks after interviewing Michael Barnecott, I spoke to Patrick Chambers, the friend with whom he shared the uncomfortably close encounter. Patrick lives in California, and was nice enough to be interviewed while traveling and switching trains.

He also remembers that night in Saugerties very clearly—they were waiting for friends who never showed up. They put out the fire and headed back down the hill.

"We had gone about 40 feet down when I got the chills and without saying anything, we both spun around and looked at the same place."

He described two "glowing green" figures about 30-35 feet away in the bushes. They were about four feet tall, and he remembered seeing the fingers of one of them, as it was pushing a branch to one side to get a better look at them. The other detail he recalls was that he couldn't see any features on their faces. In retrospect, he now believes that was due to some sort of helmet with a face shield or mask. And what was Patrick's reaction to this bizarre pair of glowing figures?

"For a spilt second I thought this was the greatest thing in the world! I wanted to run right over to them and welcome them. I started to move toward them and stopped when I got the feeling they were *not* happy I was coming toward them.

"It was like they were in my head and I got this fight or flight response, and my first thought was fight. I actually thought that because they were so small I could run right into them and tackle them both.

"But then it was like they hit my fear button and I had the most overwhelming, irrational fear and I couldn't move a muscle. I don't know if it was for 30 seconds or 4 minutes. And I got the strongest feeling that I wasn't at all relevant to them, that they looked at me like a bug, or a lab rat. It was a very, very negative feeling. Then suddenly I felt like I could move again, and I took off running down the hill.

"Mike was really fast and ran track, and I figured he was right behind me. When I got back to the street and realized he wasn't coming, I thought, 'Oh crap! Now I have to go back and get him,' which I *really* didn't want to do. I had a cigarette and waited, and then just as I decided to go back for him he came down.

"We talked about what just happened, and he didn't remember being gone that long. And I thought I was going to get home around 11-11:30pm, and I distinctly remember my parents yelling at me when I got home that it was 1:16am, and where had I been? I have no idea why I was so late."

Patrick didn't tell his parents what happened, and he and Mike only mentioned it to a couple of friends. Then for the next two years it was like "the memory of it had been diluted" and we never talked or thought about it. However, when the two friends took a cross country trip together, the memories came flooding back. They realized that not only were these two beings "in their heads," but whatever was happening had allowed Mike and Patrick to "get in each other's heads." For example, words that Mike clearly "heard" Patrick say were only thoughts; they were never spoken.

"In the beginning, I just never thought of it. Now, not a week goes by without something reminding me of that night."

And there was still more to remember. As we spoke, I asked him if any other family members ever experienced anything. At first, he said nothing had happened, but then recalled his father talking about a night of terrible nightmares. Both of his parents were having bad dreams, both woke up "totally weirded out," and both couldn't move when they woke up. While bad dreams and sleep paralysis are not uncommon, both parents simultaneously experiencing them is unusual—especially as this incident occurred around the time of Patrick's encounter.

I also asked if Patrick had any physical signs of his encounter. He began with sort of a "no"—but his memory was kind of fuzzy in the months after, as "right away" he had a very serious medical issue develop. He began having pain in his hip, and at first doctors just prescribed pain killers. As Patrick skied, they thought he may have pinched a nerve. However, the pain only increased until one day his leg was wracked with constant spasms and the pain was severe. Four doctors searched for an answer, and finally one of them found the cause.

Patrick had osteomyelitis in his hip, a serious bacterial infection that was actually eating away his bone. The doctors were all baffled as to how he contracted this hip infection, as it is rare in younger people, and is usually the result of some sort of surgery or a fracture, or a puncture or cut injury resulting in an infection, none of which Patrick had—that he can recall.

"Now you have me thinking that this was somehow related to that night," Patrick said, as the wheels of his memory inched forward. "I remember the doctors kept saying that they couldn't understand how I got that infection in my hip."

The fact that he contracted osteomyelitis right after his two hours of missing time could be purely coincidental, but Patrick is certainly not the first person to tell me about some medical condition following an encounter. The good news is that despite the long delay in diagnosis, he healed well and only now experiences some mild pain and discomfort in that hip.

One more bizarre experience must be mentioned. Years ago when Patrick moved to California and began his new job, something remarkable happened during his first hour there.

"It was an ordinary office environment. I was being trained for my new job by this guy who suddenly said, 'You've seen aliens, haven't you?' I didn't know what to say. I mean, I wasn't even at my new job for an hour, and this guy is asking if I had seen aliens! I asked why he said that, and he said that he was psychic, and he could tell. So I told him my story."

That is a bizarre way to start a new job, even for California!

I had to ask how all of this had influenced his life, and Patrick didn't hesitate to reply that the "little mundane things just aren't important. There's a lot more out there, and people should know about it. But I'm still skeptical about a lot of sightings."

As our conversation was winding down, I mentioned that I had just interviewed Florence about her family's encounter at Big Indian in the early 1960s, which sparked another recollection. His mother had a large extended family that lived in Pine Hill, not too far from Big Indian. It was 1961, she was eight years old, and the whole family was in the backyard doing various things.

Suddenly, a small creature came running out of the woods. She described it as being "like a little monkey." Chasing this creature was a small, glowing, silver sphere. The entire family watched in amazement as the sphere raced after the creature, until they disappeared back into the woods.

Then, just as if nothing had happened, everyone went back to what they were doing! Only his mother and an elderly great aunt had any

195

reaction to the remarkable sight—only the oldest and youngest of them retained the memory of what had just happened right before their eyes. Even though everyone stopped to look, no one else could remember a thing, as if the event had been instantly wiped from their minds.

Why hadn't Patrick thought to mention this incredible story earlier? Memory is a tricky thing, especially where UFOs are concerned. While some people can remember every second of their sighting even decades later, others seem to have had their memories "diluted," if not completely erased.

Is there more for Patrick to remember? Is there more that he will experience? In the UFO world, as in life, it isn't over until it's over—and I get the feeling it isn't over yet for either Patrick or Mike.

A Picture is Worth 1000 Words

In June, 2012, I received an email from a local political figure—let's call him Joe—who had lived in Putnam County for many years. He wrote that he saw a giant triangle over his house, and then described subsequent encounters with beings that looked like huge squirrels and owls! I was naturally somewhat taken aback, to put it mildly. But as I read more of his email and found out that he was a highly educated man holding important positions, I decided to give him a call and find out just what he was talking about.

His story began in the fall of 1984 while he was renting a house in the town of Putnam Valley. One night his dog, a golden retriever, began to whine. Joe assumed the dog wanted to go out, but when he opened the door to the backyard, the dog began to tremble and whine even more. Joe couldn't understand his dog's unusual behavior, and when he finally got the frightened dog out the door, it immediately curled up into a tight ball and whined even louder.

Joe suddenly had a very "weird" feeling and at that moment, the sky went dark.

There, right above him, at an altitude of no more than 250 feet, was a solid black triangle at least the size of two of two football fields. Greenish-yellow lights lined the edges of the enormous craft, and the most disturbing part was that it was totally silent and completely motionless. Joe yelled for his wife, who came running out and was stunned by a sight that was beyond anything she ever imagined. The massive triangle just sat above the house for at least five minutes, and they were both frightened by the incredible size of this unknown object so low in the sky.

Just as Joe's wife was asking what this thing could be, it started drifting slowly away, gaining a little altitude. However, it moved so slowly that it to look at least another 10 minutes for it to finally move out of sight. Once it had gone, Joe called the local police. He knew all the men on the police force and he asked them, "What was that massive triangle?"

They told him that they were getting flooded with calls, but that there was nothing to worry about, because it was just a bunch of ultralight planes flying in formation. Joe replied that it was a ridiculous excuse, as it was hovering completely motionless for five minutes, it was completely silent, it was obviously solid as it blocked out the entire field of stars, and the lights were at fixed positions and never moved relative to one another, which also meant it was one solid object.

The police response to Joe's astute observations?

"Just calm down, Joe, it's only ultralights." Then they hung up.

The next day the *Journal News* and Putnam County newspapers were filled with accounts of other witnesses seeing the same exact thing. The massive triangle had been seen throughout the region, and everyone described it as having no sound and the ability to remain motionless. As Joe put it, it was "an insult" to try to pass off the story of noisy ultralight planes for the solid, silent object that hundreds, if not thousands, of people saw that night.

This remarkable sighting, alone, would have left a lasting impression on Joe, but unfortunately, that was only beginning. Soon after the "nightmares" started.

About a week or so later, Joe was asleep in his first floor bedroom, when he suddenly awoke and felt a strong presence. He looked at the window and there staring back at him was something with big eyes. It had to have been about 4 feet tall, and its head was about the size of a child's, but much narrower. The most disturbing feature was those huge eyes, which Joe described as being as large as those of a squirrel, a very large squirrel. He woke up his wife, but by the time she looked it was gone.

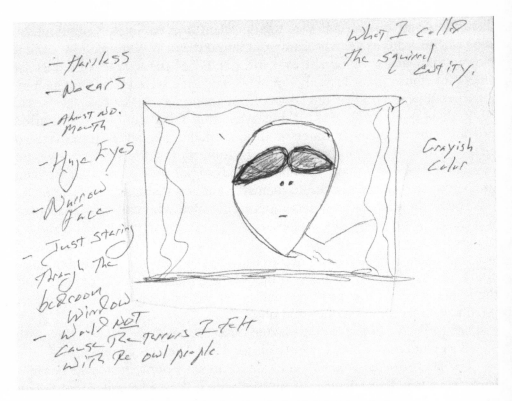

Joe's sketch of the "squirrel people" in his window.

The following week, he awoke again with a start, and found that something else was staring at him, only this time is was at the foot of his bed! He wanted to scream, but was so paralyzed with fear that he couldn't make a sound. This figure was also short, but unlike the "squirrel person" with the narrow face, this one looked more like an owl, with a large, very round head that "kind of melded into the shoulders." Once again, the most frightening feature was the eyes—"oriental or like almonds," and again, incredibly huge. Unlike the face at the window, this "owl person" terrified him. It just stared at him with those frighteningly big eyes, and then the next thing he knew it was morning.

These encounters went on month after month, sometimes only once a week, sometimes two nights in a row, but always in the same manner—the squirrel-like face looking in the bedroom window, and the terrifying owl eyes that stared at him from the foot of the bed. Then five or six hours would pass as if it was only a second, and he would wake up and it would be morning. He knew that these were not dreams, but how could this be reality?

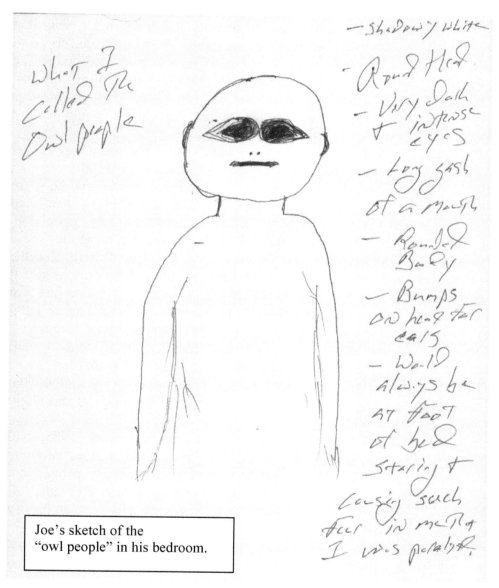

Joe's sketch of the "owl people" in his bedroom.

There was one other strange thing that began happening with the onset of these bizarre encounters—Joe started to have terrible nosebleeds. For months, his doctors were unable to find any cause, and then they finally found strange abrasions and scrape marks way up in his sinuses. They had no explanation for the odd tissue damage.

The awful stress of these encounters wore Joe down to the point that he thought he was beginning to lose his mind. He soon refused to go to bed alone. He told his wife about the horrifying things he saw, and as she never saw any squirrel or owl people, she told him they were only bad dreams. As time passed, however, she saw the effect these nightmares were having on her husband, and she, too, thought he would have a nervous breakdown.

Finally, in August of 1985, Joe couldn't stand the terror any longer and they moved out of that house. The nosebleeds stopped right away. In the new house he did have one dream about the owl person, and he woke up thinking, "Oh please, don't let this start happening again," but fortunately, that was the last he ever saw of the squirrel and owl people.

After speaking with Joe, I felt a lot better about his names for these beings he was seeing. And just for the record, I had him clarify that the squirrel person did not have fur or a bushy tail, and that he only used that term because of the narrow head and relatively large eyes. I also had him state that the "owl person" did not have feathers, wings, or a beak, and that he only used that term because of the round head and relatively large eyes. Trust me, if someone told me they were literally seeing four-foot-tall squirrels and owls, their story would not make it into this book!

For further clarification, I asked Joe if he could possibly sketch what he saw, and he provided these chilling images. A picture is definitely worth a thousand words!

I asked if anything else unusual had occurred since 1985, and fortunately, nothing had. Then I asked if anything had happened when he was younger. He replied that he didn't know if this had any connection, but he used to have terrible dreams when he was about nine. Of course, all kids have nightmares, but Joe's were a little different than most, and eerily similar to what happened to him decades later.

He used to dream that he would float out of his bedroom window and fly very quickly above the houses in his neighborhood. That was the fun part. Unfortunately, these dreams would always end with him standing in a room surrounded by figures in white robes, and hoods that had small slits for the eyes. These figures absolutely terrified him, with a distinct type of fear he was later to experience again in 1984. He felt they were somehow judging him and sensed that something awful was about to happen.

He would inevitably wake up screaming. Joe told his parents about the dreams and said he felt like he was taken out of the house at night and brought somewhere. They completely dismissed the entire idea and said if he was taken away they would know. However, despite his parents' reassurances, the terrible nightmares continued and he was finally taken to see a psychologist. He told the psychologist about the figures in white robes and hoods, comparing them to the appearance of Ku Klux Klan members. The doctor agreed that being surrounded and judged by a room full of Klansmen was frightening, but the doctor was unable to offer any solutions to the nightmares.

There was one other strange incident that occurred in 1978, soon after Joe got out of the army. He had been out with friends, and admittedly "had a few beers," and was driving home late at night. He felt very drowsy and decided to pull over on a deserted stretch of road. The next thing he knew the sun was shining. He assumed he had simply fallen asleep, which is a logical assumption.

However, soon after, he had "a dream or a vision" of that night. He was driving his 1965 red Mustang, when the engine suddenly cut out and he had to pull off the road. Then several "squirrel people" approached his car. He was terrified, but powerless to stop them from opening the door and pulling him out of the car. He then felt his body floating upward to somewhere, but he couldn't recall where he was taken.

Skeptics would say that Joe simply has an overactive imagination. Perhaps he does, and these dreams and visions of white-robed figures, squirrel and owl people are just that, dreams. But how would a skeptic then account for the massive triangle over his house that terrified his dog, a normally calm animal who never showed any type of reaction to aircraft before? How do you explain his wife also seeing the object, as well as the hundreds of other UFO sightings that night by people throughout the Hudson Valley?

Now that so many years have passed since the events of 1984-85, my last question to Joe was how everything had impacted his life. He didn't hesitate to respond:

"It makes me believe that the government is aware of it. Whether it's their own craft or something else, they know what's going on.

"And it's an insult that they try to pass these sightings off as ultralights. So many people saw it—cops, teachers, doctors—that it's an insult for them to downplay it and for us to be ignored. It's really opened my eyes.

"On the other hand, my experiences have given me a greater appreciation of the unknown and unexplained. Reality is a lot deeper than most people think. I have been increasingly drawn to the unknown, to psychic abilities, and things like that."

I have to mention that Joe has not spoken to anyone about his experiences for the last 27 years. And other than his wife at the time these events were taking place, I was the only other person he ever told. It takes courage to call up a stranger and relate your deepest, darkest secrets, and I very much appreciate that he entrusted me with his story.

I also want to point out that when he emailed me the sketches the next day, he offered to allow me to use his real name for the book. Again, I appreciated the offer, but I advised him that a man in his position would most likely take a lot of flak for claiming to have seen a UFO and aliens. It was enough that he was willing to share his story with the world, and he didn't need to jeopardize his career to do it.

Cathy Zates: Glasco, c. 1982-4

From: Cathy Zates
Sent: Thursday, September 20, 2012 8:23 PM
To: lindazim@optonline.net
Subject: lights in the sky

Linda,
Wow!! Your article in the *Daily Freeman* brought back vivid memories. I live in Glasco, NY, between Saugerties and Kingston. I live

across from the firehouse with a large field in front of my house and a large tree-lined portion of woods around the edge of the field. The first time I saw the lights in the sky was in the early 80s, it was very large, triangular shaped with white lights on the points. My children saw it also and so did several firemen who came out in the field to watch it. It stayed in the sky above us for several minutes and then slowly went to hover over the trees. It stayed there for at least 20 min. I remember that a friend of my son had ridden his 4-wheeler through the woods right before it appeared and was watching it with us. When it was time for him to go home he was frightened to go through the woods to get home.

It appeared quite frequently. I started working nights at the Hudson Valley Mall and shortly after starting, when I was getting in my car around 9:30pm I looked over the mall and saw it just sitting there again. I went down 9W and turned off 209 to RT 32 and it followed me all the way home. I was quite freaked out at first. It was there in the sky every night when I got out from work and followed me home every night for quite some time. I wasn't afraid for long and in fact, called it my friend and looked forward to having it look out for me on my way home.

When I tell people about this experience now they look at me like I'm crazy, but I know a lot of people in my area saw it and were mesmerized by it. When I read your article in the paper it brought back lots of memories of that time.

———

I admit to being skeptical about this craft following Cathy home every night, but with so many witnesses it was worth following up on her story, so we arranged to talk. I found her to be open, honest, and believable. The following is a summary of the details she provided, along with an interesting, and more recent, surprise.

I began by asking if this object was simply following the same path every night at the same time—so it only appeared to be following her home—but the more Cathy described this triangular craft moving north along the river, paralleling her course, and then always stopping near her house as she got home, it did seem that whatever was going on, it was not the result of a coincidence.

Cathy described the silent object as being at least 50 feet per side, which she was able to determine as it had hovered directly over her house during that first sighting, which was also witnessed by at least 15 stunned firemen. When the craft settled in its "usual spot" over the tree line of the field, it was about 200 yards from Cathy's house. I asked if there might be any power lines in that area, and she said that there were, about 50 yards further back in the woods.

I asked how long she would observe the triangular-shaped craft over the trees on an average night, and she said that on at least one occasion it sat there for a least an hour, and it could have been much longer, but she finally went to bed. Whenever she did witness it leave, it looked as though it would just turn out its lights and be gone.

As these sightings continued almost every night for a few months, I had to ask the obvious question—did she have any photographs? I was hoping she would say she had a drawer full of them, but was actually not surprised to find out that she "never even thought to take a picture of it."

On the face of it, this seems to be remarkable to the point of disbelief, and should bring into question the validity of any story such as this. However, this kind of mental lapse is more common than one would think. I couldn't tell you how many people have failed to think to grab a camera or camcorder and start shooting. They are often astonished that something so obvious never even entered their minds, and they later kick themselves and are unable to comprehend what happened. For many witnesses like Cathy, they often use terms like "mesmerized" to describe the almost hypnotic state they are in during a sighting. As one man told me, "If you had been there, and experienced it in person, you would understand."

Then came the night when the craft was not by the Hudson Valley Mall, nothing followed her home, nothing hovered over the trees by her house, and she never saw it again. As strange as it sounds, when the sightings stopped, Cathy felt as if she "was losing a friend."

I then asked if she had any sightings as a child, or anything since the early 80s. She thought a moment, and then said, "This is unrelated, but…" and then proceeded to tell me of an incredible missing time incident in 2008. Like the failure to think to take photographs, it continues to amaze me how people fail to connect bizarre incidents in their lives!

Cathy was driving south on 9W one night, and as she was heading down the hill by Glenerie Falls, she had a "weird feeling" like she "was in a dream." She felt like everything slowed down, like she was driving through molasses and "was never going to reach the bottom of the hill."

The next thing she knew, she was sitting in her driveway, two miles from where she had just been!

She had absolutely no recollection of driving home, and doesn't know how much time passed from the onset of the "weird feeling" to suddenly being home. I will leave it up to the reader to determine if this incident is related to all of her UFO sightings!

We then spoke of other strange things, one of which was an event in 1954 that saved her life. Cathy and her mother were moving to New York and were going to take a plane the next day. That night, her mother dreamt that the plane crashed, so at the last minute, they switched to taking a train. When they arrived in New York, they discovered that the plane had indeed crashed, killing everyone on board!

This was apparently not the first or last time her mother had displayed psychic abilities. Cathy also told me that after her sightings of the triangular craft, she, too, began to display some abilities of her own. This is also something people have told me before—that after having a sighting they have a precognitive experience or something similarly inexplicable.

So how has all this influenced Cathy's life? She feels that "anything can happen" and she is open to spiritual ideas and the concept of life on other planets. She also understands when friends are skeptical about her story.

"I know it's hard to understand. I don't push it, and I don't talk much about it anymore."

After the initial fear with the earliest sightings, Cathy doesn't appear to have any misgivings about her many experiences. Her outlook seems positive and upbeat, with no apprehension about possible future encounters. And if something does appear in the sky above her home again someday, will she grab a camera this time?

Well, that depends upon how mesmerizing a sight it is…

Gary

When I first decided to test the UFO waters and see if this was a project I wanted to undertake, I called Gary and left a message. When he called back and we spoke for the first time, I wanted to get some details about his experiences, but he replied that he didn't really feel comfortable talking about them over the phone. A moment later, there were some odd clicking sounds and the line went dead! It took ten minutes for us to re-establish our call, and we joked about someone tapping the phone and disconnecting us.

What wasn't so funny is what happened after we interviewed him at my house. Gary, Sarah, and Felix had gone by the time my husband, Bob, came home from work. We were standing in the living room in front of a big picture window, and I started to tell Bob all about Gary's experiences. Just as I started to get into the details, a van pulled up and stopped in the road, right in front of the window where we were standing. I couldn't see who was in the van as the windows had that dark film.

I joked that it must be the Men in Black, but when the van didn't move, I wasn't laughing anymore. Not many people drive down my narrow, sparsely populated street. In fact, I often say that I could take a nap in the middle of our road. Yet, here was a van we didn't recognize, with darkened windows, which for some reason decided to park right in front of the picture window where I was talking about Gary's UFO encounters.

Both Bob and I stood and stared at this van for several minutes, and Bob finally said he was going to go out there and see what this guy wanted. He went out onto the front steps and looked at the van, trying to see the driver, but still couldn't see in. Just as he was about to go down the steps and confront the driver, I stopped him. I decided that no good would come of some kind of confrontation, so Bob came back in.

Several more minutes passed as we stood inside looking out at the van, and whoever was in the van was most likely looking at us. Finally, it drove away. I might have dismissed the two incidents, had nothing else happened.

However, the next day I started transcribing the audio of the interview. I began early in the morning and worked for several hours before taking a break. In addition to the Microsoft Word software automatically saving my work periodically, I am a compulsive saver, as I write for a living and you can never be too careful.

Well, after a break for lunch, I went to get back to work, but instead of several pages of painstaking transcription, I had just a few lines. Could I have accidentally saved it all under a different file name? I searched and searched, but could only find the one file, and hours of work were missing. I could have understood if somehow the entire file got deleted, but how could only part of the text be gone, especially as I saved my work every few minutes? I checked the file properties and it said I had last changed the file at a certain time in the afternoon. I knew for a fact I wasn't changing any files at that point, as I was on the phone with Bob telling him about Gary's transcript!

I was now officially paranoid—the disconnected call, the mysterious van, and the altered file—it was all classic *X-Files* material! And there would be other disconnected calls and strange occurrences over the course of the project—including a pair of black SUVs with blackened windows that passed by Sarah and Felix's house as they worked in the front yard—twice!

In any event, these odd occurrences did not deter us from finishing the book and the documentary, and in hindsight, certainly spiced things up. So, baring anymore technical interference, I present the case that started this entire project.

Zim: First of all thank you for agreeing to do this. I just want to establish, have you ever been interviewed before or spoken publicly about your experiences?

Gary: No.

Z: OK, what has made you decide to speak out at this point?

G: I think people should be made aware of what's going on, you know. That's all I have to say about that. I don't know, I kind of feel like I'm on the spot now with the cameras.

Z: That's fine. Do you mind saying how old you are?

G: 62

Z: And how would you describe yourself? What kind of a person are you?

G: Levelheaded, honest, hardworking, family man.

Gary did not wish to reveal his identity during the interview.

Z: Okay.

G: I forgot professional.

Z: Professional, okay. How old were you when you think you had your first experience?

G: Before school. I think like maybe four or five. I'm not really sure how old I was. I have some real early memories of seeing a craft up over the mountain by our house.

Z: And where was this, Rockland County?

G: That was in Rockland County, in Congers, over the top of Trap Rock Mountain, which wasn't far from where I lived. [Note: Trap Rock is now where the Tilcon mining operation is located.]

Z: Okay. Did you understand what was happening at the time?

G: No. No, I didn't. I remember seeing this object sitting up over Trap Rock and I knew it didn't belong there, as a child. And it was in broad daylight, I don't know if it was morning or afternoon, but it was plain to see, and I think I saw it several times there.

Z: Was it resting on the mountain or hovering?

G: It was hovering above the mountain.

Z: Can you describe what it looked like?

G: It was kind of egg-shaped, but it wasn't smooth like that. It looked like it had some rough edges.

Z: Was it metallic, any lights, or anything like that?

G: It was just dark.

Z: Did you tell anyone you saw these?

G: I told my parents. I'm not sure my mother or my father, I might have told both of them. Because I remember it must have been on a weekend, because they weren't working on Trap Rock, and I told my parents, and I remember my father took me for a walk up there, just up the road and on

209

The street in Congers where Gary grew up, looking toward the mountain over which he saw and egg-shaped UFO hovering.

this back road to Trap Rock, and we got to the area that they had dug out, and my father went on alone for some reason. This is kind of vague to me, too. And he went up alone to the mountain and he told me to go home. And I walked home by myself, which was really unusual. These are some of the things I don't remember, but I'd like to.

And he stayed there and I don't know what happened, and he came home later by himself after going up there to see what this thing was. That's all I remember of that.

Z: Do you have any explanation now?

G: I have no explanation at all about it.

Z: Why would your father tell you to go home?

G: I don't know. I thought maybe I was having a rough time climbing on the rocks, but it just wasn't like him to send me home from there, because I had to walk on the road by myself and I was a little boy. But he did. But anyway, that's all I remember about that.

Z: About how long was he gone, do you recall?

G: I can't really tell now. It seemed like a long time to me. I actually made it home and he didn't come home for a while.

Z: He never told you what, if anything, he saw?

G: No.

Z: Could you talk about any of your other early encounters?

G: Well, I remember at the same time, around the same time, I remember meeting this little guy in the woods. Because our house was on, it was a dead end. I don't know if it was a dead end when I lived there, or before I moved there, but there weren't any other houses around, not next to on either side, and 9W was up behind it. So I used to play in the woods around there, and I remember meeting this little guy who was about my size, and he had like a baseball hat on, but it had a flat top to it, and there was an insignia on it. And he had like a pair of coveralls on, and I think there was an insignia on that, too.

And I just remember coming face to face with this little guy, and I don't remember being frightened or anything. And the next thing I remember is just waking up under a big tree, like curled up in the roots of it, and just going home. It was like the end of the day or something.

Z: So all that time is missing?

G: Yeah. Yeah, I don't know what that was all about.

And a lot of, I remember as a little boy, I lived, yeah, I didn't live, but my bedroom was in the front porch, which was a sun room, a sun porch, and there wasn't any heat and it was all glass windows around it. We only had two bedrooms and two girls and a boy, and so they kind of put me in there with a bed cause, you know, there was only one bedroom for my two sisters. And I remember that this light used to come every night and I told my parents about it, that there was a light that kept me awake at night. And they always, they used to say it's the street light out there. And I'd say, no, I know where the street light is and this is a different light. And that's it for that memory. It's just something they tried to explain, but it wasn't.

And then I moved to, you know my parents built on a master bedroom and I ended up taking the room my sisters had and they moved to the other bedroom. And I remember, I don't know, I guess this has to do with it, but I remember figures being floated around my bedroom at night, like geometric shapes and pyramids and cubes and formulas. And I don't know what that was all about, but I would like sit up in bed and see these things floating around in my bedroom.

And I remember floating back down to my house from up in the sky somewhere, but actually coming down over the neighborhood and seeing the surrounding road and the surrounding houses and trees and all, and like coming back down into my bedroom somehow.

Z: As if you were just passing through the roof or the wall?

G: Yeah, yeah.

Z: These shapes and these formulas that you're describing, were you seeing them as solid figures or projections?

G: They appeared to be like blocks, you know, like child blocks that were floating around. Actually, they were gray. You know, it was dark in my bedroom and you could just see shadows, and so I could just make out the shapes, and like the formulas were just dark letters that were all tied together. But I could see, you know, I didn't know what they were, but I could see them and now I know they were formulas. But I don't know what it all meant. And that's all I remember right now about it.

Z: On how many occasions, you said you saw yourself floating down to the house, was that once, or more than one occasion?

212

G: More than one, yeah, but I can't say how many. It was a very long time ago. (He laughs.)

Z: And how often did these occurrences happen to you? Was it almost every night? Several times a year?

G: I couldn't tell you.

Z: Okay. When was the last time something happened to you?

G: Probably in the eighties.

Z: The eighties. Could you tell me what that was?

G: Well, actually things happened to me in the seventies. You said the last time, but I forgot all about this as a child. I didn't think anything of it. I knew it was strange, at the time I felt that something was going on, but I had no idea. And my father worked nights sometimes and my mother was scared at night, because she said there were these lights that came down in the woods next to our house that scared her and she didn't know what they were. And she would just see the glow coming from the woods. That's all I remember about that, but she was frightened by it.

And before my father died, I had talked to them a little bit about this as an adult, maybe about eight or ten years ago. And my father, after I talked to them, my father at dinner one night said that he, when we lived at that house when we were kids, he woke up several times in the middle of the night, he didn't say how many times, and he saw these little figures around their bed. And that he pulled the covers over his head and tried to go to sleep and never told anyone about it, never said anything to my mother, and he just kept that inside all these years. And so that kind of verified that something was going on to me cause I have all these strange memories.

Z: Did he describe what these figures looked like?

G: Just that they were little, like kid-sized figures, and I think they scared the heck out him so he...

Z: Did your sisters ever have anything happen?

G: My sisters have never talked to me about them. I told them a little bit of the things that happened to me, you know, as an adult, and about the things back then and seeing that craft over the mountains there. And my older sister told me she used to feel like she was being touched at night in bed, that something was touching her arm. And my other sister hasn't said anything.

Z: What about people in the neighborhood? Had anyone ever shared experiences or said they had seen craft?

G: No.

Z: So you have seen ships on how many occasions would you say?

G: Through my life?

Z: Yes.

G: Uh, I don't even know.

Z: Many?

G: Many, because fast forward to the seventies and I had forgotten about this stuff as a child, as you would.

Z: It stopped at some point?

G: We moved, actually. We moved from that house to another house. And I remember always at night going to the window and standing at the window looking out at the moon and all as if I was waiting for something. And that stands out in my memory right up through high school I used to do that. I used to sit by the window, like late, when everybody was asleep. I don't know what I was waiting for, but it seems that I was waiting for something, but I don't have any memories of that.

214

Z: Did you have any sense of fear at these times? Or just curiosity? How would you describe your emotional state?

G: Unemotional.

Z: Unemotional?

G: Yeah.

Z: It was just something that was happening and it was just part of your life?

G: Yeah.

Z: Okay. So at no time you could really say you were scared?

G: No. Not that I remember.

Z: You say you were going to fast forward to the seventies?

G: Yeah, fast forward to the seventies, and I had moved upstate. I was in the Navy and got discharged and moved back to Rockland County. And at some point we moved to the lower tip of Ulster County. And my wife and I—for no reason—I was working in an engineering office in Ramsey, New Jersey, and I came home from work and I got my wife in the car and drove upstate and rented a house. It was just like for no reason. It was so odd.

I did this. I drove up there, and I bought a newspaper, I found a house to rent—it was a nice old farmhouse on five acres, and I rented it there on the spot. And we moved there, so now I had to commute to New Jersey every day. And I don't even know why I did that, but I did.

Anyway, I started having a lot of experiences there in this farmhouse. And one in particular that started this whole memory thing with me and I started thinking about what happened to me as a child. And one night I came home from work, it was a Friday night, and we ate dinner and were kind of watching TV and relaxing and I had a couple of beers and I went in the kitchen and I saw these lights in the woods. Around my farm I had a barn and animals and I kept seeing these lights moving around in the

215

woods and I was just curious as to what the heck it was, because I knew it wasn't a car, because there are no roads back there, there were no roads at all. And it was also freezing. It was like ten below zero, one of those really cold January nights.

And I didn't think anything of it, but something kept telling me to go to the store. And it was, you know, go to the store and get some more beer. Cause, you know, I had a few cans of beer in the refrigerator, so I didn't really need to go, but at some point, I went. And I would say it was about ten o'clock, and there was a country store a few miles down the road that closed at midnight. And so I went out and I got in my car, and I drove down this back road, and as I turned onto this road, I saw this light up over the field. It was actually an apple orchard to my left that went up a hill. And on top of that ridge there was a big, bright light up there, and as I was driving, that light followed me along the treetops down this road. And I kept watching it, and it just kept pace with me as I drove.

And at some point it disappeared from my view and when I came around a curve this light was on the ground off to my left and not very far away, and it was a big like egg-shaped light. And I couldn't really tell if it was a solid object, but it was a big, bright light sitting on the ground there. And there was like a mist swirling around it. And I remember I stopped dead in the road and I was looking at this thing, and I looked up at the moon, a full bright moon, and it was a freezing January night, and I said, it's not the moon, there's no houses there, what the heck is it?

And I just remember sitting there looking at it and I remember feeling all the hair on my head and body stand up, and the next thing I remember is seeing it disappear. It seemed to raise off the ground a bit and it was gone in an instant. I don't know whether it just flew away that fast or just disappeared, but it was gone. So I started my car up and I drove on to the store. And when I got to the store they were closing, so it was around midnight. And I went in and I bought—I don't even remember what I bought—I remember I was like buzzing, like I had just stuck my finger in a wall socket.

Anyway, I went on home and my wife was hysterical. As soon as I walked in she said, "Oh my god, where have you been?" I said I haven't been anywhere. I just went to the store and came back.

She said, "No, you've been gone for two hours!"

And I said, well, you know, I didn't go anywhere. I went to the store and I came back. And oh, by the way, I saw this light on the side of the road. And that was it. We went to bed, and that was the end of that story.

Gary points to where the egg-shaped UFO had landed, and where he lost two hours of time.

But I remember, I don't know if it was the next day, or that weekend, or another weekend, you know, same time, it might have been the next day, I don't recall at this time, but I was working on my wife's car in the driveway and I had pulled my car up next to it, cause I had to jump it, and I had to squeeze between the two cars at one point, I parked them very close. And as I did, I felt my thigh hurt.

So I went into the house and into the bathroom, cause it really hurt like I did something to it, but my pants weren't ripped or anything. So I went in and I pulled my pants down and I had this scoop mark on my thigh like

217

a piece of skin had been taken out of it. And you could actually put your finger in it like it was scooped out. But it was also cauterized—no blood. No blood or anything, just a little pain that alerted me when I rubbed it up against the car.

And I'm shaking inside right now.

Z: Well, I'm covered in goose bumps.

G: And I became very ill after that. I don't think I finished working on the car. I felt like suddenly I had the flu. And I don't think I went to work for a week, or so. My head, my head hurt, and I think I went up to bed, I don't remember. This was all the same day.

And another night, it might have been the next night, that night when I woke up in the morning and my wife woke up and looked over at me and she said, "Oh my god, I must have hit you in the face during the night." Because I had blood caked all over my face coming out of my nose, and it was all over my mouth and chin. And my head hurt, right up over my nose, and my forehead between my eyes. I went down and took a shower and washed the blood off of me and I couldn't figure out what the heck happened. I thought maybe my wife would have really had to sock me in my sleep, you know, and it would have woken me up.

At any rate, I became really sick after that. My face hurt, and I don't know if this was the next day or the same time, because I know I missed work, I really felt sick, really sick, and my head hurt, and it felt like the flu, I guess. I became very ill.

Anyway, the same house I remember—this stuff went on for while there—I remember at one point lying—it was an old colonial saltbox—and it had two big bedrooms upstairs, and you came up a big center hall staircase, and I remember lying in bed with my wife one night with my nightlight on reading a book and she was asleep next to me, and as I was lying there I was facing the bedroom door, and I saw something come out from behind the bedroom door, like a little figure popped out and looked at me for a minute. I saw it out of the corner of my eyes as I was reading. And I got out of bed, and I think I walked very slowly over to the door and looked behind it, and I don't remember seeing anybody.

Here again, I have these fragmented memories of looking at, we had these windows, the chimney came up through the bedroom against the wall, and there was a big window at either side that you could stand at, and it was practically a full-sized window from floor to ceiling that you could look out, and I just remember seeing lights out there or something.

And, oh yeah, the farmer that had the land next to my house—I was out in the yard—this was all the same time, same period when I lived at this house—I was outside and the farmer was out cutting his hay and he stopped his tractor and got off and came over and he said, "Do you know what happened to my field? What happened here?"

And he asked me if I did something, and I said, no. And they had a barbed wired fence up and I never even went over there.

Anyway, they had a crop—what would be called a crop circle now—right next to my house in that field, where the grass had all been laid down in a perfect circle—maybe a thirty-foot circle, something like that. I don't remember now. So I didn't think anything of it at the time.

I really didn't think anything of it—I thought I caught the flu, I didn't know what happened to my nose, where this mark came on my thigh—so I just said no, I didn't see anything, I don't know what happened. And he was pretty angry at the time, I just remember that.

And the whole time I lived there, I don't think anything grew anymore.

Z: In that circle?

G: Yeah, in that circle.

Z: How long were you there?

G: I was there about, oh, four years.

And my wife was trying to have a baby at the time. And this happened quite a few times. I don't know how many times, but she thought she was pregnant, and, you know, we would go to the doctor and she was indeed pregnant and she kept losing it, or having a miscarriage, or not being pregnant.

I remember one specific time, because this happened several times, where she was pregnant and then she wasn't. And I came home from work—and we were sure about it, you know—and I came home and she was sitting on the steps crying, and I said, "What's the matter?"

And she said, "The baby's gone."

219

I remember those words, because it seemed odd to me at the time. And she said, "I'm not pregnant anymore. It's gone."

And now that kind of ties in with things I've read that they take embryos and babies and stuff. That's my interpretation of it now. Back then, I had no idea. I just...she... we kept trying to have a baby and it was just always gone, was what she said.

Z: So you had actually gone to the doctor and she was pregnant?

G: Yeah.

Z: Those are pretty definitive tests.

G: Yeah.

Z: And then she would know she miscarried, or it just wasn't there anymore?

G: Uh, she just said it was...gone.

Z: And this happened more than once?

G: Yeah. And I've never spoken to her. We divorced not long after that. We moved from that house, and maybe a year later we divorced. And I've never spoken to her about it, and I'd like to talk to her about it, but I have no idea where she is. Because a lot of odd things were going on at that time.

Z: In retrospect now, when you said you have no idea why you suddenly went up there and rented that house, do you now feel that you were somehow directed to that location, to that farmhouse?

G: I kind of do, yeah.

Z: Did your wife ever speak of any other kind of experiences?

G: No. We never talked about it then. There weren't abductions then or anything like that going on. I knew absolutely nothing about UFOs or aliens or anything. I tied this together in the eighties when I started having more experiences.

Z: Okay, do you want to talk about those?

J: Yeah, fast forward to the eighties, and I'm married again, and I had a few children. At this time I was living—should I say where I was living?

Z: In general.

G: [The town of Walkill in] Ulster County. Well, actually in the same general area. Remarried, new house, and this is how this started: I was in the family room watching TV, and my wife was in bed already—I don't think she was feeling well—and she was in bed asleep, and the kids are in bed asleep, and my dog is barking frantically outside. It's like, maybe ten o'clock. And here we are in early January again, another cold, January night. This was in…1985, maybe? '84, '85?

I opened up the sliding doors and I yelled at my dog to be quiet, and I went back and sat down. And he's carrying on like crazy outside. So, I put my coat on and went outside—no, actually I didn't. I looked out the screen door, the sliding glass door again, and I yelled at him, and I saw all these lights over in the field on the other side of the road from my house. So I put my coat on and I went outside to see what the heck was going on out there.

I just saw all these different colored lights. And over on the top there was this house to the right of my house, facing the highway, and I could see over the top—this was a two or three story house—I could see over the top of it, these lights, in a field, across the street from that house was a big cow meadow that rolled down into town, and I walked up in the back of my yard—I had about an acre of land back there—and I walked up and I could see it looked like it was like a ball of lights, different colored lights, like Christmas tree lights, rolled up in a ball, except that it was huge.

Z: How huge?

221

G: Um…30 feet, 40 feet? It was a big ball of different colored lights. Green, yellow, orange, blue, and I don't remember if they were blinking or what, but they were just a mass of lights and there was a mist around it, like flowing around this, this thing. And I walked out to the road where I could get a better look at it in the field, and as I was walking this ball of lights was rolling down the meadow. And it was like the lights were turning over, slowly. And I don't think it was really touching the ground. I think it was just moving down the contour of this meadow, and I had no idea what to think of this. Strangest sight I've ever seen in my life, these lights.

And as I got out into the road, it was getting further away down the meadow, and I watched it actually go all the way down, almost to town. It would have ended up across from a high school, almost, pretty far away until it was just a small (spot) and it shot straight up in the air like a bullet when it got down towards town. It shot straight up in the air until it was a little dot and it shot back east, out of sight, gone.

And at that point I went back to the house and I went in and woke my wife up and I told her what I just saw and I encouraged her to get up and come out with me, you know, I thought maybe it would be back, and indeed it had come back. And I brought my wife out, and I brought her down to the end of the street and she saw it, too.

It had come back in the field and was doing the same thing, kind of slowly moving down the field and my wife panicked and started running back to the house. And she was screaming. And she was screaming, "I have to protect the kids!"

I stood there for a little bit watching it and then took off after her, because she was hysterical almost. And I caught up with her on my front porch, front steps, and I just kind of put my arms around her and we stood there for a minute, and I looked up, and as I looked up, I saw the peak of this craft coming over my house and this craft was huge, and we both looked up at this thing as it totally engulfed the sky. That's how big it was.

This craft came—it was a triangle, a perfect triangle shape—and it came over my house and disappeared in the trees, but it was huge. We both stood there and watched it and looked at it and it was like the ceiling right here, and I could see it, I could see appendages on it and lights. I remember there were like upside down "Ts" out of the bottom of this thing, and didn't hear any sound. I felt a vibration, like a "hmmmm," like a deep hum inside of me. I don't know if I could actually hear it or I just felt it.

And my wife and I both stood there and watched this thing come over our house. And I stepped off the porch and actually took a step to see how fast this thing was going and I had to wait for it to catch up to me. That's how slow it was moving. It was just hovering there and moving very slowly. Both I and my wife watched this thing until it cleared the house and had gone a distance away. And the back of it was just a big, like bar of light. And then it turned kind of north, it headed north away, and then it was gone, out of sight.

My wife just totally freaked and won't talk about it to this day, she's an ex-wife also, but she won't even acknowledge it to this day.

That was the time when the Hudson Valley Triangle was coming over and that's what I thought I saw. And I said well, jeez, I just saw the huge triangle I keep hearing about on the radio.

After that, I saw these craft every week, almost, around my house, my house there. At night, I would just go outside and there they were over in the field across the street, and I saw this little— not little—but a small triangle. It was about treetop level over this meadow, and I stood under it, and it was just sitting there shining lights down on the meadow. I don't know what it was doing, but I got scared because I heard something—it was pitch black out—and I heard something very close to me, coming towards me and I ran out of the field and went home.

But this went on for a long time, and like you know egg-shaped craft, different shaped craft, around my house. I would see them, I would go out, like I said, every week they came almost. I could actually go outside and see UFOs! It was very strange.

Z: Did you seem to know when they were going to be there?

G: I, I think I did. I think I felt when they were there and I would go out and look at them.

I'll tell you another strange experience that happened in the same house. I had to go up to New Paltz after dinner one night, it was during the week. It was 7:30 or so, it was winter, and I had my kids with me. And as we drove back home, as I turned onto the street that my house was on, over in that huge field where I had already seen on those strange crafts and

The field across from the school in the town of Walkill
where Gary and his family saw many UFOs.

the ball of lights, was a huge light. It looked like a fluorescent light and it
was lying horizontal above the field. And it was huge, you know, like
sixty feet long. It was a huge light hovering in the field, like a two by four
fluorescent light—not a two by four, maybe a single—fluorescent light
fixture.

And my kids are going, "Dad, what's that!? Was it that, dad!?"

And I said I don't know.

And as we approached it, it stood straight up in the air, vertical—it
moved from horizontal to vertical position over this field, just standing
there—and I'm thinking that everybody in the world can see this thing, as
well as that ball of lights that had rolled down the field, and that huge
triangle that came over my house. You know, I'm thinking nothing is ever
going to be the same, everybody's seeing these things.

Nobody, in fact, that I know, saw it.

224

But anyway, I drove home and brought the kids in the house, and they're like, "Dad, what's that!? Was it that, dad!?" And I brought them in and I went over to the field and this light was gone. That particular light, but the other ones came back to the field, the smaller triangles. And this went on for a long time.

Z: Do you have any sense of what they were doing there?

G: No.

Z: Did they appear as if they were examining things with these lights?

G: No, not really. They were looking around, it seemed to me, but at what I don't know, or why. Because, you know, a couple of them shined lights on the trees and the ground area. That's all. I wouldn't begin to understand what they are doing.

Z: There are some skeptics who would say that these Hudson Valley triangles were military craft, or stealth blimps, or something like that. Do you think that's possible at all from what you've seen?

G: Well, I don't know what the military has for real. You know they have the stealth bombers and all, that look like a triangle, but these things were totally silent. I didn't hear anything, and I was pretty close to some of them—like I said, like looking at the ceiling here. I was pretty close to them and never heard anything from any experiences that I had.

Z: From your description of that one craft that shot straight up and over, it doesn't sound like anything we could have developed?

G: I don't think so. Not that I know of, and I served in the military, too. I know we have some pretty fast jets, but—

Z: Not slow ones.

G: Not slow ones, and quiet.

Z: So how long did you live at that location and kept experiencing those crafts in the field?

G: I would say that that went on for a couple of years. Actually, I don't remember how long I lived there, in that house. I don't remember now, maybe five years, or maybe longer, maybe seven years? But starting in 1984 or 85, it went on for two or three years where I had experiences.

Another thing that happened in that house—and I had three children, and my wife had a child from a previous marriage, so we had four kids—one night I was awakened by what sounded and felt like someone kicked the end of my bed and woke me up. I just fell back to sleep.

But the next morning, which I think was an hour or two later, I got up and showered and got dressed and off to work. And the kids were still in bed sleeping when I left, and I think my wife was, too. And I went in and kissed my kids goodbye every day, as I always did, and every single one of them had dried blood out of their nose, onto their face, all four of them, even my wife's other son.

Z: Did you?

G: I did not. I had already experienced that years ago, before that. But I was really startled by that. Because when this happened in the eighties there, you know, with that huge craft coming over the house, I started remembering all the things that had happened to me, that I never thought about or put together like my previous marriage and my wife having all these false pregnancies, and the scoop mark on my thigh, coming across that odd object on the ground and losing time—it appears I lost a couple of hours' time there—and I started remembering all these things, and I started going to UFO conferences and buying books and reading about it, and kind of putting it together. It seems like it's been my whole life.

Z: Have your kids ever mentioned any experiences?

G: No, they haven't, but for some reason they are scared to death of the entire subject.

Z: Do they know of your experiences?

226

G: Well, yeah, they saw that light in the field, that lighted object, and other things that were happening all the time, and so I talked to them about it. I said I didn't know what they were, or whatever, but I certainly didn't scare them, or try to scare them about it. But they are petrified of it now, as young adults.

Z: Do they have children of their own?

G: Yes, they do.

Z: And no mention of lights or anything?

G: No. Not from any of them.

Z: Because you had experiences, your kids had experiences, and your father had experiences.

G: Yeah, I feel like they were marked, now, like I was. It was just so odd that they all had blood, you know, coming out of all their noses the same night.

Z: Was the 1980s the last time you had any encounter?

G: Yeah, I moved—actually, I got divorced again—and I moved. And I was remarried again. And a couple of things happened in the 90s—was it the 90s?—or the early 2000s, probably the end of the 90s. But I was camping with my wife up in Wilson State Park, which is up by Woodstock, and we woke up in the middle of the night—like three in the morning—and the entire wooded area around us, we were camped on top of a—well, we were camped in the state campground—but the ground went off into a big valley right, like five feet away from our tent, and there was nothing down there, it was all woods and wilderness that just went off. But like three o'clock in the morning I woke up and the outside was lit up like daytime, like it was bright like it was daytime.

I looked out the tent window and I couldn't see anything except bright lights out there, and it was down in that ravine, coming from that area. My wife and I both saw them, but we didn't hear any noise, and didn't see anything other than it was really lit up bright.

And the next morning I looked down there. Actually, my wife and I hiked down there, and hiked all around there. And there's nothing down there, there's no tracks, so no someone could drive in there. It's a mystery to me what it was.

Z: Have you ever had any x-rays or anything to indicate that something had been implanted?

G: No.

Z: Have your children?

G: No.

Z: Have you ever felt anything unusual in your body, something under the skin?

G: No. I have three triangular-shaped marks on the back of my neck, here. I have no idea--and they're pretty big, you can take a look at them. You can put your finger in one of them. I don't know where they came from.

Z: Do you know at what point you received them?

G: I think when I had the wound on my thigh, here. I'll show them to you.

Z: I have to ask, do you think this is something that's going to happen to you again?

G: (Long pause while thinking)   I get the sense, no... I think they're done with me.

Z: Do you feel relieved?

G: No, because I've always been fascinated by it, by anything that happened. I was curious. I just wanted to know more. I've never been afraid of it.

Z: So, we've just discussed well over fifty years of experiences. How has this affected your life, your outlook, what you've done, how you view things?

G: Well, I think, even from a child, I've always known that there are more things we don't know or understand, than what we do understand or what we're told. And I've always kind of known that we weren't alone. I think I always felt that way. Maybe it comes from my childhood and whatever was going on then.

Z: So, do you think this has made your life better in any way?

G: I don't know. I really don't know.

Z: But you don't feel it has ruined your life?

G: No.

Z: Or you've lived in fear?

G: No. I don't think so.

Z: So, people watching this or listening to your story, who don't believe you, what would you say to them?

G: Um...jeez...I don't know. It's difficult to convince people. It's just too hard to believe, but it's not for me. It seems like I've always been open to the possibilities that other people don't see. But like I said, it probably goes back to the fact that this has been around, I think, my family forever.

Z: So it's something you just accept?

G: Yeah, you know, I've spoken to friends about it, and some friends have embraced it, and some friends have just brushed it off as utter nonsense. So, it's really individual. I'm not here to convince anybody, but I know what has happened to me.

Z: And what would you recommend to people who do believe and may have had similar experiences? Do you have anything you'd like to say to them?

G: I think the more people talk about it, the more mainstream it could end up being, helping people. That's kind of why I'm doing this interview right now.

Felix: Even though you say you're open to letting everyone know what's going on, and everything, can you explain why you wanted to be in the shadows?

G: Well, I'm not really up to being ridiculed. I've seen so many people ridiculed and turned into a big joke, which is what happens with anyone who talks about this subject. The government, media, that's all, really.

Z: Well, I'm blown away. I've had a hard time just sitting here calmly, because it's not only listening to what you're saying, but seeing the emotion in your face, feeling how real this is for you. I mean, I was shaking at several points and I've been covered in goose bumps.

G: That's what happens when I read some of your books!

Z: Well, thank you. But this has just been an amazing eye-opening experience for me. The genuineness and the emotion—I'm covered in goose bumps right now thinking what you have experienced, what you've come in contact with, and I'm sitting across from you now. It really has been an amazing experience for me and I can't thank you enough for sharing.

G: Oh, you're welcome. My pleasure.

Gary's Mother

I was pleased when Gary said his mother was also willing to be interviewed. I thought she would just be telling me what her son had experienced in the 1950s when he was young. I had no idea she had experiences of her own, dating back to the 1930s!

Gary's mother.

Z: For the record, you are the mother of the man I interviewed on May 10?

Mrs. X: Yes.

Z: Can you tell me when you moved into this house near Trap Rock where these experiences took place.

Mrs. X: Yes, exactly. We moved in 1950, on June 14th.

Z: You do know exactly!

Mrs. X: And my son was only five months old.

Z: Do you recall your son telling you about any of these experiences.

Mrs. X: Oh, yes! He told me many times that it was all lit up on the outside of his room. We had a lot of windows on a sun porch we had converted to a bedroom for my son. And he told me that somebody was in his room at night, and I would tell my husband, and he didn't want us to be frightened and he'd say, "Oh, well there's a street light right over the garage that's probably shining in his room."
But these lights were too bright. It wasn't the street light.

Z: Now, was your husband having any experiences that you know of?

Mrs. X: Yes, but he didn't tell me until after we moved from there, because he didn't want me to get upset, being sometimes I would be alone with the children because he worked until twelve at night. He told me one night there were two of them with the oval eyes on the side of the bed, his side of the bed. And he said he quick turned over and covered up his head and put his arm around me.
And I said, "Did you look to see if they left?" And he said they didn't right away. But he covered his eyes and he finally went to sleep.
I said to him, "Weren't you afraid?" And he said, "No. What were they going to do to me, take me away?"

Z: Your son had an incident where he saw an egg-shaped light over Trap Rock.

Mrs. X: Yes.

Z: And he and your husband went to investigate, and he sent your son home alone. Do you know what happened?

Mrs. X: No, he never told me.

Z: He never told you about that?

Mrs. X: No, he didn't want me to be afraid with the children, so he would say, "Oh, it wasn't anything. It was just lights they had up there."

Z: Okay. Did you ever see anything around your house?

Mrs. X: Yes.

Z: Could you describe it?

Mrs. X: I belonged to the PTA [and she was coming home one night from a meeting]. We had long cement steps, and then a walk, and then three steps up to our house. And as I'm going up the three steps to the house, two of them were standing by the side of the, the...about 500 feet from our walk. And I couldn't wait to get in the house, and I didn't turn on any lights, because I didn't want to wake the children. My husband had gone to bed—sometimes he would wait up for me—and I told him you don't have to, because I wasn't afraid—not until I saw them on the side of the property. And when I went inside I got changed and went in the bedroom. I peeked out the blinds and they were still standing there.

Z: Could you describe what they looked like?

Mrs. X: That might have been the night that my husband saw them by the side of the bed. Their heads were real white looking, and these oval eyes. And the next morning when I told my husband, he said, "Oh, we're just below 9W, and there's the Wheel Inn up there. Probably a couple of men were cutting through our yard."
But I said they were standing there watching me. And he said they might have been afraid I was going to say something about them being on your property.

Z: About how tall were they, could you say? Could you judge?

233

Mrs. X: Not real tall. Maybe about three feet.

Z: Okay, so probably not the size of people who would have been in the bar that night?

Mrs. X: No.

Z: Did you ever see any ships or craft or anything at any point.

Mrs. X: Not when I lived at that house, but the backyard used to be lit up many times. I kept the blinds closed because I was afraid to look out.

Z: And how long did this go on that you were seeing these lights? The whole time you lived there?

Mrs. X: Most of the time that we lived there.

Z: And did it start soon after you moved in in 1950?

Mrs. X: Yes. I used to tell me husband, "Why is our backyard lit up so?" And he said, "Well, probably the cars on 9W." I knew 9W was up a ways in our back and I'm sure it wasn't cars.

Z: Did your daughters ever have anything unusual happen to them?

Mrs. X: Only my eldest daughter. She used to feel, have someone run their finger on her arm, and she thought it was either her dad or me, but that's about all she knew when we lived there.

Z: Has anything happened to her since living in that house?

Mrs. X: Up in Vermont.

Z: Currently?

Mrs. X: Her whole yard was lit up a few times. And it lit up her whole bedroom, it was so bright. And she saw two of them out in the yard. She told her husband, but he said, "Oh, you were probably dreaming after that movie we saw." I don't remember the movie, but it wasn't too recently that she saw this movie with aliens.

Z: So he tried to tell her it was her imagination, but she's certain it was not?

Mrs. X: Yes.

Z: How many times have things happened to her in Vermont?

Mrs. X: She said a few times. She also, at the first house they had built in Vermont, she used to hear all this noise. Her husband used to be away a lot. He used to work for IBM and they would send him over to Scotland or Europe, and she would be alone with her one son. But she said he told her he was hearing all this noise in the attic, and his dad said it was probably just ice on the roof. But she said it happened too many times, even in the summer. Now, there was no ice in the summer. And she was alone with just her boy.

Z: Any other experiences with your grandchildren or relatives?

Mrs. X: No, not that I know of.

Z: Do you know of any experiences by your parents or brothers or sisters?

Mrs. X: No. But when we lived on (deleted) Ave, my daughter got married in '67 and she said, "Mom, go sign up and take ceramics," because I was going to miss her because she was going to the (Midwest) to live. Anyway, I left ceramics at ten o'clock (PM) and I was crossing over the reservoir road to Congers, there was one (UFO) over the reservoir. And this ladder, like a rope ladder going down into the water. And I was the only one on the road, and it was eerie, it was silent, and I couldn't wait to get home. And when I got in the house I told my son, and our house was up high on a hill, and we could see the lights from our kitchen window. It was still there.
The next day it was in the paper that they were sighted in Stony Point.

Z: Can you remember what year this was?

Mrs. X: It had to be '67 because that was when my daughter got married and I started ceramics.

Z: Can you describe the shape of what you saw? Was it hovering?

Mrs. X: It was round with lights all around it. It looked like, to me, a big wheel from a wagon. And these lights all…[she uses her hands to indicate the lights were spaced around it like on the end of the spokes]. And I told one of the women at work the next day, and she didn't say anything, but she looked at me funny.

Z: That's a problem, people getting ridiculed. You can't help what you saw.

Mrs. X: You know I saw it. I wasn't dreaming or imagining, I said, because it was so eerie, and I was the only car on the road.

Z: How big was it? Could you judge the size of this?

Mrs. X: It was at least as big around as this room.

Z: So at least 20 feet, 30 feet?

Mrs. X: Yeah, it was large.

Z: When was the first time anything happened to you? Do you recall anything as a child, or was it just when you moved into that house near Trap Rock?

Mrs. X: When I was growing up on 3rd Street in Haverstraw. It was so hot one night that I was leaning on the windowsill to see if there was a breeze. And I saw these…two of them in the backyard. And that's the first time that I saw them.

Z: About what year was that?

Mrs. X: I told my dad. I guess I was about eight years old [in 1937]. And my dad said, "Oh, I think you were just imagining it. There was no one out there." And I didn't think any more about it, but it never happened again until I got married and moved to [the house near Trap Rock].

Z: Did you feel scared when you first saw them?

Mrs. X: Yeah, I did.

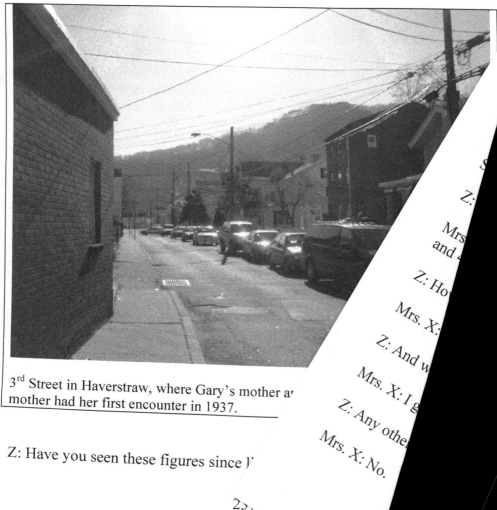

3rd Street in Haverstraw, where Gary's mother a' mother had her first encounter in 1937.

Z: Have you seen these figures since 1'

Z:

Mrs and

Z: Ho'

Mrs. X:

Z: And w

Mrs. X: I g

Z: Any othe

Mrs. X: No.

Mrs. X: Where I'm living now, standing in the hallway standing by my bedroom door. And I thought, oh, I'm back in Rockland again and now they've followed me! That's what went through my mind. And I tried not to keep looking down the hall, and they were there for at least a half hour.

Z: How many of them?

Mrs. X: Two. And then I heard my front door open and close.

Z: Did you lose any time? Did you fall asleep? Did anything happen?

Mrs. X: No. But when I was in high school and I was at my girlfriend's house, I was supposed to be home by 1:30 (PM). And I left her house at 1:30, but I didn't get back until 4:30, and I don't know what happened. And my mother was real annoyed, because she was supposed to play cards with some women and I didn't get home until 4:30, because I remember her saying, "It's too late, now. Where were you? I told you to be home at 1:30." And I said, "I did leave at 1:30, Mom. Your clocks must be wrong." he said they're not wrong.

So you have no idea what happened?

X: I have no idea where I was or what happened to me between 1:30 :30.

old were you at the time?

I think I was in the second year of high school.

hat year would that be, roughly?

raduated in '44, so that would be 1942.

times in your life you can recall having that missing time?

Z: About what year was that?

Mrs. X: I told my dad. I guess I was about eight years old [in 1937]. And my dad said, "Oh, I think you were just imagining it. There was no one out there." And I didn't think any more about it, but it never happened again until I got married and moved to [the house near Trap Rock].

Z: Did you feel scared when you first saw them?

Mrs. X: Yeah, I did.

3rd Street in Haverstraw, where Gary's mother and father grew up, and where his mother had her first encounter in 1937.

Z: Have you seen these figures since living there? Anything recent?

Mrs. X: Where I'm living now, standing in the hallway standing by my bedroom door. And I thought, oh, I'm back in Rockland again and now they've followed me! That's what went through my mind. And I tried not to keep looking down the hall, and they were there for at least a half hour.

Z: How many of them?

Mrs. X: Two. And then I heard my front door open and close.

Z: Did you lose any time? Did you fall asleep? Did anything happen?

Mrs. X: No. But when I was in high school and I was at my girlfriend's house, I was supposed to be home by 1:30 (PM). And I left her house at 1:30, but I didn't get back until 4:30, and I don't know what happened. And my mother was real annoyed, because she was supposed to play cards with some women and I didn't get home until 4:30, because I remember her saying, "It's too late, now. Where were you? I told you to be home at 1:30." And I said, "I did leave at 1:30, Mom. Your clocks must be wrong." She said they're not wrong.

Z: So you have no idea what happened?

Mrs. X: I have no idea where I was or what happened to me between 1:30 and 4:30.

Z: How old were you at the time?

Mrs. X: I think I was in the second year of high school.

Z: And what year would that be, roughly?

Mrs. X: I graduated in '44, so that would be 1942.

Z: Any other times in your life you can recall having that missing time?

Mrs. X: No.

Z: Any time you have had these sightings or incidences, have you ever physically felt anything afterwards? Any pain, or any marks on your body?

Mrs. X: I do remember one time when I was pregnant with my third baby, and I remember saying it to my husband in the morning, "You woke me up rubbing my tummy." And he said, "I wasn't waking you up rubbing your tummy!" But we never thought anything about it.

Z: So you never had any marks, any physical marks on your body?

Mrs. X: No.

Z: And none of your children, that you know of, have had that?

Mrs. X: No.

Z: Any other experiences anywhere else?

Mrs. X: No. Most of them happened at the house [near Trap Rock.]

Z: Do you have any sense what they want from you and your family?

Mrs. X: No, I don't.

Z: Okay. So your general feeling with these experiences has been that you were afraid of them?

Mrs. X: Yeah. Well after I saw them on the side of the [property], my husband decided that when I came home from PTA to blow my car horn and he would come down and unlock the garage to walk me in because I was afraid!

Z: Did your husband tell you any other stories of things he encountered, other than seeing the two of them in the bedroom?

239

Mrs. X: He saw our backyard lit up all the time and he saw this big circle up in the sky, and that's where the lights were coming from. But he didn't tell me this until after we moved because he knew I was afraid because I saw them.

Z: Did he have any experiences after leaving that house?

Mrs. X: No, not that he told me. But the first thing that came to my mind (Referring to her earlier statement that "they" had come to her again because she was back in Rockland.) —we lived up in New Windsor for 12 years—when I moved back to Rockland County where I am now, when I saw them down the hall standing in my bedroom doorway—about the distance to that doorway there.

Z: Okay, about 12 or 15 feet away.

Mrs. X: Yes. And I didn't imagine it either, because I would look away and look back and they would still be standing there. And I heard my front door open and close.

Z: And again, these were the short ones with the whitish heads and the oval eyes?

Mrs. X: Yes.
(At this point there is some discussion as to anything else she would like to add or had forgotten to mention, which led to the following question.)

Z: When your husband saw these figures in the backyard, about how many were there?

Mrs. X: He told me there were about six. And I said to him why didn't you tell me when we were living in that house and he said because the children were small and I knew you were afraid when I had to work nights.

Z: And he saw them in the yard more than one time?

Mrs. X: Yeah, I think he did, but he didn't want to tell me about it.

240

Z: So, you have had experiences since you were a child. How has this impacted your life?

Mrs. X: I tried not to think about it anymore. The only one I told was my dad and he didn't seem to think it was anything. So I just blocked it out.

Z: Did you tell your husband when you first met him?

Mrs. X: My husband lived upstairs and I lived downstairs. We were childhood sweethearts from the time we were six years old.

Z: Wow, good for you! So you didn't tell him about those experiences?

Mrs. X: No, not until he told me what happened in [the house near Trap Rock].

Z: So, are you worried, were you worried that something would happen? Was their fear?

Mrs. X: Sometimes…yes.

Z: Were you afraid for your children?

Mrs, X: Yes! Mostly when we lived there I was afraid for my children.

Z: So overall, this has been a negative thing in your life? Something you wish never happened?

Mrs. X: Right.

Z: Do you have any advice for people who are experiencing things? What would you tell them?

Mrs. X: I don't really know. But, you know, most people think you're crazy. I've told a few people and they look at me like, "What's wrong with you?"

Z: Okay, I think that's it. Well, you've been wonderful and I really appreciate you sharing these—for having the courage to share these memories, and thank you very much!

Mrs. X: Oh, you're welcome. It was nice to meet you.

Z: It was nice to meet you, too.

I don't think it was a coincidence that Gary's mother and father grew up in the same building. This was where his mother had her first encounter with the short figures with the big eyes in 1937, and has continued to see them for the next 75 years!

It's also not a coincidence that her son, daughter, and grandchildren experienced similar things. It appears as though contact with one or more members of the same family is more common than not—as if certain families are chosen for some kind of ongoing experiment.

If these stories represent just a tiny fraction of the people who heard about this project and had the courage to contact me to share their stories, how many others in the Hudson Valley have yet to speak out? How many hundreds, or maybe even thousands, of residents over the last 75 years have seen strange figures, lost time, had physical marks on their bodies or came down with mysterious illnesses? And what has the emotional toll been of these forced encounters?

Something dark and sinister has been occurring in the Hudson Valley for generations. Something beyond our control has been happening to the residents of Abduction Alley.

<u>Addendum</u>

Hypnosis:
Should You Remember?

There are few subjects that evoke such extreme responses as alleged alien abductions, and many books have been written to argue whether such cases are the result of delusions or have a basis in reality. The fact remains that many people *believe* they have been taken and experimented on by aliens. Truth or fantasy, such things are *real* to them.

Setting aside those people who have actual psychiatric issues, what is it that makes otherwise ordinary people going about their lives suddenly think they are being carried off in the night and subjected to all manner of horrible testing? What would make people jump to the extreme conclusion that *they* have been chosen by *them* for some nefarious purpose?

For starters, as this chapter has shown, there are people who witness a UFO and then experience lost time—sometimes hours or even days they can't recall. Then there are the frighteningly realistic nightmares about aliens, exam tables, and painful probes. Some people, especially after having one of these nightmares, may wake up in another room of their house, or their yard, or even another part of town. Then there are the nosebleeds, headaches, and physical marks on the body—burns, scoop marks, scars, triangular impressions or discolorations, and a host of other bizarre experiences that would test anyone's sanity.

If you truly and honestly believe such things are happening to you, who can you turn to for help? What can you do? An obvious place to begin is to stop all recreational drugs and alcohol, and check with your pharmacist to make sure you aren't experiencing any prescription drug side effects or interactions. Then it would make sense to see a physician and a psychologist or psychiatrist to make sure there aren't any underlying medical or psychological reasons for whatever you think is happening. When all conventional avenues are exhausted and people still believe they are being abducted, many turn to hypnosis.

Of course, hypnosis is as controversial as aliens, but it has been used with success to get people to stop smoking and break other bad habits. It's also very entertaining when hypnotists make people do foolish things, but here's where the danger lies—are the details recalled under hypnosis real, or false memories? Just as good hypnotists can make you think you're a rooster at dawn, can being placed in such suggestible states and then asked about your abduction experiences make you fabricate abduction memories?

Conversely, if hypnotism does truly help people unlock memories, is it better that those memories stay buried?

When I was at one of the Pine Bush UFO meetings, someone asked about hypnosis as a means of recalling details of possible abductions. Bill Wiand strongly recommended against hypnotism, as he feels it causes more harm than good. According to him, there are some things are you better off *not* remembering.

However, there are many people who desperately want help with circumstances in their lives they can't explain—things that are having serious impacts on their physical and mental wellbeing. Some of these people turn to hypnosis and regression to step back in time in their minds, to try to see what actually happened to them.

In September of 2012, I was contacted by Richard Wander of Milan, New York, who told me he had started an abduction hypnosis group in 1999. About a week later, we arranged to have Richard come by Sarah and Felix's house for an interview. He began by talking about two sightings he had when he was a kid—one in 1956, and another he saw with his sister in 1957. So, from an early age, Richard had no doubt that there were aliens visiting earth.

Richard Wander during the interview.

Years later as an adult, a friend in Wurtsboro phoned him in the middle of the night and said a UFO had landed in his yard. When Richard went up the next day, he found crushed vegetation and three round depressions in the ground forming a triangle with 9-foot sides.

Richard read a lot of books about UFOs, but one that really had an impact was *Missing Time* by Bud Hopkins, with its chilling descriptions of alien abductions. In 1996, he decided to take a course to learn how to hypnotize people, thinking that he might able to help other people with missing time. By his own admission, though, he had no idea what he was getting himself into.

He placed a small add in the local newspaper for just a week, and received 32 calls from desperate people claiming to have been abducted! Interviewing them all, he realized many of them were not credible, and decided upon the four most "normal" people for his first group. There was a married couple, Marge and Joe, and two women from Hyde Park, Karen and Joanne (these are not their real names).

Marge suspected she was being abducted, Joe suspected she was crazy. One night he awoke to someone banging on the front door, and it was Marge outside in her pajamas, with no memory of how she had gotten there. As the deadbolt locks could only be locked from the inside, they couldn't figure out how she managed to get outside and lock the doors. Another time she awoke with her clothes inside out.

While such incidents could be written off as sleepwalking, it got stranger. Even though Marge had a hysterectomy, she "felt pregnant" to the point of taking a pregnancy test, which came out positive! Then a few days before she was going to go to the doctor to see what was going on, she had another missing time incident and no longer felt pregnant. This happened to her over and over, four separate times.

Richard placed her under hypnosis, and wasn't prepared for the hysterical screaming and crying that ensued. Marge was yelling that "they were coming to take" her, and she yelled for her husband to wake up and help her. After "they" brought her to their ship, "they took something out of" her—a fetus. And what did "they" look like? Small grey beings with big eyes, and taller ones with a more beige-colored skin.

Was this all just a rehash of a Hollywood movie? Had hypnosis given Marge a venue to create her worst nightmares and bring them to life? Only one thing was certain—Marge believed it was true, and Richard was also swept up by the raw emotions and terror she displayed. After four sessions of hypnosis, Marge decided she had learned enough and decided she would not undergo hypnosis again.

The cases of Karen and Joanne were also similar. Under hypnosis, both screamed and tried to fight off the aliens taking them. Each, separately, said they recognized the other from "the exam table" next to them. Each described the experiments, the fetuses, the small and tall aliens, as well as the leader, who looked like a praying mantis.

Richard stated, "It just blew my mind that all these women said the same exact thing." It was all too much for him then, but now that years have passed and he's retired from his day job, he would like to begin to work with abductees again to see if he can help.

I had to ask what he thought about all the things these women said, and he believes that these experiments are designed to create a race of human-alien hybrids to take over the world. Again, I know it sounds like a script right out of *X-Files*, but again, these women truly believe it.

Then I asked if he thought there was any way to prevent being abducted, not really expecting an answer, but he quickly replied, "Velostat." I had no idea what that was, and he said it was a special fabric that blocked electromagnetic fields, and therefore blocked alien mind control. Richard said the fabric could be used to make hats.

At this point, I think I was biting my tongue hard enough to make it bleed. Then after a pause, Richard added, "And tin foil doesn't work." We both started laughing and I said I was glad he mentioned tin foil, because I was just about busting at the seams to bring it up.

The next day I did a Google search on Velostat and found the following description on Wikipedia: "Velostat is a packaging material impregnated with carbon black to make it electrically conductive. It is used for the protection of items or devices that are prone to damage from electrostatic discharge. It was developed by Custom Materials, now part of 3M. Other uses: It is also used in Thought Screen Helmets, claimed to block telepathy by extraterrestrial beings."

I then found a website, stopabductions.com, that tells you how to make a Velostat hat. The site also has testimonials by people who claim that by wearing a homemade Thought Screen Helmet they have kept the aliens from abducting them. The site also claims that aliens have been

246

stealing these Velostat hats, so when you aren't wearing yours (and why would you ever take it off!?), you need to keep it locked in a cabinet, as aliens don't know how to open locks.

Hey, whatever works for you, right? Live and let live, right? If wearing a hat brings you peace of mind, more power to you.

Never mind that if there are aliens who have traveled through vast distances of interstellar space who have vastly superior intelligence, they are nonetheless completely baffled by locked cabinets, and are completely incapable of knocking a stupid hat off your head!

This is just my opinion, but if wearing a fabric hat stops your abductions, maybe you really weren't being abducted in the first place. This sounds like a classic placebo effect. If you believe the hat will help, it will.

And I am poking fun at all of this because I think it detracts from cases where people actually do have otherwise inexplicable things happening to them. Like the nonsense spread about ultralights and weather balloons, serious research into such cases can be compromised by muddying the waters, and lumping all abductee cases into the same category.

So where does all this lead? Well, if you have honestly ruled out any other rational explanations, and still you are convinced that you are being taken and experimented on, you really don't have a lot of options to get help. You can seek out support groups like the one in Pine Bush. You can go to people like Richard and try hypnosis. You can try to find a doctor who will take you seriously, but you shouldn't get your hopes up in that regard.

Beyond that, if the abduction phenomenon is a reality, it is most likely a case similar to humans subjecting mice to experiments—the mice can't do a whole lot about it.

12
Strange, but True?

Air Force Secrets

Just in case there are any confidentiality issues still involved, I agreed to keep this witness anonymous. He is a Hudson Valley resident who has experienced a sighting in the area, but also had some interesting stories from his career in the Air Force. Let's just call him the captain.

It was around 1963 during the Cold War, and the captain was stationed at Mather Air Force Base by Sacramento, California. There was a squadron of B-52 aircraft at the base, and all "were kept in tiptop shape" as they had to be ready to take off with no more than a 15 minute notice. These were the days when the country kept a nervous eye on the Soviet Union, and needed to be in constant readiness to strike back in the event of an attack.

Then one day, just as group of B-52s was about to take off, one completely lost power. However, this mysterious loss of power was not limited just to this one plane—the entire squadron lost all communications for a full half an hour! In a time when any Soviet threat would have demanded an instant response, thirty minutes must have seemed like an eternity to the Air Force personnel who scrambled to find out what was wrong. Then just as suddenly as the power and communications had gone out, it returned.

The official excuse was that the Russians had some secret jamming and disrupting technology, and the incident was immediately "hushed up." In fact, I was the first person the captain had told in the fifty years since it happened! Unofficially, the captain said that Air Force personnel had reported "flying saucers" over the base during the incident. As he said it was later proven that the Russian's didn't have the technology to make a B-52 lose all power or cut off all communications in the squadron, then perhaps those unidentified flying objects are the prime suspects.

He also mentioned another incident involving a B-52 that had taken off from Diego Garcia en route to Korea. Half way through the flight, the plane lost all communications. This time, they were told it was the

Chinese who were responsible. Although none of the crew spotted a UFO, the lack of a real explanation—and the official bogus Chinese explanation—left the captain wondering.

What was really to blame for these two incidences—simple electrical glitches, Russian and Chinese secret weapons, or UFOs? The captain can't say for sure, but the sighting he had years ago in the Hudson Valley left him convinced that we are not alone.

Carol Anstey: Grahamsville, 1975

From: Carol Anstey
Sent: Sunday, September 23, 2012 6:33 PM
To: lindazim@optonline.net
Subject: UFO Sightings

Hi Linda, After reading the article in the *Daily Freeman* about your book on UFO sightings, I just had to respond. Although I live in Sullivan County I have an interesting story to tell:

One hot August night in 1975 (I was 16 years old) I was swimming in our pool in our backyard. Nothing seemed unusual at the time. I got out of the pool and went to bed, as usual that night. The next morning my father started yelling, "Hey, who let the water out of the pool?" We could not believe what we saw. During the night the pool water had disappeared. There was no water or soggy ground around the pool and we all checked for leaks/holes, but none were to be found. Normally it takes about 3 days to release the water from the pool, as we did every year before winter. After trying to figure out how the water disappeared, my father proceeded to fill the pool with water and the water stayed. It never "leaked" again.

You should know that I live in Grahamsville, which sits right in between two major New York City Reservoirs. A few days after our "incident" the local paper had a small article that someone spotted a UFO over one of the reservoirs.

Now, I can't tell you that a UFO took our pool water, but to this day we can't explain what happened to that water. Not one single explanation makes sense.

249

Feel free to contact me. Thanks for listening.

From: Linda Zimmermann
Sent: Monday, September 24, 2012 8:13 AM
To: 'Carol Anstey'
Subject: RE: UFO Sightings

Ok, so I have to admit when I first read your email I thought, "Well, now I've heard it all!" But then I started searching to see if there have ever been other types of UFO-related water draining, and found that there have actually been quite a few! And they are all similar—huge volumes of water gone overnight with no sign of damage to the pools or water tanks. Who knew?

So, let me just ask a few questions, as I would like to use this story.
1. I assume this was an above ground pool? What size was it? (I would like to estimate the number of gallons.)
2. Have you or family members ever seen a UFO?
3. Was all the water gone and was the liner dry, or were there some puddles or a few inches left?
4. Can I use you name, or just initials?

From: Carol Anstey
Sent: Monday, September 24, 2012 6:30 PM
To: 'Linda Zimmermann'
Subject: RE: UFO Sightings

Hi Linda, I have no problem with you using the story or my name. To answer your questions:
1. Yes, this was an above-ground pool - oval shaped – approximately 15 X 25 feet/4 feet deep.
2. Many years after the swimming pool incident, about 1986, my dog woke me in the middle of the night. I got out of bed to let him out and noticed a bright light outside the window. When I looked outside the window, I saw a bright spot-light shining straight down from the sky with no sound of a helicopter. I could not see any "vehicle." This light was not very far from where our swimming pool was. By the time I got outside to see what it was, it

disappeared. To my knowledge, no family member has ever seen a UFO, but a woman I work with saw the typical triangle-shaped UFO outside of Liberty, NY. She was with other family members, who saw it also.

3. The pool had a few inches of water left in it.
4. Yes, feel free to use my name as Carol Meyer Anstey.

Now that I had the dimensions, I used a volume calculator to determine that there were about 8,850 gallons of water in the pool. As Carol said there were a few inches of water left, let's knock off 850 gallons to make it a nice round 8,000 gallons removed. That makes the weight of the missing water (using 8.35 lbs/gallon) a whopping 66,800 pounds!

Carol sent a photo of the pool, taken many years after the mysterious draining. The pool was nowhere near a road, so a vehicle could not have driven up to it.

To give even more perspective, I also found that the largest 18-wheeler water tank trucks can only hold about 8,000 gallons. So, somehow, without any leaks or holes in the pool, and with no water on the ground around the pool, a huge tanker truck full of water weighing over 33 tons disappeared overnight!

I have to admit, this is truly bizarre. And I can speak personally as to the length of time it takes to drain a pool. In another of these odd coincidences that have popped up during this project, I am—at this very moment—draining water from my pool to close it up for the winter. Granted, my in-ground pool is larger and deeper than Carol's, but even with a powerful pump, it seems to take *forever* just to drain about a foot to get below the level of the skimmer opening. Even when a deer fell in the pool one night and tore three gaping holes in the liner, the water level did not go down more than two feet.

This is definitely one of those cases where you, the reader, will have to decide whether you believe a UFO drained this pool, or this story is all wet!

Another view of the pool area, since overgrown, which shows its inaccessibility.

BPA FREE PAPER   SHOPRITE 260 JFM   FOR ADVERTISING CALL 1-800-247-4793   17047   BPA FREE PAPER   SHO

==== ShopRite of VAILSGATE ====
==== Security Receipt ====
Purchased from ShopRite #260

PRICE PLUS # 48502922823
Number of items: 33
Total Amount: $185.07 +TAX

03/30/23 12:43pm S260 R3 T23 C150
Take our survey within 7 days for a
chance to win $500 ShopRite Gift Card
To get started visit
MyShopRiteExperience.com

13
Out on the Fringe

God knows I personally believe in a lot of weird stuff, so I am in no position to throw stones. However, there are just some stories that are even too weird for me. Here are several cases that fall into that fringe category. Are these stories all real, all imagined, or half-real and half-imagined? I know there will be believers who will take their every word as gospel, and skeptics who will take their every word as utter nonsense.

With these cases I will simply report and let you judge for yourself where the truth and fantasy reside.

The Mystery Caller

On June 7, I received a mysterious phone call under strange circumstances. Bob and I had gone to see—fittingly—*Men in Black 3D,* and when we got home I checked my phone messages. There was just one, from someone I will call Andy from the Pine Bush UFO group, and the message went as follows:

Hi Linda, this is Andy. I was at the meeting last night, and I have some things I want to talk to you about. I know what you are trying to do, but I gotta tell you some things you need to be careful of—

At this point, the message became garbled and unintelligible. Then there were some clicks and the message ended. It sounded like some sort of interference, and it certainly could just have been a bad cell phone connection. However, given that the call to Gary was also disconnected, this seemed to be an unsettling coincidence, especially as the interference began just at the point where he was trying to warn me. Paranoia is a potent force!

I tried to call Andy the next day, but had to leave a message. When he returned my call the following day, one of the first things he told me was that, due to his research into UFOs, he was being watched and his phone was being tapped. Normally, I wouldn't put much stock into such an idea, but there was that interrupted message…

He didn't want to discuss much over the phone—for obvious reasons—but the gist of his claims was that certain sectors of the government were not pleased with his articles about UFO activity and photographs of strange aircraft. In addition to the surveillance, Andy also claimed that the government had somehow blacklisted him, making it impossible for him to get a job due to a "questionable" background check. And, he was in the process of moving to the Hudson Valley to get away from some of this surveillance.

It was all extremely difficult to believe, but the story became even more incredible. Andy stated that one potential employer looked at his background check and asked him, "What did you do, photograph a UFO?"

I tried to process all this and make some sense out of it. Had Andy actually inadvertently photographed sensitive or experimental U.S. airplanes or space vehicles? Was he somehow exposing military secrets? Or had he truly seen something extraterrestrial? And finally, was he one of those people who constructed their own altered reality?

After the phone call, I felt like I was stuck in the middle of an episode of the *X-Files*! (Unfortunately, without the devilishly resourceful and handsome Agent Mulder.)

It was clear I would have to interview him in person and we arranged to meet at the Goshen Diner for lunch. It was a long, strange meeting, to be sure, filled with stories of alien contact, implants, messages from ETs, hybrid offspring, government harassment, conspiracies, cover ups, and assertions about the true nature of the human race: 90% of us are good people who have some type of ET connection, while the remaining 10% of the population are the selfish, negative power brokers running the show— for now.

My head was spinning as I drove away; one of those "What just happened!?" feelings. I admit I was really "weirded out" the rest of the day. Was Andy purely delusional? Or had Andy actually been subjected to so many alien experiences that now his every thought and action was influenced and tainted? Or, was every word he said the truth? Only one thing was certain, *he believed* everything he said.

As many of the details of his encounters he told me that day were to be kept confidential, we arranged to have him interviewed on camera, keeping his identity hidden. This would give me the ability to get all the information he would allow to be public for the book. It would also give audiences of the film the opportunity for a better insight into the man himself, by listening to his actual voice as he told his stories.

It worked out that after interviewing Debbie about her Pine Island experiences, we drove over to Wurtsboro to meet Andy at the Crystal Connections store. If you like rocks, minerals, and eye-popping crystals—some the size of people—all in the beautiful setting of an old church, then you must make a trip there. The owner was extremely accommodating when we took over part of the store as Sarah and Felix set up all the cameras and lighting equipment.

I was anxious to hear just what Andy would divulge on camera. Would he be reluctant to share personal experiences and stick to generalities? Or would he spill all of the alien beans and then some, including dropping some bombshells? The following is the transcript of that interview.

Zim: Thank you very much for taking the time. You have an amazing story and I'm just going to let you begin wherever you like.

Andy: Okay. It all started when I was two years old. I was in my bedroom. It was in Elsmere outside of Wilmington, Delaware. All of a sudden this white, bright light shined through my window and the toys in my toy chest were thrown all over the place. I had a favorite toy. All of a sudden these beings came in through the window and took me out, and I have no idea what happened to me. I was taken up into a craft. All of a sudden the next morning around 5am, here I was walking on the railroad tracks, and some person—entity—pulled me off the tracks, and I could have been hit by a train and killed, but they saved my life.

The switch man at the railroad station that I was near said there was no one on duty, did not know who he was, and my mother wanted to thank him for saving my life. But he was a person who just appeared and disappeared.

This was my first experience and it started here and it never stopped. Periodically things happened. The next time it happened was when I went to my father's friend at work. It was up in Landenburg, Pennsylvania, near the Delaware-Pennsylvania state line. It was a known place for having UFO sightings, and I spent the night there. Of course, I was out on the farm, and you know on farms they leave the doors open, the windows open, everything is wide open. And they raised cows and cows were in the pasture. Not at night, of course, but they had cows, they were on the farm.

So during the night that I spent, the night over with his son, my father's friend's son, I had a cot right next to him, all of a sudden this bright, white light shone in the window. I was a little apprehensive, and I kind of figured out that this was what was going to happen again. I'm going to be taken up again, or am I? I didn't know what was going to happen. I couldn't wake my friend, because he was sound asleep like a rock. I could not wake him up.

All of a sudden I heard something open the door and come in, and it started up the stairs. I was really scared. This wasn't my own house. I wasn't familiar with this place. Like I said, the doors were unlocked and it was a farm. I like the city where you lock your doors and turn out the lights.

The lights were turned out and I ran into the bathroom. Usually when I get scared like this I ran into the bathroom and turned on the light. Unfortunately, the light would not go on. So I ran back to my cot, and wouldn't you know it, my flashlight wouldn't work either. But this bright white light was there and this thing, this entity, kept walking up, and all I did, I was so scared, I just covered myself up, and then something eerily tapped my shoulder.

256

And it said, something like, something about "You've been chosen." And I wondered why, and I had enough guts to look what it was. To me it looked like a Frankenstein, that's all I could identify it with. And it took me up into the ship, and I don't exactly remember what happened, but when I returned it was time to get up. My friend's son was waking me up telling me it was time to get up.

Zim: So at least several hours were missing?

Andy: Yeah, well, I wasn't in the bedroom for those hours. I don't know where I was. I don't know what they were doing with me. I was evidently brought back, and whatever it was forgot to put the covers back on me when I was returned. But I don't know what else to say about that.

Zim: How old were you at that point?

Andy: At that point I was about 8 years old. See, it does follow you the rest of your life. So, if others have experiences like this, don't think it's going to go away. Maybe temporarily or periodically it will go away, but it's still with you. If you have that ET connection, it will always be with you. You can deny it all you want, or you can accept it all you want, or you can just do what I did, try to live your life and just deal with it as it comes.

So when I was ten years old, this was after I went up to a camp in Hughesville, Pennsylvania, around Williamsport, Pennsylvania. Isn't it funny that they have also had a lot of UFO sightings up there as well?

Zim: Around this campground?

Andy: Around this campground, this area. And I think it's called the Susquehanna Watershed up there, but I'm not sure. Anyway, I was in this cabin, and we just had a party—and no, it wasn't anything that was put in our punch. I wish I could say that. I wish I could really say that, but no, it was all non-alcoholic stuff, though, unfortunately. That was not the answer to whatever happened.

Anyway, we were in a cabin, and there were two sides to the cabin. And in the middle was the luggage, that's where we stored the luggage,

257

and the rest was just bunk beds. And afterwards…uh…I'm not going to say little green men, but these were sort of a green color, and they were alien-type. And actually, they were throwing the empty suitcases at us on both sides of the cabin.

Zim: They were throwing suitcases at you?

Andy: And they were not human. They were not shadow beings, but they were light beings. And they had been seen at the camp before. I was not familiar with it. And that was another experience I had with these entities, only I had company this time.

Zim: How many people witnessed this?

Andy: Eight people. Eight people were in the cabin, including the counselor.

Zim: And what was their reaction?

Andy: The campers didn't know what to think of it. They were not used to this subject. They thought that they were ghosts. I don't think they were ghosts. Apparently I've had a transplant, and again-

Zim: What do you mean a transplant?

Andy: Perhaps when I was up in the craft, the ship.

Zim: A transplant or an implant?

Andy: An implant, excuse me.

Zim: So if you want to start that over.

Andy: So evidently I've had an implant, and the campers were wondering why one of these green beings took my hand and walked me out of the cabin. I don't remember going in to anywhere. I just remember walking out of the cabin into some kind of dimensional space. And then all of a sudden I woke up with all the rest of the campers in the morning.

Zim: Did they recall this happening?

Andy: Some of the campers said, "Where did you go?" I said, "I don't know." So that was when I was ten. And let's see, for a couple of years they let me live my life.

And then when it came to, let's say, uh, I can't remember exactly. So anyway, when I turned 16, I had another experience. I was out driving, and I don't remember what happened there.

Zim: You just lost some time?

Andy: Lost some time.

Zim: Okay.

Andy: And then we bring it all the way up to when Reagan was president. I heard Tom Brokaw on the television say something like, uh, let me back up on this. One night I had an entity come in my bedroom where I was living. This was not in Elsmere, this was more toward Stanton, Delaware. And I was in my bedroom and a bright white light shone through and the same type of beings came in when I was two.

Zim: And how old were you at this point?

Andy: I was...it was about...the late 1980s. [He is currently 60 years old.] So I don't remember what age I was then. I know Ronald Reagan had just become president, or he had been president for about a year. What the message was that I had gotten from that experience, that encounter, was that they were doing a lot of nuclear testing in Nevada, and they asked me, they were telling me to do something to stop it. The ETs were telling me to do something to stop it.

Zim: What did they think you could do?

Andy: Well, what I did was write President Reagan a letter, telling him to stop the testing in Nevada. So a couple of days later, or weeks later, or a week later, Tom Brokaw was on NBC and he had said something to the effect that they were doing nuclear testing in Nevada, and you know how Tom Brokaw is, he said, for some reason or other, a lot of people had been writing him [Reagan] and as a result, this testing for some reason has been temporarily stopped. So I may not have been the only one that was contacted by the ETs.

Zim: Did you ever receive any sort of response from the White House?

Andy: Yes, the typical general letter, thank you for your concerns. It wasn't a personalized letter, other than my name and address like normal form letters are. Uh, so, I knew there was something to do with that. Then later in 1982 there was something else that went on. I was-

Zim: This was after this event?

Andy: Yes, it was after this event.

Zim: So then was it 1992 then? You said this event happened in the late 1980s.

Andy: The late 1980s, I can't remember when it happened.

Zim: Okay.

Andy: It was when President Reagan started his term.

Zim: So then the next episode was after this?

Andy: It was after this. It was in '82. So this was evidently when 1980 when Reagan started and this one was, I know this one was in 1982. So this was before that. And then I got a message from an ET about there being a crop circle out near Limerick, Pennsylvania, and a friend and I took a ride out there to see if there was one, and there was. It was the shape of a unicorn. And what happened is that I went back and talked to a

260

friend that does aerial photography and, lo and behold, she, this person, was doing something for a client out in that area the next day. So she went out the next day and she took a picture of it. The news media was trying to discount it as pranksters and everything, but I had a message from an ET that this is for real and the ET told me that this really happened. At this point a lot of people didn't believe me, they thought it was a prank, so I contacted Linda Howe, she was still in the Philadelphia area at the time. And she presented it to a bunch of people to do a scientific research on this to prove or disprove it, because I asked her, I said, "Prove me wrong." And so this study lasted for a year. After a year it came back that that was for real and it had all the scientific evidence of a crop circle like the one in Stonehenge. It was one of the most legitimate. It was an event crop circle here in the United States and on the North American continent.

Zim: So, they did scientific tests to find that somehow the crops had been somehow altered by either heat or chemicals, or something like that?

Andy: Yeah, their cells had been changed, just like the one in Stonehenge in England. Their scientific proof was proof that it was for real. Of course, when I said to them that an ET told me, you know what their reaction was, "Sure, right." But I knew that it was for real and now it's further confirmed that what I had been told was not a dream. It was true. It was something that was really happening. I was really getting contacted by ETs.

And so I just decided, when in the beginning I couldn't give pictures out because it was a hoax, a bunch of pranksters.

Zim: Pictures of the crop circles?

Andy: Yeah, they didn't believe it. A year later they looked at it differently, it was looked at differently, and people were offering money for the pictures. And I just decided it was not my photograph, it was an aerial photographer's photograph, they should get the money. So, it's now published in one of Linda Howe's books of crop circles. I think it's volume number one. I forget the exact name of her book, but it's now published in that book, and it's the Limerick crop circle.

Zim: So you were the one to discover this one?

Andy: Yes. I think the government wanted people to believe it was a hoax. It was a real thing. Unfortunately I spilled those beans.

Zim: Have there been any repercussions from you spilling the beans?

Andy: Yes, there has been, but I didn't really feel them the most until after 9/11 happened. Why? I guess because they were watching people more closely or whatever. I've had trouble getting work. I've lived on all my own resources, but in the early 2000s I had to go look for work. The stock market went down and my investments went down and it was time for me to get back to work. My own resources were running very low.

And I still have these contacts today, and I just want to say they are for real. It's not a dream. Sometimes I wish it were a dream, but on the other hand, I have learned a lot from it. What I have learned, I don't know. I mean, I can't sum it up, but I've learned that evidently I've had many experiences, many learning experiences.

So I moved up to New Jersey. I moved up to Franklin, New Jersey first, in a mobile home park. I did have an ET contact experience. They didn't disseminate any information to me. Specifically they are trying to keep track of me. I don't know.

Zim: About what year was this?

Andy: This was the year 2010. And then the next year I moved to Branchville, New Jersey. I just sold my mobile home and I was just renting an apartment, and I've had some contact there, as well.

Zim: A similar nature--

Andy: A similar nature, yes.

Zim: Any messages with those?

Andy: Evidently, they are keeping track of me for some reason. And they are moving me around for some reason. No, it's not the government that's moving me around, it's them, the ETs that are moving me around. They have a reason behind it. And at this point it's for security reasons. I don't know, and I don't really want to know at this point. But I've continued to channel beings and channel messages. I've written several channel messages in the Star Beacon Newsletter out of Colorado. And in Delaware I've been on WILM radio with John Watson several times, talking about UFOs. It's a call-in talk show. And also once or twice on a cable TV show, my friend's cable TV show talking about UFOs and ETs and crop circles. And I also talked to a paranormal group in Pennsylvania about crop circles, as well. So I have been around, I've talked about these things. I've been at several conferences.

All I can say is I know these things effect people's lifestyles. I didn't expect it to start hitting my career and me having trouble getting a job.

Zim: Can you elaborate on how it's keeping you from getting a job?

Andy: Evidently, I am on a Homeland Security list, or somehow on there. And when people do background checks I don't get hired. It's not because of my lack of skills or lack of experience or lack of education, I've been told that. So it's just that they get scared when they see that I've been on the list or have done these things.

Zim: And you have no criminal background?

Andy: I have no criminal background. No, none whatsoever. Unless contact with ETs and seeing UFOs is a crime. At this point I don't know why, or if it is, but I have no control over it. And yes, they are still in contact with me and I'm still getting messages. At this point I have not published anymore.

Zim: What do employers tell you then, why you aren't getting the job?

Andy: The Homeland Security issue. It comes up that I have a questionable background.

Zim: Has anyone told you anything specific?

263

Andy: Two or three it doesn't scare away. They have an idea what it might be that I'm getting and it doesn't scare them away.

Zim: So you definitely see a direct correlation between your connection and your work in the UFO field, to be considered some sort of threat by Homeland Security?

Andy: Yes, and this is very, very unusual. I don't know of anybody else who is going through this. However, recently in the past two months, I have talked to a friend who knows several people who have had their careers affected by it. So do I feel relieved I'm not the only one? No!

Zim: It doesn't help you.

Andy: No, I don't feel relieved at all. I never felt like I was the only one, but I didn't know why. Because I don't have a criminal record, I've done nothing wrong. And this has happened throughout my life, it's not something I can control. Yes, I have an ET connection. Am I happy I have it? Well, yes. I'm not ashamed of that at all. I think it's a great thing to have contact with beings from other star systems and everything. It's like a neighbor, only it's in another star system, another planet, another star. I am not uncomfortable about that. What I am uncomfortable about is how it's affected my career and my job searches. And I feel like I've done nothing wrong.

By the way, I would like to point out that there are 90% of the people in this country, and the world, who have an ET connection. Only half of them have reawakened to the fact. The other half of you still have to reawaken. Just because you deny it and don't reawaken, doesn't mean that it's not a part of you. You still have that connection, it's still there. It's just like a bad habit, you can deny it every day that you don't smoke, and if you smoke you can still deny that habit. But if you still do it, you still do it. It stays with you.

Zim: Can you clarify the ET connection, this 90% of the population, have they had actual contact, or seen things, or received messages?

Andy: Yes, I do, because there is 10% of the population for some reason who are not in contact with ETs, and they are the ones who are mostly in control. That's why we have all this pollution, that's why the planet is going the wrong way, that's why there's all these economic issues.

Zim: So then, according to this idea, this 90%, would you consider them a little more enlightened, more open, more favorable for the planet?

Andy: I would say they are, but they don't know why, and they also don't know their connection, they have to be reawakened.

Zim: So then the 10% you're saying are the ones in power, and they haven't had the benefit of this ET connection, so they aren't working for the benefit of the people?

Andy: They have another type of connection.

Zim: And what would that be?

Andy: Well, there are positive ETs and there are negative ETs. The 90% are the positive ETs and the 10% are taking their orders from the negative ETs.

Zim: So they still have the ET connection, but it's the negative.

Andy: Correct. And they're like renegades and they're still trying to hold on.

Zim: Okay. So where do you see all this leading? Or do you see some sort of conclusion or this all coming to a head at some point?

Andy: I think it will come to a head by 2013. Everything will be out and it will be known. Whether the government and those in control disclose the existence of UFOs and ETs that is to be seen, but the people themselves will find out, either on a one to one basis or in several groups or in several areas. And it will not be by faked and staged things, it will be by the real thing.

Zim: Can you elaborate on the faked UFO sightings?

Andy: Yes, mostly if you could see the craft, and can really see all the technical details and everything, it's probably a government black project that looks like a UFO. And I don't think the government likes you seeing top secret projects, either. And they don't know what you've seen, but if you've seen that it's one of theirs. Theirs are the ones that usually crash and something goes wrong with.

And I'm a little bit concerned with them sending these drones out. I don't know what they plan to gain from those.

Zim: You want to elaborate on that? Sending out drones in this country?

Andy: It's this country. It's to control the rest of us 90%. I don't know why. I guess the renegades, the 10% are scared they're going to lose power and lose control.

Zim: So, what can the average person do?

Andy: Try to remember your dreams, because most of the information comes to you in a dream state, and it is not a dream. Think back, think back to your own experiences, think back to strange things, even strange lights, anything that you could think, oh maybe that was a dream, well maybe not. Just think back and try to recall your dreams and your memories, and the things that have happened to you in your waking moments and sleeping moments. And you, too, may have an ET connection and not realize it. And you need to learn about it so you can correct all these things in your life. There may be something that's not going right, or whatever, and there might be a reason for that.

Zim: Anything else you want to cover? Anything about the government or disclosure?

Andy: I don't think they want it disclosed, but unfortunately the ETs are forcing it be disclosed. And again, I have nothing to do with that. And I know ETs do not like nuclear weapons and nuclear missiles, and they

266

neutralize them or destroy them. I have nothing to do with that. That is their agenda, it is not my agenda. Just because I'm in contact with them it doesn't mean I'm involved with that at all. It doesn't mean that anybody involved with an ET connection is involved with this.

Zim: When was the last time you believe you had contact that you can recall? Was it anything recent?

Andy: Back in November of 2011.

Zim: What occurred at that point?

Andy: I had a channeled message, it was an urgent type of message. Basically, all I can tell you is that I got a directive that on the clock it has now struck midnight. It was kind of like a warning.

Zim: So we are coming to a critical time?

Andy: Yes we are. That's what that was signifying.

Zim: So, do you believe that from the very beginning, since you were a kid, you were receiving messages? Or is that something that didn't happen until later on?

Andy: I could have been subconsciously receiving messages and not realized it. And now that I'm used to the experience, and grown in the experience, I know what it is and I'm able to channel some messages and get some messages.

Zim: Anyone else in your family have any kind of remembrances or contact?

Andy: No, not that I recall.

Zim: Other than your career, which is obviously distressing to you at this point, what's your overall feeling that you've had, now that this has been happening for so many decades?

Andy: Well, I know this is for real and it's not a dream, because it's happening to me for real. It's not my imagination. It happens to me in my waking moments and my sleeping moments.

Zim: And so, have you lived in fear of it happening again? Anticipation? How would you characterize it?

Andy: I don't live in fear, not fear of them. And I'm not really now afraid of the government and the Homeland Security people anymore, because I know the real situation.

Zim: If you had the power to go back to the beginning would you choose to not have any of this happen, or would you let it all happen again?

Andy: The things that I have learned have really benefitted me, also, not just have hurt me. It has benefitted me as a person, growing in many ways, spiritual and otherwise. It has helped my growth and helped my progress.

Zim: So overall, you're glad this has happened? Even with all the unpleasantness?

Andy: Yes, I don't regret it one bit.

Zim: Okay, anything else you want to cover?

Andy: Yes, I just want to tell everybody if you have an ET connection to do something about it, to find out what it is. That may solve some of the problems in your life. It may disrupt your lifestyle, but at least you'll know why, and you'll be able to continue living your life normally.

Zim: Where would people go to do something like this, or should you do this on your own, or seek out other people who have had these experiences?

Andy: Seek out other people who have had these experiences that can help them along. You know, from my very first experience, if I had not sought the help of people, older people who had had experiences, if I had not had their help and counseling, I would not have been able to deal with it as well as I have today. So yes, you do need to go to somebody that has had experiences so they can help you deal with it.

Zim: And there are groups around the area that can help you with that?

Andy: Yes.

Zim: All right, thank you.

[Author's Note: The only Limerick crop circle report I could find was from 1992. The following is from the ICCRAA (Independent Crop Circle Researchers Association):
Limerick Township, Montgomery County (May 26, 1992)
    Three circles 5' in diameter arranged in a triangle amidst at least 12 "matted down" or "randomly-downed" areas; one area "t-shaped". Discovered by a police officer the day after a heavy rainfall and strong winds that lasted until the early evening, he reported finding no tracks leading into the circles or downed areas, and reported no broken stalks. Geiger counter readings were normal.
    Dr. Bruce Rideout from Ursinus College noted node splitting and cracking as well as a 'reorientation' of the growth nodes. A second formation near Linfield was also reported.
    W.C. Levengood reported finding significant node bending and lateral node splitting as well as increased cell wall pit diameters of plant cells from the circle formations. He also reported finding reduced embryo development from formation samples as compared to control plants.
    The Miami Herald reports on May 29, 1992 that a dozen circles were found and that the farmer believed it was caused by excess fertilizer and wind that combined to produce the flattening.
    Two additional reports of RDF-type flattening from nearby Linfield and Royersford, PA (both in Montgomery County) which may have been related to this event.
    Eyewitness report only.
    Crop type: Wheat]

Phil Coseski

On Monday, September 10, 2012, Sarah, Felix, and I arranged to meet Phil Coseski at the Cup & Saucer Diner in Pine Bush. I knew this wasn't going to be a typical interview because of the email I had received from Phil describing his experiences. They were unique, to say the least, but I contacted Felix anyway to see if was interested in filming an interview.

Here's Phil's initial email of August 11, and my response:

My name is Phil Coseski age 52, I recently heard from a friend about your intentions to interview those who have had UFO encounters/sightings in the Hudson Valley of New York.

I'm one such person that has had such UFO sightings/encounters starting from 2007 to 2012 near Pine Bush, NY. I have some very interesting videos I shot of various UFO craft over the Walden area. I would like to relate to you what I've seen and filmed in the area. I also want to say up front that I believe I was contacted by one of the pilots of these triangular craft I filmed. I know this may sound a bit suspect, but it's true, please let me briefly explain it. I was contacted by a female pilot who disclosed the identity behind who are flying these triangular craft over the Orange County, NY area. I was told that they are ETs from the constellation of Orion, they are human looking like us though a bit taller. Anyway, I can understand if you may suspect this and doubt it. But I do have evidence in the form of multiple sightings/videos filmed of the same craft performing various plasma sightings for me. Please have a look at one such video below. If you would like to interview me and would like to use some of my video in your new film? I consent to it and would like to share what I know and have as tangible evidence of my sightings.

My response:

Well, I have to admit that's quite a story, but I spoke to the production team and they would be interested in interviewing you at the Pine Bush location where you have these sightings. They have to get back to me with some possible filming dates and I will let you know.

Clearly, this was a tough story to swallow, and one that could easily be filed away in a Tin Foil Hat folder, but if this man was willing to go on camera to tell his story, I was willing to listen.

We more or less took over a corner section of the diner with all of the cameras and equipment, and when Phil arrived we sat in one of the booths for the interview. I certainly had a lot of questions, but I thought the best thing to do was to go chronologically and see what unfolded. I have to say I was a bit apprehensive at the start, but found that Phil was open, pleasant, and well aware that I was skeptical, so I was able to concentrate on the business at hand.

His first experience was in 1993. He had just read Ellen Crystall's book, *Silent Invasion*, in which she claimed to have numerous encounters in Pine Bush, and he wanted to go to those exact spots mentioned in the book—the Jewish cemetery, Hill Ave., Searsville Road, etc. Phil didn't live in the area, but he hoped the long trip would at least produce a glimpse of something unusual. He caught more than a glimpse. A horseshoe-shaped craft suddenly rose up above a farmhouse. It had pulsating lights and was visible for at least ten minutes.

The Jewish Cemetery which has been the focus of UFO sightings over the years.

Convinced that the Pine Bush UFOs were real, he knew he would return one day. That day didn't come again until 2007, however, when "an intense interest" brought him back to the same farm fields where so many people had sightings over the decades. Once again, he was not disappointed. Orange, pulsating lights hovered low just above the tree line. Phil also saw a triangle about 200-feet long and decidedly to try to mentally communicate with it. The craft did seem to respond to his thoughts, moved toward him and stopped. Was it just a coincidence?

A few days later, Phil was meditating when he heard a female voice communicating telepathically. It was a female ET named Abena, and she was not only one of the pilots of the triangle ships, she was a commander in the alien base that was underground in Orange County.

Of course I had to ask if he knew what she looked like and why aliens had any interest in Orange County. Phil didn't hesitate to say that Abena was blond and attractive, with almost cat-like eyes, and her race—the Oxicarians—were here to protect mankind from the evil reptilian aliens. They were also mining rare minerals to make alloys for their spacecraft. In appearance, they looked very much like humans, except they averaged 6.5-7 feet in height.

And how did Phil know this? He claims that while walking down a street in Pine Bush one day he saw her. She was dressed in regular human clothing, and while she didn't speak to him verbally, she communicated telepathically.

Over the next few years he received many more telepathic messages and had many more sightings. He says he learned things, such as the massive underground base was actually as old as the pyramids. In fact, it was the Oxicarians who built the Sphinx and the pyramids. Our government knows of their existence, but it is a "strange relationship" between us and the aliens, but that certain Black Ops groups do deal with them. They traveled in faster-than-light ships that used plasma core drives, and in 2008, Abena demonstrated this incredible speed by zigzagging across the sky so quickly it "gave the illusion that there were two ships." They also had the ability to "cloak" their ships, turning the "scary-looking batwing" craft into something that looked like a conventional plane or helicopter.

At this point, I had to bring up what he had written in his first email—that he basically wouldn't blame me if I doubted him. I essentially said

272

that this was hard for anyone to believe, and what could he say to try to convince people that there was any shred of truth to his story?

He said the video evidence he had would show that something inexplicable was indeed still occurring over—and under—the fields of Pine Bush. For example, he said that while filming a craft he started talking to it and the lights intensified in response. And he had many other examples, which he had put on a DVD for me. I deferred to Felix's video expertise, and let him take the DVD to review first.

Phil Cosecki at the Cup & Saucer Diner in Pine Bush.

I then had to ask why he thought aliens would be communicating with him—was he special, or did they simply respond to someone earnestly trying to make contact with them? Phil said it was both, because he had sought them out, but also because they had "scanned" his blood and found out that a paternal ancestor in Poland or Lithuania had mated with an Oxicarian, so he carried their DNA.

So why didn't they reveal themselves to all the people? "Because of mankind's destructive tendencies."

What should the average person do to try to see a UFO? "It's not a right, it's a privilege," to glimpse one of their craft, Phil replied. He also said that people should "meditate and drop religious formats."

And how have these experiences changed him? They have "intensified" him "spiritually" and he has become much more "calm and tranquil" from the meditations and communications.

I was pretty much out of questions by this point, but Sarah asked an excellent question. Were these aliens aware of this documentary, and if so, what did they think of what we were doing? Phil replied that they were monitoring us, and most likely approved.

To conclude, I asked if he could request that Abena give us a sign. He said he had already asked, but as she had been recalled to her home world in March, she wasn't around as much anymore.

And so ended the interview. I have to admit that as bizarre as it all sounded, I found Phil to be quite likable. I wished there was some shred of evidence to back up some of the sightings he claimed to have, but I didn't hold out much hope.

Then the next day I got an email from Felix. He had watched the DVD and said there was some interesting footage on it that I had to see. Had Phil actually filmed genuine spacecraft? I was anxious to see it, but rather than email me the footage, Felix asked that I come up to the studio the following week to view it, so he could film my reaction.

Felix and I sat in front of the TV while Sarah filmed us. When the first of Phil's videos came on the screen, it only took a moment to see—and hear—that it was a conventional aircraft, most likely a commercial jet headed for Stewart Airport, or one of the many other airports in the area. The next video was more of the same. Then came the video of another jet that clearly looked and sounded like a jet, but according to Phil's commentary on the tape, was Abena's ship *disguised* as a regular airplane.

How do you fight that argument? If you truly believe that, you can film planes all night and claim every one of them is an alien spacecraft with the technology to mimic a human airplane in its appearance and sound. It was extremely frustrating to watch this DVD, and know that if you tried to argue that there was absolutely no evidence that these were

274

alien spacecraft, the response would be that it was because the aliens were so good at disguising their ships.

Exasperated, I finally said, "It *looks* like an airplane, it *sounds* like an airplane—"

"So it must be a duck," Felix interjected, as we both started laughing.

Has Phil Cosecki witnessed spacecraft over Pine Bush and seen the alien pilot Abena? Does he have some sort of telepathic connection with extraterrestrials?

If he has, we haven't seen any proof of his claims.

Are such things even possible? Well, Phil certainly wasn't the first person to tell me he could communicate telepathically with aliens, or at least seem to have had their thoughts read by extraterrestrial beings.

As I stated in the first chapter, I won't tell you what to believe. In this case, I can only say that anything is possible, but I remain skeptical.

Star Nation Sacred Circle

There is another support group in the Hudson Valley that welcomes UFO witnesses and abductees. The Star Nation Sacred Circle approaches the subject of UFOs—and all other subjects—with a spiritual approach. For many, this adds another layer of strangeness to an already strange subject, and therefore puts it out on the fringe.

The following is what appears on their website, followed by interviews with two of the founders.

STAR NATION
SACRED CIRCLE
with Barbara Threecrow, Melissa Reed & Jim Marzano
CONTACTEES & EXPERIENCERS OF
EXTRATERRESTRIALS*UFOs*THE PARANORMAL
WE KNOW LONGER NEED DEFEND OR PROVE
WHAT WE KNOW TO BE

~All that science concludes as baffling and inexplicable~
-Out of Body-Astral Projection-Lucid Dreaming-Parallel Realms-NDE-

275

ESP-Clairvoyance-Spirit Visitation/Communication-Light Beings-Angels-
Past Lives-Star Children-
First Friday of Every Month at AIR Studio Gallery, 71 O'Neil St,
Kingston, NY Contact: 845-331-2662
$5 donation, bring a snack to share
Barbara Threecrow: www.BarbaraThreecrow.com
Melissa Reed: www.MReedArtworks.com
Jim Marzano: www.AirStudioGallery.com

We are determined to clarify, offer support and to shed light upon the urgent questions we each have and together discover the answers to such questions as: Why me? What does it all mean? What do we do now? We each have some significant purpose, as it relates to any paranormal phenomenon such as extraterrestrial contact, dreams, visions, intuitiveness & a search for the truth. We consider ourselves to be Light Workers, those that focus on the Light & Positive, & dismiss the fear & anxiety that keeps humanity in a primordial state of fight or flight. There is something growing in each of us that destiny is meant to fulfill regarding these times of transition into the new paradigm. Something that together we could make a difference & help change the world. Join us each First Friday of the month to share knowledge, experiences, stories, art & anything of interest. We are a group of Hudson Valley Contactees and Experiencers of the paranormal who believe it is time to begin an open, honest dialogue.

Jim Marzano

Jim Marzano has had "a number of sightings" in the Hudson Valley since he moved to Kingston in 1982, but far more intense encounters began when he was just a child.

"I had abduction experiences starting when I was about five years old," he began as we interviewed him in his art studio. "And they went on until I was about 25. Through my Carlos Castaneda dream warrior training I finally beat them back and told them to leave me alone and they stopped coming."

Jim was born in the Bronx, but first remembers "experiencing abduction syndrome scenarios" when his family moved to Carlstadt, New Jersey. When he was 10, they moved again to Monroe, New York, and the "experiences continued there." His last abduction occurred in nearby Sugar Loaf.

I asked what one of these typical "abduction scenarios" entailed, and he replied, "I was terrified as a little kid of dark figures coming into my room. And the classic sleep paralysis of not being able to move. And actually being floated out the back window of the house in Jersey. I never went along willingly, I was always fighting to break loose."

Jim also described swirling lights and sounds, "as if I was being sucked into a vortex." The scariest part "was not having control of my body."

I asked if he recalled where he was taken.

"No, it was all very vague. I just felt I was in a huge, dark room with a bunch of dark figures."

Did he ever have any physical repercussions as a result?

"In my last battle that sent these guys on their way, I woke up in the morning with what looked like a bite mark on my chest. It was a ring of whiteheads, like whitehead pimples on my chest. And that was my last encounter. And that was the first and only physical sign that something had happened."

What had been the emotional impact?

"I don't think it ever really affected me emotionally—and mostly because I had been dealing with it since I was five. When I was five I complained to my parents about these figures coming in the room and they took me to a doctor. The doctor told them I was having nightmares and they shouldn't feed me after five o'clock. So I learned how to deal with it on my own from the get go. So I didn't really have a lot of choices."

I asked if his parents ever came around to believing him.

"No, no, but after 50 years I just recently found out that my brother had similar experiences. We recently spent some time alone together and he told me about it, and I was like, 'Really!? Wow, we have to talk about this.' Similar experiences—dark figures coming into the room in New Jersey. I was surprised to hear it."

As for the non-abduction sightings, Jim "has been seeing strange lights in the sky" most of his life. "I never thought a whole lot about them, thinking they were planes or satellites, for the most part. But in 1994, I did the ET Ambassador training with Steven Greer, in a week-long session in Pine Bush. After that, I started seeing much stranger, obvious sightings, including the one we had on graduation night.

"We had 20 of us in a cow pasture in Pine Bush and watched a huge triangle moving across the sky and disappear over the western horizon. Then there were two fighter jets that took off after it. Then after the fighter jets disappeared, then like a Black Ops helicopter came over the field with a big spotlight and found us in the middle of the field. So it's like they knew where we were and what we were up to. So that was a really strange experience."

(Later in the interview, Jim felt that this had been "a show" put on by the government, and that triangle-shaped craft are actually built and flown by us, not aliens.)

Jim Marzano

As for the support group he helped form, Star Nation Sacred Circle, it all began in 2010 with "movie night" in the studio. They showed "What on Earth," a film about crop circles, and realized there was a need to "have a safe, nonjudgmental place where people could go to speak about metaphysical and paranormal experiences in general—not just UFO, ET stuff. But I think they are all related, and that's the basic thrust of the group, acknowledging the extraterrestrial presence on the Earth."

The group is rather diverse, not just from the Kingston area. People from around the state, and even around the country, have come to tell their stories. Another thing that has been surprising is just how many sightings there have been in Manhattan.

"I think right from Manhattan to Albany the whole region is pretty active."

Jim has no theory as to why this area is so active, but in general, he feels that ETs are so interested in us because of the "latent DNA"—the extraterrestrial DNA that is in humans.

"We are the children of God—God being the extraterrestrials, and I think that extraterrestrials consider us part of their progeny."

"So do you think they're just observing us? Studying us? Testing us?" I asked.

"I think that Earth is a kindergarten of souls," Jim replied. "That they are cultivating our souls for future reincarnation into extraterrestrial bodies. I believe that's the goal, that they are maturing our souls, so that when we reach a state of enlightenment we will be peaceful enough for an extraterrestrial form. As soon as we got rid of all the monsters from the id."

"That's going to take a while," I interjected with a smile.

"Yes, it's going to take a while," Jim agreed, laughing.

As for advice for people who have had sightings or contact, Jim recommends that they "talk about it, and find people who have had similar experiences. It never ceases to amaze me how many people come to our meetings and have had sightings or experiences and they stuff it—they don't talk about it, they haven't talked about it for 10 or 20 years. And they never talked to anyone about it because they are embarrassed, and they don't want to be ridiculed and made fun of. At the same time, they can't deny their experience."

Jim can sympathize with their plight, as "Even my own wife thinks I'm nuts!"

As for the future, Jim would "like to help lay the groundwork for first contact." And he believes that there are "dark, selfish, extraterrestrials who are exploiting for whatever reasons, and we have the light and positive extraterrestrials who are much more compassionate, altruistic"— just as on Earth we are deciding whether mankind will go to the light or the dark.

And despite the early years of terror with his abduction experiences, Jim has now come to believe that the extraterrestrials actually saved his life. He likened it to bringing a sick puppy to the vet—the puppy is terrified, but you are making him well. Jim says he "was very sickly" as a child, to the point of death "on a number of occasions," and he "would like to think" that the extraterrestrials "helped keep" him alive. It is an interesting perspective on the abduction scenario—that ETs are actually helping those they are taking!

We then discussed the function and power of dreaming, precognition, what the future may hold, and the many positive experiences that have come from their Star Nation Sacred Circle. While Jim and this group takes a more metaphysical approach to the UFO experience than the Pine Bush group, their goal is ultimately the same—give people a place to speak up and be accepted.

Barbara Threecrow

Barbara Threecrow is an artist and the author of *Mending the Hoop* and *Four Sacred Shields Twelve Sacred Paths*. According to her website, "She has created the Star/Indigo Children workshops to help guide teachers and parents. Since 1989 she has gathered women from all walks of life to teach the Grandmothers' Ways, the Return of the Feminine… Barbara's heritage is Irish, [and German] and her Native American heritage is Nanticoke/Delaware. She was a long-time student of the late Lakota medicine man Wallace Black Elk."

Barbara joined us at Jim's studio in Kingston to be interviewed.

Barbara Threecrow

"My first memory of an experience was when I was five," she began. "I grew up here in the Hudson Valley, and I had two visitors. Of course, during that time—being just five years old—they appeared to me like they were alligators. It was quite a frightening experience. And they had me by the thumbs and they were pulling me off the bed. And that woke me up, of course, and I started screaming. And they disappeared and my family came running in and told me I was having a nightmare. And I knew it was

281

not a bad dream. I felt the energy, the remaining energy on my thumbs. And it was many years after that, that this is how I went to sleep." [She demonstrates that she tucked in her thumbs and kept them covered by her fingers.]

"I found out many years later that they were not alligators [she laughs] but that they were reptilian. I had no idea there were all these different entities—12 to 13 groups. Grays, blues, malevolent, benevolent, reptilians, and so on."

"What did you think their intent was?' I asked.

"At that time, at five years old? You know from very early on, before I was even five, I had communication with beings. Years later I was told by my father that I was born with a caul. In ancient beliefs it means that child is a visionary. So my psychic abilities were very highly developed, so I had a lot of communication with other beings, a lot of insight and abilities to understand people's feelings and thoughts. Clairsentient, clairaudient, and the various sensory perceptions were very heightened.

"So I had a relationship with other beings, and they were not these particular beings, these reptilian beings. And the relationship then, and still remains to be, those with the light. I call them the channels of light or the beings of light. So that was my beginning experience, so these were other entities that I didn't really know anything about till much later when I stated to explore the UFO and ET phenomena.

"I had profound experiences in my childhood, throughout my life, but I've also had UFO experiences—sightings, lost time, spheres, beings coming in my house and so on. So I've had a lot of phenomena like that."

I asked if they happened quite often, and Barbara responded that they did, but to her they were just normal experiences. However, she never really spoke about these things with anyone. When she did share her "prophetic dreams" with her mother, her mother told her "to stop, because she couldn't handle it. So I was left to my own devices to try to figure out what was happening."

The only family member to be supportive was her grandmother, but she died when Barbara was ten. Now, approaching the age of 70, Barbara can look back on her life and appreciates that all of her experiences were an opportunity to learn and grow, even if she didn't understand what was happening at the time.

One of the things she didn't understand at the time, was when she was young and one of these beings told her that she was "a star child." I asked her to explain what that was, and Barbara said that she always "had a deep longing to go home." She would spend a lot of time outside looking up, feeling as though she "didn't belong here and wanting to go home." She even felt as though she must have been adopted "and her real family would come and pick" her up. "I've spoken to a lot of people who are star children and they all have similar experiences. I know now that it is all a part of a star child's journey."

I asked if she thought that star children were the result of alien DNA or something more spiritual, and Barbara said there are many different aspects to it. She then alluded to the fact that many ancient and indigenous people believe their ancestors came from the sky. She also spoke about some Native American beliefs, as well as the references in the Bible that she interprets as aliens breeding with human women, thereby imparting their reptilian DNA.

As for the future, she feels that many more people are becoming aware of our ET connections, but that there is a lot of intentional misinformation and "the fear factor" that is engendered "by the Illuminati" in order to try to maintain control. The best thing the average person can do to combat this "is gain knowledge. Knowledge is power. But find your own truth. That is very important."

She also emphasized the importance of the Star Nation Sacred Circle group, and hoped that more people would start attending. It's "all about having people feel safe to share their experiences and to hear another viewpoint."

Barbara also wanted to stress the fact that just because you haven't seen a ship or ET, it doesn't mean you haven't been visited, as that "can come in many ways, such as dreams." The fact that you are drawn to this subject or this group may indicate you have had some sort of visitation.

14
Stone Chambers

The stone chambers of Putnam County may have absolutely nothing to do with the UFO sightings in the area. Then again, they may have some strange connection. Whatever the case, these chambers do have something in common with the Hudson Valley UFO phenomenon—they are largely ignored or misinterpreted by scholars, officials, and the general public.

This lack of respect for these structures is due in part to three major issues: 1) Lack of formal archaeological surveys and studies, 2) Outlandish claims as to the nature and origin of the chambers, prompting one academic to state it would be "professional suicide" to even attempt to study them, and 3) Greedy landowners and developers who would prefer to bulldoze something rather than take the time to understand it.

This is neither the place nor the time to explore the lengthy arguments on both sides of the chamber debate. In brief, many historians and scientists dismiss them (without any study) as simply colonial root cellars. Suffice to say, there are many reasons why these suppositions are wrong—the sheer number of chambers (over 100) in Putnam County far exceeds the needs of the number of colonial farms, they are built in a manner that would cause vegetables to rot, some are built on rock ledges in areas with no farmland, and there are documents going back as far as the 1600s that speak to stone structures in New England that predate the arrival of European colonists.

On another side of the debate, there are those who claim the chambers were built by aliens, are portals to other dimensions, or vortexes in the space-time continuum. Obviously, such people have even less evidence to back their theories.

Let's just take a deep breath, step back, and examine what we do know.

- Columbus was not the first European in North America. Norse explorers visited at least 500 years earlier. If they could do it, then it is possible other cultures visited, perhaps even much earlier.
- Hundreds of stone structures and inscriptions can be found throughout New England which cannot be attributed to the Native Americans since the time of Columbus.
- Many of the stone structures and inscriptions resemble European structures and writing.
- Both the standing stones at America's Stonehenge in New Hampshire and some of the chambers of Putnam County have celestial alignments, indicating they may have had ceremonial purposes.

So, without resorting to dismissing every stone chamber as a vegetable bin, or ascribing it to extraterrestrial masons, we can at least state that it is possible they are ancient, as well as constructed by travelers from outside of North America.

Bill Pollard, a Ferrari mechanic and restorer by trade, has been examining the stone chambers in Putnam County for many decades. He first became interested as a child when his Irish grandfather told him about the Irish stone structures in Putnam. His grandfather assumed they were made by the Irish because they looked just like ancient structures in Ireland. It was a very astute and innocent observation—one which has somehow alluded many "experts."

As Bill grew up and reached adulthood, his fascination for the chambers increased, so much so that he actually moved to Farmers Mills Road in Kent because of all the chambers nearby. He carefully studied their construction and tool marks, and came to believe they were many thousands of years old, and therefore he was horrified by the dozens that were being bulldozed during construction projects. He wanted to try to preserve these chambers, but repeatedly hit a wall of ignorance.

Then the UFO flap of the 1980s hit Putnam County. Bill had has own sightings (see the Triangles chapter), and as a result, was contacted by none other than Dr. J. Allen Hynek. Dr. Hynek wondered why there were so many sightings in Bill's locality, and asked if there was anything unusual about the area. While Bill didn't think the chambers were in any way related to the UFOs, he nonetheless mentioned them to Dr. Hynek.

Dr. Hynek was so fascinated by the idea of these mysterious chambers, he came to Bill's house to learn more, and to see them for himself. Thus began the association of the stone chambers and extraterrestrials, although Bill still does not believe there is any connection.

Again, without going down the road of cosmic vortexes and portals, could there be some other reason that UFOs seem to have appeared frequently in areas where there are stone chambers? Perhaps, but I will have to launch into some pure speculation.

According to the publication *Magnometric Survey of the Mahopac Magnetic Mine, Putnam County, N.Y.* by the U.S. Department of the Interior in September of 1948, in 1880 there were 26 operating iron mines in Putnam and Orange County. The iron ore from the Mahopac mine was high grade magnetite, which of course, has magnetic properties. Unfortunately, this mine had to close, as a fault had displaced the vein of iron ore, and they were unable to find where the vein continued.

This is not just a history and geology lesson, and here's my point. What if:

A) Some ancient culture did come to North America and found that there were stones in the Putnam County area that had "magic," i.e., magnetic, properties. Would they consider the land special enough to build temples or ceremonial sites? Also, it is known that areas that have faults can produce perfectly natural, but eerie-looking lights, which could have further added to the mystical appearance of the land.

B) Some types of UFOs could use electromagnetic fields for propulsion. Perhaps the mineralogy and fault lines in Putnam provide electromagnetic fields these craft can utilize, so they just happen to frequent the same spots where these stone chambers were built.

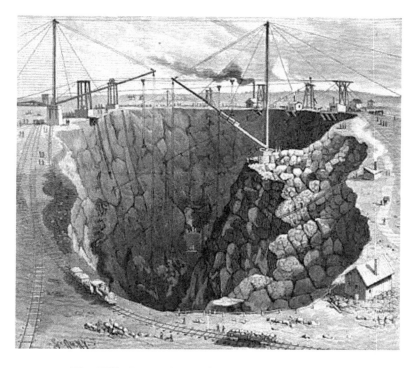

The Tilly Foster iron mine near Brewster, NY,
from an 1889 issue of *Scientific American*.

Again, I am not making any claims that this is anything but speculation on my part, and I'm certainly not stating that this solves the UFO/Stone Chamber mystery, if indeed, there is any mystery at all. But now that I have dispensed the suitable disclaimers and tried to at least attempt a rational hypothesis, let me relate my personal experiences with the stone chambers.

When I was about 18, there was an episode of *In Search Of* which examined Mystery Hill in New Hampshire, now called America's Stonehenge. The site comprises about 30 acres, with a central complex of stone buildings and walls, surrounded by standing stones that point to celestial events, such as sunrise at the winter solstice. Carbon dating indicated that the site may be at least 4,000 years old.

Part of the central complex at America's Stonehenge in New Hampshire.

I was astonished. I spent countless hours learning about ancient cultures around the world that had megalithic sites, but no one ever told me there might be one in New England! I learned all about Columbus sailing the ocean blue, but nobody ever said that the Celts, Vikings, or other cultures beat him to it by hundreds, or even thousands, of years. Within a year I was standing at the central complex at Mystery Hill,

288

wondering what else my teachers and text books failed to tell me about the history of North America.

A standing stone at America's Stonehenge,
which points to the sunrise on the winter solstice.

I can't recall when I heard about the stone chambers of Putnam County, but at least a decade or two had passed since I had first heard about the New Hampshire site. I remember trying to get some information from libraries and historical societies on the chambers' age, construction techniques, and who could have possibly built them, and universally was told I didn't need to waste my time on these colonial root cellars.

About the same time, people coming to my lectures started telling me strange tales of things that happened in and around these chambers—glowing lights, hooded figures, a feeling of being disoriented. Taking these stories with a large grain of salt, I nonetheless became even more intrigued, and started visiting as many of the stone structures as I could find.

Some were in very good shape, some had collapsed, some had been converted to use by farmers by adding doors and concrete. But they all had the same type of construction—corbelled stone walls with massive stone slab roofs. When I started bringing along a compass, I also found that several had the same alignment, and later learned about some that had the sunlight of the winter solstice shine through the openings onto the back walls. I also noticed that while some were near houses and farms, others were in remote places, in areas not easy to access.

I personally never had anything strange happen on any of my expeditions—no hooded figures, glowing balls of light, or vortexes. However, I did get the impression—both intellectually and just a gut feel—that these were truly ancient sites. These were not simply potato bins for Joe Colonial (a name I'm borrowing from Bill Pollard!), they did resemble European structures, and the wealth of other sites throughout New England gave considerable weight to the argument that at the very least, these chambers should be preserved and studied, not obliterated to put up another convenience store.

So, when this project began, I knew I would have to at least devote a chapter to the stone chambers, and suggested to Sarah and Felix that they somehow weave them into the documentary. We had our first opportunity the day of the Lake Oscawana interviews, as there is a double chamber by the south end of the lake.

We found the site across from a school, but I was disappointed that most of the stone walls were clearly of modern construction. However, the double chamber was of a different type of construction—more in line with the other, single chambers—so either this was a newer site added to some old chambers, or the land owner had copied the old form of construction.

As we were leaving, as if on cue, a man pulled up in a pickup truck and shouted to us, "You know, that's not an ancient Druid site or anything." We went over to talk to him, and he explained it was the site of an old barn and silo, and he had similar remains on his farm just down the road. Apparently, some fringe groups claimed that the rounded base of the old silo was a Celtic or pagan "baptismal font," and while the man was good-natured, he clearly had no tolerance for such foolishness. It was another reminder that we were treading on a very polarizing topic—as if we didn't have to be careful enough with the UFOs!

It turned out that Scott Dilalla also had an interest in the chambers. He had heard about them, but had never seen one for himself, so we arranged an expedition. Scott, Sarah, Felix and I met at the Anthony Wayne Recreation Area in Harriman State Park one cloudy and humid morning, and I drove us all to a semi-secret parking area where we could hike back to the King's Chamber, so called as it was one of the largest chambers, and also had a standing stone in front of it.

My husband and I had first tried to find the King's Chamber (located in Fahnestock Park) a year earlier, but floods and sticker bushes thwarted our attempt. Then Christine Leonard (of the Lake Oscawana sighting) told me about this other parking location, although once we arrived we had no idea which way to go. By sheer dumb luck (or was it!?), we happened to stumble upon the site of a small chamber, then continued on and found the large and impressive King's Chamber.

The partially collapsed smaller chamber nearby the King's Chamber.

291

So on this expedition, I already knew both where to park and what direction to hike. It was fun to see Scott's reaction to the King's Chamber—that same excitement I had when I first saw it, when I couldn't resist running the last few hundred feet. We poked around, took some measurements, and actually got some readings on the EMF meter— although whether they were caused by minerals in the ground, or the approaching thunderstorm, I couldn't say.

Speaking of that thunderstorm—we had to use that stone chamber as shelter to ride out that storm, as none of us was crazy enough to hike back through the woods in lighting and heavy downpours. It was kind of fun sitting in the chamber during the storm, imagining how many people before us had done the same thing.

Felix saw the thunderstorm as a great opportunity to get some cool footage.

The standing stone at the entrance to the King's Chamber.

Scott and Sarah in the interior of the King's Chamber.

The rain abated long enough to get back to the car, but our plan of hiking to several other chambers was changed to the two by Meads Corners, as we could drive right up to them. Unfortunately, the rain soon became torrential and we decided to just head home—although I honestly don't know how I managed to drive in such relentless and blinding downpours. Of course, as soon as I pulled into my driveway, the sun came out!

So, what can we conclude about who built these stone chambers, and what their connection is to the numerous UFO sightings? Well, as I stated before, we just don't have any information to really conclude anything. However, we do have a couple of mysteries that need solving, which will require some serious, organized research.

In the meantime, if there is even the slightest chance that UFOs are somehow drawn to the areas where there are stone chambers, plan a little expedition of your own. There are websites that list locations of some of the chambers, but please don't go traipsing around people's backyards and private property.

Bring a compass, bring a tape measure, camera, and notebook, and look for any similarities or differences. Check for tool marks, inscriptions, and watch a solstice or equinox sunrise from a chamber entrance. Unleash your inner Indiana Jones, and perhaps you will help solve the riddle of the mysterious stone chambers.

In Europe, these are called dolmens—massive rocks propped up on smaller ones. Some are many thousands of years old and are thought to be ancient grave markers. This site is in North Salem, NY, and until recently, the "official" explanation was that a glacier just happened to drop this granite bolder on these limestone supports! The new sign at the site finally concedes "this may be a dolmen—a Celtic stone used to memorialize the dead."

15
Casebook

The cases in this chapter either involve sightings of irregular-shaped UFOs, multiple sightings of different shapes, or the witness couldn't determine the shape—in other words, it's a mixed bag.

Elizabeth Butler: Peekskill-Cold Spring, August 1969

At the age of 75, Elizabeth Butler says that she has no reason to make up stories. And, after 43 years, she was grateful to finally find someone who would listen to the truth—the truth about a very close encounter she had one hot, Friday night, driving north from Peekskill, NY to Cold Spring.

"I had just gotten married in July, and I was at my mother's house picking up some presents. I was alone, and it was a very warm night so I had the windows open. Off to the right side of the road, about four cars were pulled over. The people inside the cars all either had their heads leaning out of the windows or were looking through the windshield."

Elizabeth slowed down as she didn't know why all those cars were off the road. Then she saw what had stopped traffic.

"Right smack in front of my car was a large UFO with lights blinking and there was this humming. I can't recall if it was round or had points, but it was so low it looked like it was practically sitting on the treetops."

At first she couldn't believe what she was seeing, but she knew everyone else there was seeing the same thing. But there was one big difference between Elizabeth and the other eyewitnesses, "They stayed, and I gassed it and took off!"

She doesn't "even want to guess at the size" of the UFO. All she knew was that it was very big, hovering over the middle of the road, and definitely "too close for comfort!" The entire sighting for her lasted about 15 seconds, but obviously it had been there for a while; at least long enough for four other cars to arrive and pull over. It was admittedly nerve-wracking that she had to drive directly under the massive UFO to get away, but she was glad she did because she "didn't know what the thing would do" if she stayed.

On Monday she went to work and told everyone what she had seen, and no one believed her. It was obviously disappointing that her coworkers doubted her story, but later one of the men spoke to her in private. He revealed that several years earlier, he had seen the same UFO over his backyard in Hyde Park, NY. At least one person believed her, but realizing what the general opinion was regarding people who claimed to see UFOs, she decided not to talk about it again.

Fast forward 43 years, and as Elizabeth was reading the *Poughkeepsie Journal* article in June of 2012, she thought that here was finally someone who would listen to her, and appreciate the experience she had. And I most certainly did appreciate it. I asked her how the experience influenced her life, and she quickly replied, "Do people really think that Earth is the only planet that has life?"

Still, Elizabeth retains some healthy skepticism. Over the years she has seen many lights in the sky, but nothing that couldn't be explained as a plane or a jet. She also doesn't "believe that UFOs kidnap people and do all kinds of things to them."

While she doesn't really fear UFOs, and whoever is piloting them, she does admit that her very close encounter in 1969 was simply "too close for comfort."

Sandra Wheeler: Barrytown, 1968 and Rhinebeck 1998

The first one I recall was when I was a kid in 1968. I grew up in Barrytown, NY. We were outside one evening after dinner playing on a swing set. We heard a whirring noise that got louder by the minute. When we looked up in the sky there was a huge cigar-shaped object circled by several pastel lights. It was probably the size of a small plane and was up in the sky a few hundred feet. It stopped directly over us and my mother freaked and made us run into the house, so I don't know what it did after that.

My second sighting was probably around 1998. As a friend and I were coming home around 11:00 pm from working second shift at Ferncliff

Nursing Home in Rhinebeck, NY, on River Road, we saw a huge silver triangle-shaped object dart very rapidly down towards the front of the car and stop dead for about a second, then it darted away rapidly in a flash. It was about 50 feet above the front of the car and maybe the size of a medium sized car.

Very Large Tinker Toys
Peekskill, late 70s-early 80s

After reading the article about our project in *The Northern Westchester Examiner* on June 12, 2012, Mr. K. of Buchanan wrote me the following letter. *This was the first time he told anyone about this.*

1. The object I saw was not boomerang shaped as mentioned in the article, but more like something built from a Tinker Toy set.
2. It was traveling at a high rate of speed in an even, straight direction.
3. It was traveling approximately from NW to a SE direction.
4. It seemed to have colored lights in a set pattern.
5. Sighting was in the evening just before darkness.
6. Size of object was difficult to determine, as was altitude which was steady.
7. No noise was detected from the object.
8. Location of this incident was Lakeview Ave. W., Peekskill, NY, my residence at that time.
9. This happened in the 70s or 80s—not sure.
10. I did not report this at the time. This is the first time being mentioned to anyone.

I gave Mr. K. a call to get more information. The following is a summary of that conversation:

He was alone, and the sighting lasted about one or two minutes. His feeling during the sighting was one of surprise. The object was irregularly shaped, and the lights were stationary, indicating it was one, solid object.

The reason he referred to it as being like from a Tinker Toy set is that there appeared to be all sorts of beams, like the underside of a bridge.

When I asked what he felt the object was, he replied, "I would think it was from somewhere a little bit strange." He laughed, and then added, "Somewhere *very* strange."

Norelco Razor
Lagrange, c. 1976-80

Somewhere between 1976 and 1980, James K. and a few of his buddies were sitting on the hood of a car one night by an apple orchard off Bushwick Road in Lagrange, NY. They were near what they believed was a government radar installation for the Dutchess County Airport. The site was composed of a large, white, cone-shaped object behind a chain link fence that had all kinds of official warning signs on it.

"It kind of looked like an Apollo space capsule," James explained.

An interesting choice of description, as he and his friends just might have seen a real spaceship that night.

As the friends sat there listening to the car radio, they suddenly saw in the distance "three lights spinning, with a haze or fog around them." Then "just like that, they popped in front of the cone about a quarter of a mile in the air and jumped around each other."

As we spoke on the phone, I was having trouble visualizing what James had seen, so I asked for a more detailed description. His response immediately gave me a clear view in my mind.

"Have you ever seen a Norelco razor? That's just what the spinning lights looked like."

He further described the motion of the lights to be something like shining a flashlight on your ceiling and then jerking the flashlight back and forth. The lights "always darted in unison and kept the same distance from one another, so they could have all been attached," but he couldn't be certain whether they were separate craft or part of the same one. He and his friends watched in amazement as the spinning, multi-colored lights made impossibly rapid motions and instant changes of position. The sighting lasted about 30 seconds, then the object "shot away" and out of sight.

"What the hell was that?" one of his friends asked.

As they tried to make sense of what they had just seen, a report came over the radio. It was WPDH from Poughkeepsie, and they were apparently being flooded with calls about a UFO in the area. The following day, the *Poughkeepsie Journal* had a small paragraph about the sightings, "but they downplayed the whole thing as if it was nothing."

However, James has no doubt what he saw, and you can still hear the excitement in his voice.

"I saw a UFO! I never saw anything else on Earth that moved that way. It's real, UFOs exist!"

Did this 30 seconds of his life change anything, and does he still think about it more than 35 years later?

"It's always on my mind for some reason. It made me truly believe that there is life on other planets. UFOs are real, and we are not the only species in the universe. I was never afraid, I was in awe. It was inspiring. It was *so cool!* I've seen one. They *are* real!"

Nancy Hewitt: Garnerville, mid-70s to early 80s

From: Nancy Hewitt
Sent: Monday, July 16, 2012 2:50 PM
To: lindazim@optonline.net
Subject: rockland ufo story

I don't know exact year that this happened, but it had to be around middle 1970s to early 1980s, anyway it was myself and my sister Karen who is now deceased, we were in our house and she went outside it was a clear night that I do remember, she told me to come outside, I was young I remember and we walked out our house and looked up in the sky to the right of our house, and we saw all these lights in the sky, there was no sound etc, we were both wondering what the hell it was, we turned to look at each other for a split second and boom when we looked back that thing just took off and was gone, we knew then that nothing can move that fast where we couldn't see it in the sky anywhere....I remember that a lot of people saw the same thing we did that night.

I know that my cousin's husband also had an experience also here in Rockland, I am not sure if it was the same night as when I saw it or not, but if u would like I can contact her and see if he can email u what happened to him etc.

I hope what I saw helps I know it's not much but it's what I saw that night, I wish I could tell u more like the exact year and date etc.

I responded by asking:

A few questions: What town was this in? Were the lights in any pattern—round, triangle, etc.—and were they white or colored? Any sense of size or distance?

Nancy's response:

It happened in Garnerville, New York in Rockland County. If I am not mistaken they were colored and I believe round, and as for distance I honestly can't say, I do know it wasn't too far up in the sky cause I would have thought it was a plane or a helicopter, as for size I honestly don't remember that.

Phil: Brewster, 1980

"As we did often on Sunday early in 1980, after church, we went to visit my stepmother, Helene, who lived in Lake Carmel. My late wife, Hazel, and our three kids [ages 7, 9, and 11] had a nice dinner with her and as it got dark we headed for home.

"Our destination was Purdys, about 10 miles south, so after a short trip on a local road we had an easy drive down Interstate 84, with a final connection to Interstate 684. As we drove on I-84, Hazel said, 'Look at the long string of lights west of the highway, way up in the sky.' Some little lights seemed to fall off, she said. As we proceeded south, the kids in our station wagon lay down in the back and watched the lights. As we approached the exit to 684, the kids started yelling, 'The lights are over us. They are OVER US!'

"Well, as I used the ramp to Interstate 684, I noticed that cars and trucks had pulled off the road. So I stopped, too. The lights had returned to their position to the west and then were gone. They were gone in a flash. It was dark.

"Shaken, when I got home I called WHUD, the only local station (FM-music) on the air at that time. I explained what we had seen and they wanted to record my experience, but I declined. Listening to WHUD a few minutes later, they interrupted their programming to indicate that many had seen something strange in the sky as reported to the Putnam County Sheriff's Office.

"An all-day program was scheduled at the middle school where they tried to explain what we saw was just some stunt pilots who glide without any sound in formation…hmmm.

"All I know is this was an amazing event I shall not forget. I wish I had more details, but this is what I remember."

Two things to note with Phil's story: The intersection of I-84 and I-684 is in Brewster, New York, where many sightings (such as Dennis Sant's) took place. Also, it is interesting that the radio station reported that the Putnam County Sheriff's Office stated that "many people" had called about the lights, although today the Sheriff's Office can't find any records of anyone ever calling to report strange lights or UFOs:

Putnam County Sherriff's Department

As so many UFO witnesses over the years had called various law enforcement agencies to report their sightings—and were treated with various levels of response including ridicule, skepticism, or complacency, I thought I would give law enforcement a chance to tell their side of the story. I also hoped at the very least to find stacks of old reports from some of the mass sightings in 1983. And what better place to turn than to the Sheriff's Department of one of the hottest of UFO hot spots in the Hudson Valley in the 1980s, Putnam County.

I spoke to a very experienced member of the department, and I must say he was polite and courteous at all times, and was kind enough to take the time to answer all of my questions. I was curious to know what the

302

protocol would be if a UFO call came into the Sheriff's Department today. The officer explained that the first step in any call of suspicious activity was to dispatch a patrol to make observations at the scene. From there, the level of activity—if any—would then dictate the next action.

As far as reporting goes, if the officer saw nothing and there was only one call, very little, or perhaps nothing at all, would be written on the blotter (the daily record). If 50 or 100 people called, there would further investigation and more detailed reporting.

From a historical perspective, while old blotters are retained, the more detailed records are only required to be held for five years, which certainly but a damper on my hopes of finding UFO reports from the 1980s. Also, about 20 years ago, the department changed over from paper to an electronic system, no doubt losing a lot more of the old records in the process.

Then there was one more wrinkle—they only had the blotters for calls placed to the Sheriff's Department, not those calls to local police, and as of 1985, to 911. For example, any UFO calls made today could be placed to the towns of Carmel or Kent, the State Police, 911, the FAA, or the Sheriff's Department—each of which keeps their own records under their own retention policies.

So, while my hope of making one phone call and unearthing a treasure trove of detailed UFO reports was shot down, I still hoped that the old blotters would at least give some tantalizing clues as to the number of calls and the response to the major sightings on March 17 and 24, 1983. I was hoping I could spend the day in the records room poring through 30-year-old blotters, but I found out that wasn't happening, either. However, the officer said he would have someone check the blotters for at least those two dates and get back to me.

Anxious to hear what would be found, but fully realizing they had a lot more important things to do, I waited a month for a response. I finally called and left a message, and received a message back a short time later. "After an exhaustive search," not even one single mention of a UFO report was found in the blotters of those two days, or any other days, for that matter. I was very disappointed, and somewhat skeptical as to the lack of results, given that many hundreds—if not thousands—of people witnessed the massive triangles or boomerangs at that time. However, after talking with another member of law enforcement it made more sense—something that *isn't* reported *doesn't* require further investigation or paperwork!

I know for a fact that Dennis Sant called the Sheriff's Department on March 18, 1983 to report his sighting of the night before, but that call apparently did not make it into the blotter as no patrol was required. How many other calls had been made to other law enforcement agencies that either didn't write anything down, or has since purged their records?

It was all rather disheartening, but fortunately, such reports were not essential to my research. There were enough living, breathing witnesses to tell their stories in detail, in a personal manner no written report could hope to duplicate. It would have been nice to have some official records to go along with the testimony, but the firsthand accounts were the most important things.

Do I have any confidence that UFO reports made today to the police or Sheriff's Department will be taken seriously and duly recorded? No, not really. But then again, what can they do about these craft anyway? If they are government black ops vehicles, they will be told to look the other way. And if they are not government vehicles that are violating our airspace, a patrolman has no jurisdiction over that kind of illegal alien!

Karen Gibbons: Stony Point, 1983

In August, Robert Vanderclock was kind enough to let me speak about the project for a few minutes at his UFO lecture at the Garnerville library. During the break, I spoke with Karen Gibbons, and she let me videotape her account of her 1983 sighting.

"I saw a UFO over the Farley School in Stony Point in 1983. It was round on the sides, flat. It had all white lights, but when it started to move it had red, green, and white lights like triangles going all around the sides of it, and then it started to move very slowly. I saw it for…I don't know, maybe five or ten minutes.

"And then I started to leave and I couldn't find it, and I went like this [she shows how she leaned out the car window] and I saw it go right over

304

my car. I thought I was in the *Twilight Zone* or dead, or something, really!"

I asked if she was scared, and she replied, "Oh, yeah! I was scared to death. I went home and I didn't stop for any red lights or anything. And it was in the paper the next day. A lot of people saw it."

Delia S.: Tomkins Cove, 1980s

Facebook message:

Rockland UFO sightings: My mom and sister were driving on Mott Farm Road one night in Tomkins Cove, NY. They came around a turn and saw something hovering over power lines. They opened the car windows heard no sound coming from it. That happened around the UFO sightings in the 80s. On that turn u can get a view of Indian point. The next night my mom was driving us home from religion class and the power lines were sparking. For my mom to say something about that stuff it was true. Just something to look into.

AJM: Wappingers Falls, 1983

In 1983, AJM was driving home in Wappingers Falls when he saw strange lights in the sky. He pulled into his street and got out to get a better look. There was a circle of lights—red, blue, and green—and they were not flashing. It was an overcast night, and the silent object hung below the clouds.

AJM determined that what he was looking at was one solid object—not individual craft flying in a circular formation—because he couldn't see the clouds through the inside the circle. Also, the lights remained in steady, fixed positions from one another without wavering, and moved as one object.

His neighbor and two other people stood and watched this object for at least 20 minutes, before it slowly moved to the southeast. As they watched, the neighbor said, "This is what my kids must have seen last night!" Apparently, this same circle of lights had been over the street the night before, and while they couldn't say what it was, at least the neighbor now knew his kids weren't making up the story.

How does AJM feel about the entire UFO experience? He is convinced we are being visited by alien space craft, and our government knows and is covering it up. In addition to his sighting, he is certain of these things because of the stupid official excuses for such sightings.

"What I saw was not a weather balloon, the planet Venus, or planes in formation," he said. "I know what I saw, and those kinds of excuses are just an insult."

Christine: Peekskill, c. 1983

From: Christine
Sent: Wednesday, June 13, 2012 9:44 PM
To: lindazim@optonline.net
Subject: looked like a ufo to me

My friend Neil told me about your FB page and thought I should tell you what I saw.

The year must have been 1983 or 84. I was driving in a car with my boyfriend on route 202 near the Peekskill hospital. I remember it was a warm night, summer maybe. It was a dark sky with many stars. As we turned the corner we saw lights in the sky that seemed pretty far away, he pulled over and we got out and now the lights were a little closer. They were in the shape of a diamond. At first we thought it was planes flying in formation, but the lights just looked like they were floating. No sound at all. We watched for about 5-10 min and then the lights began moving very quick in a sideways direction. We lost sight of them behind the trees. The lights were mostly white with a few green ones. I remember noticing that I couldn't see the stars between the lights as if it was solid, if it was a solid object it was gigantic. It was fascinating and creepy, I never saw anything like it.

The next day we heard of some others seeing the same thing at Caldor department store parking lot (now I think it's a Kohl's). We were told by authorities that it was planes flying in formation running a test. I can't remember if it was in the paper or not, but I think it was. The whole thing seemed very weird.

I haven't thought of that night in a really long time.

Jeff S. : Vassar College Alumnae House, Poughkeepsie, Mid-1980s

The following are the series of emails I received from Jeff S. about his sighting.

From: Jeffrey S.
Sent: Sunday, September 23, 2012 7:25 PM
To: lindazim@optonline.net
Subject: UFO

1) Hi Linda, I read your article in the paper, and I would like to share an experience a few coworkers and myself had. It was in the mid to late eighties I can't remember the exact year however, I worked at Vassar College Alumnae House in Poughkeepsie then. I would like to tell you about it please reply if you are interested.

I replied that I was interested and asked for the details.

2) Linda, like I said it happened in the summer in the mid to late eighties, I was in my office at the alumnae house not sure of the exact time but it was dark maybe 8-10pm when I heard a noise coming from outside my window sorta like a humming I can't really describe the sound, so I walked outside to check it out. I looked up and saw a large object in the sky directly over our parking area about a hundred feet above the tree tops. It had lights along the perimeter of it. I would say it appeared to be round or even an oval shape. It seemed almost motionless with a faint noise, even almost quiet, hard to explain. I just stood there staring at it for a minute or so, it was so close I thought I could throw a stone and hit it. I ran back inside the kitchen and told one of my waitresses to

307

hurry and come outside and check it out. I was afraid that people would think I was kidding them unless I had a witness. When we came back out she saw it as well, along with a few customers that were walking out the front door of the restaurant. I then called the Dutchess County Sheriff's office and told them I just saw a UFO and they replied that they received many calls about it already. This was an experience that I will never forget

I asked how people reacted, the duration of the sighting, and whether the craft moved away slowly or quickly.

3) No one seemed scared. We were more in awe or mesmerized. It lasted less than 2 minutes, and slowly moved away.

Doris Jean Kolarek: Peekskill, 1980s

From: Doris Jean Kolarek
Sent: Monday, June 25, 2012 12:22 PM
To: lindazim@optonline.net
Subject: 80s ufo sighting

I was very young when the big sighting happened in Peekskill, NY and I cannot remember the exact year, but I'm sure you'll have no problem figuring it out. It was the year everyone in the area saw a UFO. I had just been put to bed and, being young, had not yet fallen asleep. I heard a commotion downstairs and went to see what was going on. I found my father and sister outside on our front lawn looking up at the sky. I went to them and my father picked me up, not saying a word.

Neighbors had come out of their houses and cars had stopped along the road, people getting out and standing next to the doors looking up. You could hear a pin drop. A man riding a bicycle down our street looked back to see what was going on and rode directly into our bushes. He climbed out and stood with us. No one said a word or made a peep.

Right above us, not far from the tree tops (it was very, very low) was a huge white ship, slightly rectangular in shape with black windows. I

308

remember seeing a pattern of some kind on the ship also in white. It glided by very slowly with another much smaller ship behind it that looked like a large glowing ball of red light. There was absolutely no noise at all coming from the two UFOs, none.

Once they glided by, people made their way back into their homes and cars and the man on our lawn got back on his bicycle. No one talked about it, my father and sister chatted a bit, but didn't say much in front of me. Perhaps they were trying to keep from scaring me, although I wasn't frightened at all. My father put me back to bed and that was that. I heard that it was covered up as being an ultralight I believe, in my opinion those ships were not [ultralights].

I also remember seeing the famous boomerang shaped ship that went through our area. I was at the end of our driveway with my mother that time, but do not have as clear a memory of it as I was still quite young. I just remember it being very low and black in color with very bright lights.

My mother and I also saw another UFO years later when I was a young teenager. We were driving around at night and stopped to admire the stars when we noticed four stars which appeared to be in a square pattern start to spin and move. Being UFO enthusiasts we followed it out to the Croton reservoir. We were the only car on the road when it stopped not far from us, then flashed brightly and took off so quickly it seemed to just disappear.

Those are my experiences with UFOs in our Hudson Valley. I had hoped to see more, but count myself lucky I've seen what I have. I think the work you are doing is great!

Peter & Lorraine Rodgers: Stony Point, 1984

Peter Rodgers doesn't mince words. He knows what he and his wife, Lorraine, saw from their Stony Point home the night of October 30, 1984. The following day, the *Journal News* ran an article which explained the object was nothing more than a formation of ultralights.

"That's completely bullshit. That's not what it was," Peter told me over the phone when we spoke in August of 2012.

The Rodgers' home was overlooking the Hudson River, and on that night Peter was in the driveway taking out the garbage.

"It was a clear, crisp night," he explained. "I looked out toward Indian Point and there where these whitish lights. I watched them for a couple of minutes and said to myself 'What the hell is that?' Then I yelled to my wife to get out here. She came running out in a just a shirt and her underwear and we just stood in awe and watched this thing."

The single, solid object was very low and consisted "of a series of round lights that did not rotate or flicker. It was moving super slow down the river heading south to Indian Point. There was no sound. It stopped directly over Indian Point for about 20-30 seconds. Then it started moving ever so slowly to the east. Then *pffft*, it was gone!"

The object accelerated so quickly they couldn't believe their eyes. They had never seen anything move so fast. Seconds later, a helicopter was over Indian Point in pursuit of the object, but it had already taken off.

The view of Indian Point from the street where Peter and Lorraine lived.

I asked if he could judge the size of the lighted object, and his answer was astonishing.

"Take a typical shade of a table lamp and then imagine a fly landing on it. That was the difference in size between this object and the helicopter."

The next day the news had reports of many people seeing the object throughout the area and calling the police. Peter calls the lame excuse of ultralights "an insult" to anyone who actually saw it.

The excuse is even an insult to the authorities who appear powerless to stop a bunch of reckless pilots from violating the airspace of a nuclear reactor! Couldn't this helicopter have followed the alleged ultralights until they landed and then had all the pilots arrested? This absurd excuse continues to make fools of anyone who repeats it.

For Peter and Lorraine Rodgers, they have no doubt that what they saw was a single, massive object that had the ability to silently hover and accelerate with blinding speed. They were never scared at any point, only "in awe." And if you doubt their story, I'm sure Peter would be happy to tell you what he thinks about your skepticism.

Cesar Padilla: Verplanck, July 1984 and Hopewell Junction, 2012

Every July, there is a festival in the town of Verplanck that thousands of people attend. In 1984, there were approximately 2,000 revelers in the streets eating, drinking, and having a good time. Cesar Padilla was one of those people enjoying the entertainment on that warm July night, and when he caught sight of some lights in the sky, he thought at first it was all part of the show—until he took a closer look.

Cesar is an amateur astronomer who loves looking at the night sky. He also has a "fascination for aircraft," and could easily identity various commercial, civilian, and military planes. However, this massive boomerang-shaped object low in the sky above him wasn't like anything he had ever seen before. He ran into his house on Broadway to get his 7x50 binoculars. He thought when he looked at the object with the binoculars the dozen or so large white lights would resolve into individual aircraft, as stories of the ultralights flying in formation had been circulating.

Instead, he saw one solid object, although he couldn't make out the structure. In between the large white lights were smaller, pulsating yellowish lights. There was also "a red, fuzzy, blinking light trailing behind," but he couldn't tell if it was part of the craft or simply following it. "If it was part of the structure, then it was incredibly huge. Even if it wasn't, you would have had to put at least three C5 Galaxies next to one another to equal the size of this thing." (Note: The Lockheed C5 Galaxy is a large transport plane with a wingspan of 222 feet, 9 inches. Three together would equate to the length of two football fields.)

The craft came from the direction of the Indian Point nuclear facility, less than a mile from Verplanck, and only when it was directly overhead did Cesar hear "the faintest humming sound." It was also right above him that the craft turned. "It didn't bank into the turn," Cesar stated with assurance. Instead, the massive craft simply spun around as if on a pivot and began to head back toward Indian Point.

Many other people in the crowd also saw the object, but apparently between the level of alcohol consumption and the stories of ultralights, a lot didn't really pay any attention. Another person that did pay attention, however, was Cesar's father-in-law, who commented that, "Those guys are crazy. They'll be lucky if no one shoots at them with a rifle!" An amusing remark, but one that actually raises the question of how this huge craft was allowed to violate the airspace of a nuclear facility without getting shot at!

What did Cesar think he had witnessed? "Well, it was obvious it wanted to be seen," he said, making it unlikely it was a secret military craft. Also, he finds it hard to believe that we had the technology in 1984 to build such a ship, and doubts that we have the ability even today. And, considering he recently had another sighting, he is leaning toward an extraterrestrial explanation.

It was August 18, 2012, and Cesar was sitting on his porch in Hopewell Junction, enjoying the evening sky. He was "looking at the star Vega near Cygnus" when he saw a large, fast-moving object high in the sky. Despite the altitude, the craft had the apparent size of three feet—in other words, if you held a yardstick at arms' length, that was how enormous the object was.

312

Cesar "couldn't make out the leading edge," but it gave the general appearance of a disc shape. There were three white lights on the bottom "at a crazy angle, set about 45 degrees to the direction of flight." There was no sound, no visible exhaust, no wings, no visible engines, and "nothing natural" about it. The speed was also startling, as in just a few seconds it traversed the sky in a straight line and he lost sight of it behind the trees.

Its speed and strange appearance admittedly scared him. "I felt as though I had seen something very unusual...not ours." However, despite the fear, he wishes he could see it again. And maybe someday Cesar will have another sighting, as he and his daughter and grandson now make trips to Pine Bush "looking for UFOs."

While he may never find out what it was he saw, that won't stop Cesar from looking.

Lenore.: Wappingers Falls, May 25, 1985

Facebook message:
The area was on Robinson Lane, my neighbor was on Paulette Lane and we are next door... I went out to call in my cat and it was just too dark for 8-9 pm in May. When I looked over towards Louise's house there was a huge, huge circular dark thing just sitting there above the trees...came back in to call her, not knowing she was in labor at the time with the twins, pulled the cord to the glass door (old phone with curly long line) and while talking to her the thing started to slowly move more towards my yard...the cat ran in all pissed off, and it just slowly moved out back over the property that's not built on...about 30 acres of open land... closed door, made stiff drink...

In response to some of my questions:

Forgot to say...Wappingers Falls/Lagrange line. May 25th, 1985 there was a HUGE round silent UFO over the trees between my property and my neighbors... around 9:00 pm...remember because my neighbor who also saw it was in labor with her twins...

Lou didn't really remember much... she said she looked out the side window...saw it...ran to the other end of the house scared... she left for hospital shortly after, she did look up from car, but it had already moved over me and out back...always interested in this and ghosts... seen them both...and no, I'm not nuts...

The yard where Lenore saw the huge UFO hovering above the trees.

And does anyone else find it kind of creepy that this UFO was hovering over her friend's house as she was in labor with twins?

314

Irish Green
Donna Parish-Bischoff: Yonkers, late 80s

From: Donna Parish-Bischoff
Sent: Thursday, June 14, 2012 1:00 PM
To: lindazim@optonline.net
Subject: UFO story

Hi Linda

I know I mentioned this to Sarah & Felix ... But not only am I a paranormal investigator ... I had an experience in the late 1980s.

I lived in Yonkers NY at the time. It was St. Pattys night (NO I was not drinking) LOL*. It was approx 10pm. I lived across from a baseball field. I looked out the front screen door and I almost dropped to my knees. I called for my mom (she is deceased now).

But this ship was silent, as big as two football fields and had bright green lights. It was beautiful to be honest. It was low enough for me to see all the mechanical detail underneath it. It looked as if it were not moving for 20 minutes. Then it went up then disappeared.

The next day I knew two other people that were driving on the Major Deegan who drove following it as well.

I asked a few questions and Donna responded:

It was long and angular no lights were shined on me. ..but the green lights were brilliant and I loved it--I was not in fear...I was amazed and in awe.

I then asked if she could sketch it.

I am doing that now before I read your e-mail
I am not an artist ...a five year old would draw better...
Here it is if you want me to try and draw it better...I will try but I stink at drawing :(

My next message after seeing the sketch:

315

I assume the circles were lights, but what were the wavy lines, like seams in the metal?

Yes, exactly, circles were the brilliant green lights and the wiggly lines were the mechanical hardware looking structure/metal or whatever they used to make the ships. It looked charcoal underneath, in color like gun metal in tone almost.

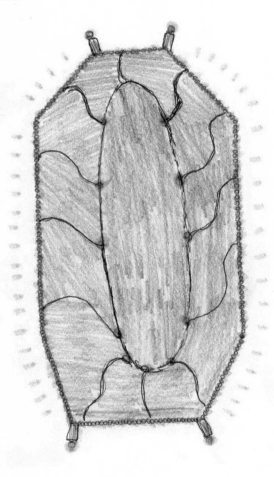

Donna's sketch.

Linda R.: Scarsdale, 1986

From: Linda R.
Sent: Wednesday, June 27, 2012 11:15 AM
To: Lindazim@optonline.net
Subject: UFOs

My name is Linda R. I live in Tarrytown, NY. A friend of mine mentioned you are looking for local people who have seen UFOs.

In 1986, we were living in Scarsdale. One evening in October, I noticed a UFO flying over our house. It was very large with lights outlining its shape which was somewhat irregular. It was flying very low, a little higher than treetop level, and made a soft whirring sound like a fan or a sewing machine. My husband and my mother also saw it. We called the police department to report it but the lines were all busy. We never could get through. It traveled to the southwest, toward the Hudson River.

I had several minutes to study it. It was not any kind of plane or ultralight or anything else I have ever seen. Anything I know of that was that large would have had to make a much louder sound to stay in the air.

A friend, who at the time was a Town of Greenburgh police officer, also saw it. He said he saw it again on another occasion when he was driving on the Taconic State Parkway.

That's my UFO story! If you need any more information or would like to talk about it, please let me know. Hope this helps your research.

From: Linda Zimmermann <lindazim@optonline.net>
To: 'Linda R.'
Sent: Wednesday, June 27, 2012 5:00 PM
Subject: RE: UFOs

Thanks for your story. I do have a few questions.
Could you give me an idea of the size—as big as a house, a plane, a football field? Also, what color were the lights, or were they all white? How did you all feel when you saw it? Scared, excited, or just curious?

From: Linda R.
Sent: Thursday, June 28, 2012 7:15 AM
To: Lindazim@optonline.net
Subject: UFOs

As I recall, it was probably about the size of a jumbo jet, but not the same shape. You can imagine what a jumbo jet at treetop level would look like! It was huge. The lights were all the same color. I believe they were white. I was very curious when I saw it, not scared. I had no idea what it was. I remember going into the house and telling my mom to come look, and, if I were going to see a UFO, this is what it would look like!

I guess it wasn't that scary because it made so little noise. It just sort of floated off to the northwest. We just kept looking at it, trying to believe our eyes. I don't think it occurred to me to be scared! The feeling throughout the whole thing was, "What could this be?"

Karen F. : Shrub Oak, 1986-88

It was somewhere between 1986 and 1988, and Karen was returning home from work one night. She was driving north on Route 6 between Mohegan Lake and Shrub Oak when she saw a bright light in the sky around the Strawberry Road intersection.

"It was very solid—I mean no blinking, no wavering. It was white and very round."

The light was some distance away, but suddenly it began to descend rapidly right in her direction.

"I never saw anything move so fast! As I looked down the road the light was right in the middle, in front of me."

The speed and brightness frightened her, and she admitted she "drove through the 35 mph speed zone in Shrub Oak at 75 mph." [Which is another reason her full name isn't being used!] As the light drew closer, she turned down a street perpendicular to the path of the light, and fortunately it didn't follow her, and she lost sight of it.

What could have been so bright, so round and so "solid," and move "faster than any jet" or anything else she had ever seen? Whatever it was, it frightened Karen, to the point where even decades later, she is still uneasy about driving alone at night. More than once she has seen a light in the night sky while driving and been "freaked out" enough to take a detour to avoid it.

When I asked if she hoped to someday see something like it again, she quickly replied, "No! I hope I never see anything again!"

David G: Amawalk Reservoir, Somers

The following is an email I received from David G. on June 19, 2012. I spoke to him the next day to get some additional information. My questions and his responses are below.

I lived on Lake Road in front of the Amawalk Reservoir in Somers...in the early 80s I saw a bright white full moon shaped object around ten o'clock pm with a dark key slot cut out at about six o'clock...I watched it for a long time, it was stationary and I went inside to get my wife and it was gone when we returned outside.... also...when we moved in we put a huge antenna on the roof facing at NYC...the reception was amazing...every now and then every station went to total snow....one day my tv went to snow and my daughter came running in from the reservoir saying she saw a UFO over the lake...maybe this is why my reception was lost many times???? This was probably 1992. But the one UFO that I saw that was totally mind boggling was about 8 years ago....I was driving south on the Taconic Parkway at 2am...just as I crossed route 84 I saw a huge dark object in front of my windshield that spanned the valley with about 8 or 9 bright lights on its edge...it must have been a few thousand feet across...long and thin....it filled my entire windshield and was possibly a thousand feet ahead of me...I pulled over and got out of my car to get a closer look....When I got out to look, it was gone...my background is a highly educated science guy...I am 65 now and certainly of sound mind...I have a background in bio, astronomy, chem, ecology, and spend a lot of time looking up at the stars, shooting stars, and satellites passing over.

Zim: Where was the moon the night you saw the full moon-shaped object?

319

David: That object was definitely was not the moon, because the moon was further west in the sky at the time. The object was to the east, and there was that dark, rectangular slot about 1/3 of the way into it from the edge.

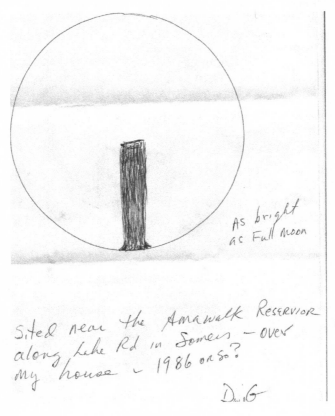

As bright as Full Moon

Sited near the Amawalk Reservior along Lake Rd in Somers - over my house ~ 1986 or so?

D.G

David's sketch.

Zim: How old was your daughter when she saw the UFO over the reservoir, and did she describe it?

David: She was 14, and she didn't describe it, she just said there was a UFO. This was about 6pm on a summer evening. It was freaky, because usually I got studio-quality reception, but I got several seconds of snow.

Zim: The large UFO you saw on the Taconic, what color were the lights?

David: White, all white. It filled the entire windshield, it had to be thousands of feet across. It looked like it filled the entire valley. It was like this looming, dark line, but it wasn't perfectly horizontal. It was tilted down maybe five degrees on the eastern side. And it was stationary.

Zim: Could you tell if it was solid?

David: There was darkness between the lights and you couldn't see any stars. It was solid. I know what the planets and other things look like. I love sitting outside looking at the night sky, and this object wasn't anything I'd seen before. And I wasn't drunk or anything.

Zim: So it wasn't planes or ultralights flying in formation?

David: Three times I saw the ultralights in formation at night. Each time there was a loud sound, and you could also see stars between the gaps in the planes. Also, their pattern was clearly wavering.

David also said that if any of these enormous craft were U.S. experimental craft, the government must love all the disinformation created by the hoaxing pilots.

And if they weren't from our own military, or from this world, the government appreciates the disinformation even more.

Robert Jacaruso, Harriman State Park, 1984-85

After the *New City Patch* article appeared online on August 9, 2012, I received a lot of emails from people who had stories to tell of their sightings. I always respect requests for anonymity, and I always double check with everyone who tells me I can use their name. One of the best responses to my question of whether or not it was okay to use their actual name came from Robert Jacaruso of Nyack, who replied, "You can use my name. At my age I don't care what people think or say, I know what I saw out there."

Here's his initial email:

In 1984 or 85 I saw a UFO one night in Harriman State Park. I was in an old unused parking lot at the old Silver Mine Ski Center. I was with my girlfriend at the time and as we were sitting there we looked east and up over the mountain rose this orange light shaped round and flat but higher towards the middle. There were no red or green lights on it and no engine noise at all. It moved slowly as if looking at us, then went behind one mountain and came out on the other side closer to us. It went up and down and sideways as well as hovering during this viewing. We were both scared and as we were looking it just zoomed off until it was out of sight. It went real fast like you see in the movies. It was a UFO, I don't know what it was, but it was not making any noise at all. Not a plane or jet or helicopter. Maybe the whole viewing lasted 10-15 minutes. And I did say to her, it's a UFO and they're here to take us away, but we were scared.

I thanked him for his story and responded with a few questions, such as: Do you have any idea how big this object was? How did this sighting affect you and your girlfriend? Is there still fear, or just curiosity? The following is his response.

Not really sure how big it was and I think the closest it came to us was maybe a football field length away. When we first saw it, it came up real slow from behind a mountain that looked like a sun rising, then stopped, then came towards us. Then it went to our right and went behind another mountain and we lost sight of it. Then it came up from this other mountain and that is when it was closest to us. We felt we were being watched by it, after about 5 minutes of it looking at us from this range it slowly began moving away from us and picked up speed until it just zoomed out of sight almost disappearing before our eyes. We both thought it was pretty neat that we just saw a UFO and to me it was just as if I saw a famous person walking in Nyack, I enjoyed the sighting, minded my own business and just kept going on. We're not kooks, she is a social worker and I worked in the health field right up until I retired last year. Also we were not drinking or using any mind altering chemicals, so that's what we

322

saw, an unidentified flying object exactly. As a matter of fact, being up there at night you hear all kinds of noises from the animals that come out at night. I didn't notice any animal noises when that thing was close to us, whether or not they were quiet or we were just so focused that we didn't hear anything I'm not sure. I am sure of one thing, the UFO made no noise at all during the whole time it was in view. Me and my girlfriend broke up and I haven't seen or heard of her since. Hope this is of help for you.

Bob Strong: Pearl River, NY, Thursday, March 17, 1988

This story is of particular interest to me for a couple of reasons. First, Bob Strong happens to be my husband, and I had no idea he had a UFO sighting until I started this project!

Also, this is yet another St. Patrick's Day sighting. Do the pilots of these aircraft know that so many people drink heavily on that day, that no one would believe any reports of UFOs?

Finally, there were numerous other reports of UFOs that night from Westchester to Manhattan.

The following is in Bob's own words:

Early in the evening, I was driving east on Orangeburg Road, heading from Pearl River to Piermont, NY where I lived at the time. I had just passed Blue Hill Plaza, a large office complex on the right, when I saw something to my right; it was big and round, with many flashing white lights circling it. It was off to the south, maybe a half-mile to a mile away, and it was fairly low in the sky, but considerably higher than tree-top level. It was hard to judge its size, but it was big. Really big. I pulled off to the side of the road, and was quickly joined by about 3 or 4 more cars. "What IS that thing?" was our common response to seeing this object. Nobody had any answers, and we all grew very quiet as we watched.

My first thought was that it might be a blimp, but it was moving much too fast. Then I thought it might be some planes flying in formation, but it was going too slow for that. Plus, I could not hear any sound whatsoever. Even then, Rockland County did not have the darkest skies, but there were still a few stars visible, and when the object passed in front of them, the stars were blacked out. So I knew it couldn't be planes flying in formation. The lights each kept the same distance from each other, never wavering at all - an impossible feat for planes flying in formation.

"Yeah, maybe it IS a blimp, after all," I thought. Then I realized it was way too big for a blimp, and there were no green or red flashing lights, like you'd usually see somewhere on an aircraft. The more we watched, the more mesmerized we all became; nobody said a word.

Then a very weird feeling crept over me as I thought, "UFO? No freakin' way!" Then, "Well, what the heck else can it be?" That's when my heart stopped for a second. I got the impression we all felt that at the same time, although nobody was speaking. We all just stood there, staring at it as it moved further to the south, heading towards New Jersey and New York City.

We could see it through the trees for a few minutes, as there were no leaves, and we watched it till it went out of sight. Nobody said anything else; we all just got back into our cars and left. I think the whole episode lasted less than 10 minutes. I don't recall anything else about it, no loss of time or anything like that; nor did I see any mention of it in the newspaper. It just seemed so utterly strange, so foreign. I had no other life experience to compare it to. Looking back, I still feel lucky that I was at the right place, at the right time.

Kevin Carey: Holmes, 1991

It was August of 1991, and Kevin Carey was 12-years-old and living in Holmes, NY. It was after dark when his 2-year-old brother pointed up to the sky and asked, "What's that?"

It was "an oval of lights," but not a complete oval, and it seemed to be about the size and shape of a blimp. It was only about 40 feet above the treetops and was "casting light down on the trees." The object was "silent and motionless." Kevin, his brother, and mother all watched the object for several minutes, and although they assumed it was some sort of a blimp, his mother went to get her camera.

324

At this point the oval of lights started "moving west at a decent speed" and was quickly about two miles away. They decided to try to follow it, "but it picked up speed" and took off out of sight "faster than any blimp."

Kevin recalls his mother reporting the sighting to the radio station Magic 105.5, but "they didn't do anything" about it. Kevin also clearly remembers that a red Honda Prelude with a woman and her daughter stopped in front of their house, and the woman asked if they had seen anything, so he knows there were at least two other witnesses.

I asked if Kevin was afraid at any point during the sighting, and he replied that he might have been if it was much closer to him, or if he had been alone. The overwhelming feeling he did have was that of being "awestruck." Overall, he views it as a positive experience, and one that has piqued his curiosity in UFOs. Over the years, it has also made him contemplate the question of "where did we come from?"

When I asked if he had anything else he wanted to add, Kevin said that he worked for many years by the National Guard facility at Stewart Airport and saw a lot of aircraft, "but never anything like" that oval of lights that could hover silently, yet also take off at high speed.

Also, over the years when he has tried to tell people about the sighting, he could "see them pulling away in their eyes." Kevin appreciated finally being able to tell someone his story without fear of ridicule, and I told him how much I appreciated him sharing his story, and also having the courage to do so using his real name.

Eric

In the fall of 1996, Eric was sitting in the front seat of a car being driven by his uncle on Route 84 in New York. It was about 2am, and his wife and parents were asleep in the back seat. Suddenly, a bright light appeared floating alongside the car, no more than 100 feet away. The light "was so bright it was hard to look at. And it stayed with us for what seemed to be a lifetime, but was probably about two minutes."

Neither Eric nor his uncle said anything as this mysterious light followed them, and they didn't say a word to each other for the remaining one and half hours of the trip. Finally, when they arrived at their destination, Eric asked his uncle, "What did we see?"

"I don't want to talk about it," his uncle replied.

"He was crazy scared out of his mind," Eric explained. "And to this day he still won't talk about that light."

About two years later, Eric had another strange sighting. He had just dropped off his wife at Blue Hill in Pearl River and was driving east on Orangeburg Road. As he approached the intersection of Route 303 he saw something "very shiny and reflective over Clausland Mountain." All of the traffic had slowed to look at this object and Eric also noticed a pedestrian had stopped on the sidewalk and was staring at it, too. Eric opened his car window and asked the man what he thought it was.

"I don't see anything," the man replied, putting his head down and walking on!

A third incident occurred just a month or so ago. After work, Eric went to visit a friend in Haverstraw. While driving home along Route 45 near New Square, he stopped to urinate along a wooded section of the road. As he stood there and was about to do his business, he looked up and saw a "triangle bigger than a house" floating silently above him. "It had a flat front, it was dark, and it had two sets of three lights each that were round like old car headlights. Needless to say, I pissed myself, jumped back in the car and took off!"

While I appreciated Eric's honesty, I have never ceased to be amazed by what people have told me about their experiences!

Is seeing believing for Eric? Yes, coupled with the stories he has heard from other UFO eyewitnesses at meetings that used to be held in Nyack, he does believe we are being visited. Despite the recent startling (and messy) incident, he is not afraid, just very curious. Like so many others like him, he simply wants answers to the inexplicable things he has witnessed.

Jon F.: Orangeburg, 2010

Jon works as a television director in New York City and he first emailed me on August 10. In another case of it being a small world, Jon had gone to school with one of my brothers! We emailed back and forth a

326

couple of times, and I spoke to him on the phone to get a few more details. The following is his first email with some of my additions with information I received from our conversation:

Saw your article on the net and thought I'd share my sighting with you.
I was driving home on the PIP N. [Palisades Interstate Parkway North] at approximately 1100PM, it was a very humid night with very low visibility, as I was going down the large hill from NJ into NY I noticed a bank of very bright white round lights, about 8 to 10 of them all in a row, to my left. I thought it was a new athletic field that was all lit up on top of one of the mountains [and he wondered when they could have built it as he never saw anything there before], as I was progressing down the hill the lights moved to the center of my windshield and then after a few seconds disappeared in a small ball of bright yellow light. There was just a "squiggle line" of yellow light where it was. All the cars in front of me slammed their brakes on!! It was very strange in the way it just disappeared in that flash of light that just circled around it. I was shaking like a leaf the rest of the way home and called the local and State Police when I got to my house in Orangeburg. They, the State Police, said that they had received a couple of reports of strange lights. I filed a report with MUFON [Mufon: UFO Report ID:89420] and was interviewed by a NYS Field Rep about a month later.
My mother had a strange experience in 1996 in Pearl River. She was pulling into the Pearl River Hilton Hotel, where she used to swim every morning with a couple of women that would meet her there. One of her swim mates pulled into the parking lot next to her and got out of the car all exited and out of breath. She asked my mother if she just saw that thing up in the sky. My mother, who saw nothing, asked her what she saw. The other woman described it as a huge "ice cream cone-shaped" object with strange green lights all around it. She said it was just hovering in the sky above Lederles [Laboratories] while she was waiting for a light on Middletown Rd. She said that from a still hovering position the object just arced to the horizon like a shooting star in just an instant!! As she was finishing her story the other friend pulled up all exited and described the same exact thing. The hair on the back of my mom's neck stood up on end after hearing this!

327

The two women were both MDs and said they could not possibly comprehend what they had just seen. My mom checked the *Journal News* that night and there was indeed reports of a sighting in the area that morning.

I asked Jon how he felt during his sighting, and how he feels today. He replied that there was never any fear and that even today he is always looking up in the sky. As soon as he got home that night he told his wife.

"At first she thought I was just nuts," he explained, "but then she saw how nervous and excited I was, and she said I must have seen something."

The lights were not separate, they were all connected on the same object, and Jon still can't believe "the way it disappeared, from standing still" to literally shooting off in a flash.

The following is Jon's actual NUFORC report he filed that night:

NUFORC
Occurred : 7/10/2010 23:20 (Entered as : 071010 2320)
Reported: 7/10/2010 10:35:44 PM 22:35
Posted: 7/19/2010
Location: Orangeburg, NY
Shape: Cylinder
Duration:1:00

Long cylindrical row of round white lights observed for about 1 minute. Object disappeared in a flash of yellow light.

I observed one object a long cylindrical row of round white lights about 10 in all. The object was in a stationary hovering position about 1000 to 2000 feet high. I saw it as I was traveling North on the Palisades Interstate Parkway at the New Jersey / New York border. As I was traveling downhill I saw a row of lights at what I thought were on the mountains/ hills ahead of me. I thought it was a new building or athletic field all lit up at night. As I was descending the hill I realized it was in the sky. All of sudden there was a flash of yellow light and the object was gone. The flash was just centered around the object. It did not light up the whole panorama of the sky like a sudden flash of lightning does. That's when I realized I had probably just seen a UFO. I traveled another 15 Minutes on the same road and saw nothing in the way of lightning or flashes in the sky. I am a 55 year old Television Director that lives in Rockland County, New York. I have a BA degree in History and Art. I was not drinking prior to the sighting and was fully alert.

The Best for Last?

Dr. Art Donohue: Chester, October 18, 2012

Thursday, October 18, was a windy day—really too windy to rake leaves. As fast as Dr. Art Donohue would try to rake the leaves into a pile, the wind would just as quickly blow them all around his Chester, NY yard again. By 11:30am, Art was about to give up when something odd in the sky to the north caught his attention.

"Even without my glasses on, this object appeared strange, as it was very bright, silent, and it wasn't moving. It looked as if it was just pinned to sky."

Before continuing with the description of Art's sighting, it's important to note that he is an aviation enthusiast, with a particular expertise in helicopters—so much so, that long before he actually sees a helicopter, he is able to identify its type just by its sound. So, when he sees something in the sky he's never seen before, it clearly warrants special attention.

After sighting the silent object, Art ran into the house to get his glasses. When he came back out, the object was still in the same exact spot, and he could now see that it looked like a vertical cylinder. He ran into the house a second time to get his 8x40 binoculars, and fortunately the object still hadn't moved when he returned, so he got a very good look at it.

The cylinder "was shiny and metallic," and as he described to a friend, "as if it was a telephone pole covered in chrome." There were no wings, no propellers, and no signs of any manner of propulsion, and absolutely no indications that it was any kind of conventional aircraft.

It appeared to be reflecting sunlight, rather than generating light of its own, and the intensity of the reflected light changed as clouds moved swiftly by *above* the cylinder. It was difficult to judge the distance and size of the object, but it was most definitely *below* the clouds. And as the clouds were quickly blowing by in the stiff winds, and the object never once wavered, it was obviously not any type of balloon, either.

Once again, Art ran into the house, this time to get his wife. She also looked at the cylinder through the binoculars, and had no idea what it could be. She suggested he set up his telescope to look at it, but as minutes had already passed and he didn't know from one second to the next how long the object would remain, he instead opted for his camcorder. More precious minutes ticked by as the battery in the camcorder was dead, and Art had to find one that was charged. Then he tried to find a blank tape, but couldn't locate one, so the first tape he grabbed was already used—and contained his sister's wedding! Clearly, this object needed to be recorded, even at the expense of an important family event.

Running back outside, he struggled to get the object in the viewfinder, as the bright sunlight was making it difficult to see the screen. Once he zoomed in on it, he made sure he panned back to get the large oak tree in the field of view to get some perspective, and to show how windy it was that day. Although the camcorder was not high definition, the resolution was sufficient to show that the object was indeed an upright cylinder, highly reflective, and it stayed pinned to the same spot in the sky for the entire two minutes of recording.

Art shows us where he stood while filming the object.

331

Once he had the object on tape, he tried to get more witnesses to see it. He ran to a couple of the neighbors' houses and knocked on their doors, but no one was home. Unfortunately, by the time Art got back to his house, the cylinder was gone, so he has no idea how the object left, at what speed, or in what direction.

All in all, from the first moment Art saw the object to his last view of it "was conservatively at least 10 minutes, probably more like 15"—an extraordinary amount of time for any type of sighting, let alone one in broad daylight. He has since shown the video to many people, and no one has yet to offer an explanation. He doesn't claim that what he saw and taped was extraterrestrial, but it is certainly unexplainable at this point.

Fortunately, Art knew that I was working on this project, so he called me about 4pm that afternoon. It was exciting to hear about such a fresh local sighting, and I was anxious to see the video, which I arranged to pick up at his office the next day. I immediately checked the wind conditions on Weather.com, and found that there were 14 mph sustained winds in our area, with gusts to 23 mph. Of course, winds are stronger at higher altitudes, so it only emphasized how remarkable it was for this object to stay in place and not ever waver.

As I also live in Chester, as soon as I finished speaking to Art, I ran outside to scan the skies, but unfortunately saw nothing. However, shortly before 5pm, I left to go to a lecture I was giving that night in Putnam County. As I was getting on Route 17 by Museum Village in Monroe, I saw a bright point of light flash in the sky to the north. It was far more intense than sunlight reflecting off of an ordinary plane—which is why it caught my attention— so as I was navigating the on-ramp with my left hand, with my right I was trying to get my camera out of my briefcase, all the while trying to keep an eye on the object.

It appeared to blink out for a few moments, but then flashed brightly again. I pulled the lens cap off my camera and was preparing to attempt some photos while driving, but the light winked out, and did not return. I had hoped to get a view of it again at the top of Route 6, but clouds were rolling in and I didn't see it again. Was this light related to Art's sighting, or just a highly reflective aircraft? I have no way of determining that, as my two glimpses were so brief. Perhaps it was more wishful thinking on my part, but still, it was unusual.

In any event, the next day I went to Art's office to pick up the DVD he had burned for me, and popped it into the player for the big screen TV the instant I got home. I had no idea what to expect, but as I had been so disappointed by other photos and videos of alleged UFOs, I didn't get my hopes too high. The video began with a few seconds of some clouds and shaky footage as Art tried to get the object in the viewfinder. Then the camcorder steadied, and as he panned back to get the tree in the field of view, the extremely bright object snapped into focus. Slowly zooming in, the object goes in and out of focus, and finally resolves into a highly reflective, upright cylinder that is absolutely motionless as though "it was pinned to the sky."

"What the hell..." I said out loud as I hit replay to watch the fascinating two minutes of footage again, and then again. I honestly couldn't even offer an explanation as to what the object *was*, I could only offer an opinion as to what it *was not*.

1. It was not any type of blimp, weather balloon, or any other type of lighter-than-air craft or inflatable object. The winds were very strong and this object *did not move* for 10-15 minutes.
2. It wasn't a helicopter, airplane, or conventional aircraft. It was an upright, highly reflective cylindrical-shaped object, with no protruding wings, engines, propellers, or anything else, and it didn't make any sound that could be heard at that distance.
3. It wasn't a geosynchronous satellite, or anything else in orbit, as it was *beneath* the clouds.

Much past these conclusions, I can't say anything more with any degree of certainty. All I know is that in my experience and knowledge, I know of no cylindrical aircraft that can hover motionless and silently in strong winds for over 10 minutes, but I would certainly love to learn about the technology that made it possible!

On the cold and windy afternoon of November 5, Sarah, Felix, and I met Art at his house to film an interview. As Art provided more details of the sighting, his succinct and insightful descriptions showed that he was much more than just an ordinary observer. And again, he makes no claims that what he saw was extraterrestrial—but it certainly wasn't anything of terrestrial origin that he can explain.

In conclusion, for this project, at least, this case has proven to be the most credible sighting in terms of both the witness and the video evidence!

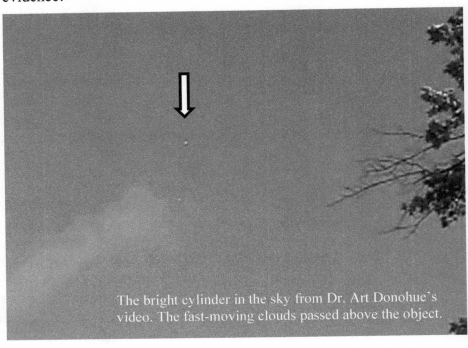

The bright cylinder in the sky from Dr. Art Donohue's video. The fast-moving clouds passed above the object.

Note: Art gave copies of the footage to two airline pilots he knows, hoping to get an explanation. The first one I spoke to said right up front, "I have absolutely no idea what it was." He said the only possible explanation he could offer was that it was some sort of tethered weather balloon or experiment. He was very knowledgeable about FAA regulations, citing that anything over 18,000 feet is controlled airspace, and had this object been above that altitude there would be records of it. However, I asked if he could determine the object's altitude by the clouds that were moving above it, and he said those clouds were *under* 10,000 feet, so that is uncontrolled airspace.

In any event, the next day I started poking around the Internet looking for any records of weather balloons or atmospheric experiments. Instead, I found another video on Youtube of the same exact object, filmed over 50 miles away in Wingdale between 3-4pm on the same day. It was also seen in Beacon, Fishkill, Poughkeepsie, and Hopewell Junction.

It was filmed for 15 minutes by a pilot and professional aerial photographer in Gardiner, using a special high definition camera, and it was witnessed by three dozen people who said the object never moved. The pilot contacted air traffic control and the FAA and no one seemed interested. First sighted around 3pm, it remained stationary for *two hours*!

It was videotaped again in East Durham about 3:45pm, and witnessed by 20 people, and remained stationary for at least ten minutes.

So much for the tethered balloon theory!

But balloon excuses die hard, and further research uncovered more videos purporting to solve the mystery—it was a Mylar balloon that had been witnessed in Kentucky two days earlier and eventually traveled up the east coast up to Maine. Someone even posted photos of the balloon taken through a telescope. All very convincing—unless you were one of the dozens of people who watched it "pinned to the sky" in high winds for as long as two hours. Is the Mylar balloon excuse the modern-day equivalent of the formations of ultralights, designed to muddy the waters and spread disinformation?

It is certainly fitting that this book ends with something like this—highly credible eyewitnesses seeing and filming an object that doesn't move, and a ridiculous excuse being "floated" about a balloon. Unfortunately, it's all par for the course with this highly controversial subject—witnesses knowing what they saw, and skeptics trying to tell them they saw something else.

Am I surprised that this is going on to this day? No, but I guess I am somewhat disappointed we still haven't learned to treat the subject with respect.

So, as the book draws to a close, there is another emotion I am experiencing—anger. I'm angry by the way witnesses have been mistreated. I'm angry at the official government response—or more accurately, their lack of response. And I'm angry that something has been going on in the Hudson Valley that has been affecting people for generations, and it's all been mocked, ignored, or generally swept under the carpet.

I have no illusions that this book will change anything in that regard. Skeptics will still be skeptics, believers will still be believers, and the government will keep doing whatever it is they have been doing. But what I do hope will happen, is that people who have had experiences will realize they are not alone—in fact, they have quite a lot of company in the Hudson Valley!

I also hope that this book will inspire you to get outside and look for yourself. UFOs have been here for many decades, and they are still here right now. If you are patient, and maybe just a little bit lucky, there's no telling what you might see in the night sky.

Places Index

All locations are in New York unless otherwise noted.

IN THE NIGHT SKY
I RECALL A UFO

In The Night Sky: I Recall A UFO
the documentary, is the companion to this
book. It is directed by Felix Olivieri and
produced by Big Guy Media. For more
information on the documentary please visit:
www.BigGuyMedia.com

About the Author

Linda Zimmermann is a former research scientist and an award-winning author of 30 books on science, history, and the paranormal, as well as several works of fiction (including her sentimental favorite, *Hudson Valley Zombie Apocalypse*.). She enjoys lecturing on a wide variety of topics, and has spoken at the Smithsonian Institution, Gettysburg, West Point, the Northeast Astronomy Forum, and national Mensa conventions. Linda has also made numerous appearances on radio and television.

When she isn't glued to her computer writing books, Linda goes cycling, kayaking, cross country skiing, and snowshoeing. She is a lifelong NY Mets and NY Giants fan, so don't even think of trying to call her when a game is on.

http://www.facebook.com/pages/Linda-Zimmermann/116636310250

www.ghostinvestigator.com
www.hvzombie.com
www.badsciences.com

Linda Zimmermann's books are available from her websites, Amazon, Barnes & Noble, and most major retailers. They are also available for Kindle, Apple, NookBook, Kobo, and other E-book formats.

Bad Science:
A Brief History of Bizarre Misconceptions, Totally Wrong Conclusions, and Incredibly Stupid Theories

Winner of the 2011 Silver Medal for Humor
in the international Independent Publisher Awards

Amazon.com Review:

"*Bad Science* is simultaneously informative and ever-so-entertaining. Riveting! Enthralling! Hilarious! I highly recommend this book if you like a jaw dropping read that is a LAUGH OUT LOUD."

HVZA:
Hudson Valley Zombie Apocalypse

Amazon.com Reviews:

"GREAT book. Buy it; you won't regret it. Well... except maybe for at 3 AM when you're either A) still up reading because can't put this page-turner down or B) waking up out of a zombie nightmare because the characters and situations in the book can seem so REAL. But buy it anyway."

"You relate, you get sucked in, seriously it's been a while since I enjoyed a book so much."

"The author has an uncanny ability to pull you into the story and make you feel like you are there."

"Zimmermann really hits home with her depiction of life during the collapse of civilization, and the heart wrenching losses, choices and sacrifices that people must make in order to survive. Zimmermann is a master manipulator of emotions: the love, fear, sadness, pain, and suffering of the various characters are surprisingly real. Set in the Hudson Valley, the authentic locations and settings lend an additional layer of realism that so many other works of fiction neglect. These just are not zombies that are attacking people - these are zombies that are attacking your neighbors and family and friends."

Dead Center
A Ghost Hunter Novel

When one of the country's largest shopping centers is built in Virginia, rumors abound that the place is haunted by ghosts of Civil War soldiers. Ghost hunter Sarah Brooks must uncover the truth, and come face to face with the restless spirits that walk through the *Dead Center*:

Okay, Sarah Brooks. This is what you do, she said to herself. *This is who you are.*

Closing her eyes, Sarah spun around and counted to three. When she opened her eyes, she had to clamp her hand over her mouth to stifle a scream. There was a pale, misty shape of a man drawing closer. It was like an image being projected into a fog, and it rippled, wavered, then slowly began to take on a more defined shape. The wounded man behind her screamed as if Death himself was coming to take him…

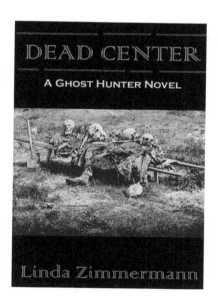

Ghost Investigator Series

Ghost Investigator Volume 1:
Hauntings of the Hudson Valley

Ghost Investigator Volume 2:
From Gettysburg to Lizzie Borden

Ghost Investigator Volume 3

Ghost Investigator Volume 4:
Ghosts of New York and New Jersey

Ghost Investigator Volume 5:
From Beyond the Grave

Ghost Investigator Volume 6:
Dark Shadows

Ghost Investigator Volume 7:
Psychic Impressions

Ghost Investigator Volume 8:
Back Into the Light

Ghost Investigator Volume 9:
Back from the Dead

Ghost Investigator Volume 10

Ghost Investigator 10th Anniversary Special Edition:
Favorite Haunts

Ghosts of Rockland County:
Collected Stories Edition

Hudson Valley Haunts:
Historic Driving Tours

New York's Hudson River Valley is a place of captivating beauty and fascinating history. It is also one of the most haunted regions in the country. From ancient Indian spirits at Spook Rock, to soldiers still walking the battlefield of Fort Montgomery, to the many haunted houses that line the streets of the old Dutch settlements in New Paltz and Hurley, this book has something extra to offer tourists—ghosts that still make their presence known to those who dare to visit.

What greater adventure can there be then to go to such a site, explore the rich history of its people and the events, and then see if you can discover any deeper secrets from the other world, where a passing shadow or faint whisper may signal that you have just had an encounter in the haunted Hudson Valley.

America's Historic Haunts

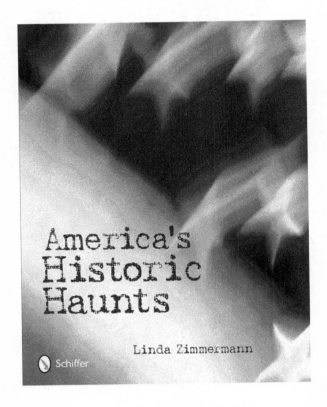

From remote villages in Alaska, to ancient Native American settlements in the southwest, to an old Spanish town in Florida, and bustling metropolitan areas in the northeast, follow the fascinating trail of historic haunts across the country. Test your ghost hunting skills in an old prison or fort, dine in restaurants where paranormal activity is on the menu, and sleep in some of America's most haunted inns. Whether you're a frequent flier or an armchair adventurer, this book will take you on a journey of discovery into the people, places, and events that led to the spirits that still walk among us in some of this country's greatest travel destinations.

CPSIA information can be obtained
at www.ICGtesting.com
Printed in the USA
BVHW080815130219
540160BV00002B/85/P